HABITS OF THE CREATIVE MIND

ABOUT THE AUTHORS

Ann Jurecic and Richard E. Miller have, between them, more than sixty years' experience teaching writing. They've taught in high schools, community colleges, and public and private universities. They've trained undergraduates to be writing tutors and graduate students to teach first-year writing; they've participated in the administration of writing programs; they've run immersive writing seminars for experienced teachers. Ann works at the intersection of writing studies, literacy studies, and medical humanities. She published *Illness as Narrative* in 2012 (UPitt) and is currently at work on a new book about the essay, *Society of Outsiders: Women and Political Nonfiction, 1960–2000*. An award-winning teacher, avid blogger, and poet, Richard has an abiding interest in both apocalyptic literature and apocalyptic thinking. Richard recently published *On the End of Privacy: Dissolving Boundaries in a Screen-Centric World* (UPitt 2019) and is currently at work on a book-length project on poverty and trauma tentatively titled, *Please Write*.

PREFACE

Ann and I were team-teaching when we realized we had to reimagine our approach to teaching writing. We'd been aware, separately, that teaching in the new millennium was somehow different from how it had been before, but we hadn't had the time or the shared experience to think through what had changed and why it was significant. But, working together in the same classroom with the same students, we began to be able to put into words why the teaching practices we'd used with success in the twentieth century no longer worked as well in the twenty-first century. We knew that our current students, with their laptops and their smartphones, weren't quite like the students we taught in the 1990s, but we couldn't really say precisely what the differences were. Our vision wasn't clouded by nostalgia; we could see that our current students were dutiful and eager to get good grades. And yet, something was missing.

What that something was came into view when we created a pair of assignments for the students to complete in the run-up to their final essays. The first, "Be Interested," asked the students to look into the events going on at the university—lectures, art openings, concerts, job fairs, protests, club meetings, etc.—and attend something that they wanted to learn more about. The second, "Be Interesting," asked the students to then place the event they had attended in conversation with a larger set of issues to demonstrate just how interesting their own thoughts could be. (As you'll see, one of our working definitions for the essay is "the traces of a mind at work on a problem.")

Many of our students struggled to find something going on at the university that was of interest. We expanded the field of places they could explore: TED talks, long-form essays, YouTube videos. These widening circles captured more and more of the students, but there was one student—let's call her Cassandra—who declared that no matter how hard she tried she simply couldn't find anything that held her interest—on campus, on the internet, or in the library. Cassandra wasn't happy with her plight; indeed, as a graduating senior, she was embarrassed to find herself so at sea when it came to engaging with the world. But writing this essay for us wasn't going to help her get a job, so the challenge, as far as she was concerned, was finding a way to fake interest in something well enough not to hurt her GPA.

Cassandra and her peers are members of the most tested generation in human history. They've sat for more high-stakes tests than any previous generation; they've been taught by teachers whose success is measured by their students' performance on these tests; they've gone to schools whose funding is dependent upon their test scores. There is nothing in this educational regime that prizes interest, curiosity, creativity, or ingenuity. It is a system that equates learning with following rules, with conforming to expectations, with doing as one is told. ("Just tell me what to be interested in," Cassandra said, "and I'll write about that.")

We came to see that Cassandra and her peers struggled with being interested in ideas, not because of some personal deficit, as they feared, but because they didn't know how to be interested. Or, to be more precise, they didn't know that being interested in the world of ideas takes practice and that if one practices being interested in that world, being interested becomes a habit.

The first edition of *Habits of the Creative Mind* was born out of this realization. We wanted to give students license to be curious and a structure within which to practice an approach to writing as a technology that enables the writer to think new thoughts. Because we see ourselves as writers and teachers, we wanted our book to be a collection of essays about writing that embody our vision of writing's power to self-educate: our essays don't contain templates or fill-in-the-blank formulas or diagrams for how to create a tasty "quote sandwich"; our essays look at the myriad ways writers use the act of writing to confront the unknown, to think new thoughts, and to imagine new possibilities.

As we settled into working on the second edition of *Habits*, we were fortunate to be able to draw on all we learned from teachers who used the first edition. We also had the advantage of returning to our own writing with fresh eyes and so were able to see all sorts of ways we could improve the book. So, instead of merely tweaking the first edition, with the full support of the amazing editorial team at Bedford/St. Martin's, we embraced the challenge of revising the entire text. Line by line, word by word, we practiced the habits celebrated in this book: orienting, beginning, paying attention, questioning, exploring, connecting, working deliberately, reflecting, persisting, organizing, speculating, and playing. Throughout, we've aspired to the same standard we have for our students. We've sought to produce writing about writing that is interesting in itself, that rewards rereading, that gives our readers access to the transformative powers of the imagination.

Redefining our work in the classroom as cultivating the habits of the creative mind has led to the most rewarding teaching of our careers. It has required that we rethink every aspect of what we do: what we put on our syllabi, how we sequence our assignments, how we grade, and how we respond to student work. Teaching *Habits* has allowed us to reconnect with the very part of teaching that most attracted us in the first place—the creative act of helping our students to access the imagination's transformative powers. If this resonates with you, we hope you'll join us in the work of training students how to use writing in ways that allow them to embrace complexity, to accept ambiguity, and to enjoy nuance. We believe practicing the habits of mind that are characteristic of speculative, meditative, and deliberative thought can pave the way to mutual understanding and the making of a better world. And that is the goal of higher education, properly understood: not the production of credentialed individuals, but the cultivation of creative, curious minds working away on problems big and small.

Key Features of *Habits of the Creative Mind*

The creative mind thrives on making connections. We want our students to be able to make connections with texts they share in common, and we also want them to have the opportunity to follow their curiosity wherever it might lead. To support both focused and open-ended acts of connection over the course of a semester, we designed the book based on the following principles:

The Twelve Habits of Mind Are Both Teachable and Flexible.
These habits, which we identify as the central practices of strong writers, offer a path to learning that feels anything but rote. One way to define creativity is the ability to look at a problem from multiple perspectives. We know that there is no right way to learn, so we offer three original essays on each habit, sharing different ways to think about each of the twelve habits of mind. Our approach to teaching habits of mind aligns with the *Framework for Success in Postsecondary Writing*, a document jointly produced by the Council of Writing Program Administrators, the National Council of Teachers of English, and the National Writing Project that identifies eight habits of mind that are "essential for success in college writing."

Creativity Takes Practice. Lots and Lots of Practice.
Learning how to write well requires an openness to change, a tolerance for ambiguity, and resilience when what has worked in the past suddenly stops working. Such habits can be learned when teaching both supports and celebrates the production of writing that attends to nuance, explores complexity, and moves across multiple perspectives. To this end, *Habits of the Creative Mind* includes ninety-seven practice sessions that ask students to do all sorts of writing—note taking, recording daily observations, reflecting on a selected reading—and all sorts of research—in the *Oxford English Dictionary*, online, and in the archives of their own school papers. The practice sessions also invite students to draw pictures, sketch idea maps, and visualize color-coded representations of how complex pieces of writing are composed. The practice sessions that follow each of the essays in *Habits* focus student attention on the mental operations that drive the work of the intellectually curious and creative mind—connecting, reading, reflecting, and researching, as well as writing and revising.

Reading the Words of Thoughtful Minds at Work Facilitates Discussion and Exploration.
Each of the five readings at the end of *Habits* is the result of a curious and creative mind working on a problem; as a collection, they provide a suggestive spectrum of the many ways that writing can be used as a tool to generate new thoughts.

New to This Edition

....

For the second edition of *Habits of the Creative Mind* we have revised, based on feedback from instructors who used the first edition, by making it even easier to teach with and by adding new essays and practice opportunities that explicitly cultivate critical, creative, and curious writers.

Twelve new instructional essays both explain and model habits of the creative mind. These essays, including "On Habits," "On Letting Go of Writing-by-Formula," and "On Imagining Alternatives," explore the complex issues that are raised when writing is understood as a way of *making* meaning. Written to intrigue and inspire students, as well as to guide them, these essays will launch meaningful discussions, powerful questions, and interested, nuanced writing.

New practice sessions encourage curiosity and help students integrate the habits into their routines. More than a dozen are sequenced assignments that span multiple practice sessions, including an extended project on "the question you want to make sure to have thought seriously about before you graduate from college." These staged assignments begin with low-stakes explorations and build naturally to longer, more complex writing goals. In addition, each practice session now explicitly links habits with the kinds of activities that support them in order to make students more aware of their learning goals and the benefits of engaging with a particular writing challenge. At a glance, both students and teachers can see, for example, how the habit of exploring is enabled by the practices of observing, note-taking, and drafting.

An expanded and entirely new Readings section provides examples of curious and creative minds at work. Five new readings now replace the three readings in the first edition. Pieces by Danielle Allen, Rachel Aviv, and Rebecca Solnit serve as foundations for writing projects on the goal of education in a democracy, the fragility of identity, and the gendering of public spaces. Montaigne's short essay "How the Mind Tangles Itself Up" gives students a chance to think about the productive powers of confusion. And *Habits* explores the *Declaration of Independence* as a collective writing project and the result of a great deal of conscientious revision, reminding students that even a foundational text like the *Declaration* is the result of a creative and deliberate writing process.

A new Instructor's Manual ensures that *Habits of the Creative Mind* will be a catalyst for invention and innovation for teachers as well as students. The manual includes sample syllabi and case studies from a variety of different programs using *Habits of the Creative Mind*. It features essays by ourselves offering practical suggestions for incorporating *Habits* into your composition course, including "On Teaching Creativity in a Screen-Centric World," "On Linearity and the Syllabus: Notes against an Orderly Writing Process," and "On Best Practices," which includes our criteria for assessment. We also provide a sample, semester-long syllabus, which points to assignments within the book and suggests potential due dates. In addition, the instructor's manual provides three case studies by teachers from very different schools showing how they adapted *Habits of the Creative Mind* to work with their students. (One of these case studies is titled "How to Use *Habits* When You're Really Not Supposed To.")

Acknowledgments

This book is the result of decades of teaching, thousands of hours of contact with students in all sorts of classrooms, hundreds of presentations at conferences, and extended conversations with the teachers and colleagues who have most shaped how we think about how to cultivate the habits of the creative mind. We want to single out Roxanne Mountford and the teachers and students in the Oklahoma State Writing Program. Roxanne was one of the very first people to get what we were after with *Habits* and she and her staff have provided us with invaluable feedback, making certain that the second edition of *Habits* is even better than the first.

Habits is also the direct result of our good fortune working with the gifted and forward-thinking publishing team at Bedford/ St. Martin's who believe in our project and who model the arts of creative collaboration. Joan Feinberg, who has provided Richard with career-long support and guidance, played a key role in the early acquisition process. Laura Arcari and Leasa Burton, publishers and friends, put together the best editorial team we've ever worked with for this second edition. Sherry Mooney, our editor, is wise beyond her years: we are grateful for her shared vision, her consistently good advice, her creative suggestions, and her good cheer in the face of our concern for details big and small. And we are grateful for the other members of the editing, design, and marketing team: Edwin Hill, Matt Glazer, Annie Campbell, Vivian Garcia, William Boardman, Kalina Ingham, and Angie Boehler.

We want to thank Robert Maynard Miller for granting us permission to use his painting "Use Case" on the book cover for this edition. We also want to thank the students who gave us permission to use their writing in our essays: Chris Osifchin, Erik Rose, Julianna Rossano, Donald Shimazu, and Annie Stiver. For their invaluable feedback as our manuscript took shape, we thank Roxanne Amico, Cedar Crest College; Jeffrey Basile, Kent State University; Michael Burke, St. Louis Community College–Meramec; Lauren Fortenberry, Georgia Southern University; David Green, Howard University; Sara Harrell, Indiana University–Purdue University, Indianapolis; Tim Jensen, Oregon State University; Burney Marsh, Georgia Southern University; Timothy McAlpine, Lindsey Wilson College; Shirley Smart, Lake Superior State University; Brian Zimmerman, Boston College. For their contributions to the instructor's manual and showing that there are as many ways to teach the habits of the creative mind as there are creative teachers, we thank Elizabeth Boquet at Fairfield University, Kelly George at Immaculata University, and David Green at Howard University.

Finally, we want to thank the members of our local community who inspired us to stay committed to this project: the students in the spring 2019 Reading in Slow Motion course at Rutgers; Radcliff Bent III, Paul Bielecki, Beth Bouquet, Peter Breslin, Richard Dienst, Jerry Floersch, Kelly George, Madison Gulbin, Debra Keates, Lauren Kimball, Tom Laughlin, Jeff Longhofer, Ben Machlin, Dara Regaignon, Ana Valens, Amanda Irwin Wilkins . . . and, of course, thanks always to Cara and Rachel, Quinta and Jack.

—Richard E. Miller
—Ann Jurecic

Bedford/St. Martin's Puts You First

From day one, our goal has been simple: to provide inspiring resources that are grounded in best practices for teaching reading and writing. For more than thirty-five years, Bedford/St. Martin's has partnered with the field, listening to teachers, scholars, and students about the support writers need. We are committed to helping every writing instructor make the most of our resources.

How can we help *you*?

- Our editors can align our resources to your outcomes through correlation and transition guides for your syllabus. Just ask us.
- Our sales representatives specialize in helping you find the right materials to support your course goals.
- Our *Bits* blog on the Bedford/St. Martin's English Community (**community.macmillan.com**) publishes fresh teaching ideas weekly. You'll also find easily downloadable professional resources and links to author webinars on our community site.

Contact your Bedford/St. Martin's sales representative or visit **macmillanlearning.com** to learn more.

Print and Digital Options for Habits of the Creative Mind

Choose the format that works best for your course, and ask about our packaging options that offer savings for students.

- *Paperback edition.* To order the paperback edition, use ISBN 978-1-319-10396-5.
- *Popular ebook formats.* For details about our ebook partners, visit **macmillanlearning.com/ebooks**.
- *Inclusive Access.* Enable every student to receive their course materials through your LMS on the first day of class. Macmillan Learning's Inclusive Access program is the easiest, most affordable way to ensure all students have access to quality educational resources. Find out more at **macmillanlearning .com/inclusiveaccess**.

Your Course, Your Way

No two writing programs or classrooms are exactly alike. Our Curriculum Solutions team works with you to design custom options that provide the resources your students need. (Options below require enrollment minimums.)

- *ForeWords for English.* Customize any print resource to fit the focus of your course or program by choosing from a range of prepared topics, such as Sentence Guides for Academic Writers.

- *Macmillan Author Program (MAP).* Add excerpts or package acclaimed works from Macmillan's trade imprints to connect students with prominent authors and public conversations. A list of recommended titles and corresponding course themes drawn up by the authors of *Habits of the Creative Mind* is available upon request.

- *Bedford Select.* Build your own print handbook or anthology from a database of more than nine hundred selections, and add your own materials to create your ideal text. Package with any Bedford/St. Martin's text for additional savings. Visit **macmillanlearning.com/bedfordselect**.

Instructor Resources

You have a lot to do in your course. We want to make it easy for you to find the support you need—and to get it quickly.

Resources for Teaching Habits of the Creative Mind is available as a PDF that can be downloaded from **macmillanlearning.com**. Visit the instructor resources tab for *Habits of the Creative Mind*. The instructor's manual includes essays by Richard E. Miller and Ann Jurecic on everything from syllabus design to assessment, as well as a sample fifteen-week course plan. The instructor's manual also includes case studies from instructors who have used *Habits* successfully in a range of writing classes. Each case study is accompanied by a sample of that instructor's syllabus.

An Instructor's Edition containing *Habits of the Creative Mind* bound together with *Resources for Teaching* Habits of the Creative Mind is available. To order this edition, use ISBN 978-1-319-25628-9 or speak with your Macmillan sales rep.

BRIEF CONTENTS

CONTENTS

HABITS OF THE CREATIVE MIND

1

ORIENTING

orient, *verb* (*Oxford English Dictionary*)

2. To bring into a defined relationship with known facts, circumstances, etc.; to give orientation or bearings to. Frequently *refl[exive]*.: to put oneself in the right position or relation; to ascertain one's bearings, become familiar with one's situation. Also: to give a specific direction or tendency to (chiefly with *to, toward(s)*).

Y ou are about to enter unfamiliar territory: *Habits of the Creative Mind* isn't like any other book that has ever been written about learning how to write. We don't claim that there's only one way to write or one set of steps in the writing process or one fill-in-the-blank formula for every writing situation. We don't try to sell you on the idea that writing is fun and easy if you just know the right tricks. And we don't narrow our focus to the modes of writing typically assigned in college: persuasion and argumentation. Our work on this book began with the premise that the best writing develops from the exercise of habits of mind that include curiosity, creativity, attentiveness, openness to new ideas, persistence, flexibility, and reflectiveness. Starting with this premise compelled us to rethink both what writing is for and how writing can best be taught. As you'll see throughout *Habits*, we insist that writing is a technology for thinking new thoughts and that the only way your writing will serve this function is through deliberate practice of the myriad mental activities — the habits of mind — that make creativity possible.

We know this is disorienting, so we've written three essays to help you get your bearings. "On Finding Your Feet" offers our thoughts about the lifelong consequences of equating education with test taking. "On Habits" distinguishes between writing memos or reports for one's job and using writing as a technology for thinking new thoughts. Finally, "On Thinking New Thoughts" provides a set of examples of how real writers create conditions that help them return again and again to the challenge of exploring the unknown.

On Finding Your Feet

"Curiouser and curiouser!" cried Alice (she was so much surprised,
that for the moment she quite forgot how to speak good English);
"now I'm opening out like the largest telescope that ever was!
Good-bye, feet!" (for when she looked down at her feet, they
seemed to be almost out of sight, they were getting so far off).

Alice's Adventures in Wonderland begins with our heroine having nothing to do. It's not that Alice is alone: she's with her sister and could choose to do what her sister is doing—reading silently. But the book her sister is reading doesn't interest Alice because it has no pictures or dialogue. Alice has a problem—she's bored.

The resources we have for relieving boredom were not available to Lewis Carroll's Alice one hundred and fifty years ago: she can't text a friend or stream her favorite videos out there on the grass. Uninterested in reading, Alice lies in the sun, trying to get up the energy to pick some daisies, when a rabbit wearing a waistcoat runs by. In an instant, Alice is transformed: "burning with curiosity," she races after the rabbit, commencing the "adventures in Wonderland" that continue to attract readers to this day.

How does this happen—the jump from idling in listless boredom to embarking on a curiosity-driven exploration of the unknown?

Both as writing teachers and as parents, we have heard a lot about boredom. The assigned readings are boring. The writing assignments are boring. School is boring. No one willingly seeks out boredom; it's just out there, waiting to overwhelm the idle. And once you are bored, then everything is boring.

Look at Alice. The rabbit runs by her and at first she thinks nothing of it. Indeed, she doesn't even "think it so *very* much out of the way to hear the Rabbit say to itself 'Oh dear! Oh dear! I shall be too late!'"

A talking rabbit? Whatever.

It's not until the rabbit stops and looks at his pocket watch that Alice snaps out of her torpor, jumps to her feet, and, in an act that has since entered the language as a synonym for plunging into another world, goes "down the rabbit hole."

There is, of course, no such thing as a talking, waistcoat-wearing, pocket watch–checking rabbit. The sister sitting on the bank, the book without pictures, the rabbit, the rabbit hole: these ordinary — one might even say boring — things are made extraordinary by Lewis Carroll's creation of a world of wonder. How did he do it? How does any writer make the jump from being bored (and boring) to being creative? From writing sentences no one would willingly read to thinking thoughts of interest to others?

Habits of the Creative Mind is based on a simple premise: no one wants either to be bored or to be boring. Entire industries are founded on this premise: show business, video gaming, the 24-hour news cycle, gambling, online shopping, theme parks, social media, wine and spirits. These industries keep boredom at bay by offering entertainment in one form or another; but, as soon as the entertainment comes to an end, the ever-present threat of being bored makes itself felt again. Education, properly understood, isn't in the entertainment business; its job is to encourage students to cultivate creative and curious habits of mind. And these habits, in turn, make the world shimmer with possibility.

Nothing is inherently interesting — not the weeping willow in the park, or the lecture on global warming, or the Monet water lily painting hanging in the gallery, or the rabbit scampering into the bushes. Everything in the material world of objects and in the immaterial world of ideas can be tuned out, mocked, or trivialized. Everything we experience through our senses or gain access to with our minds can be dismissed by someone else as *boring*.

So nothing is inherently interesting; but everything — from the ways single-celled bacteria communicate, to the back-channel chatter in the brain, to the evanescent patterns made when smoke rises from a candle's flame — has the *potential* to be made interesting. The mind can be trained to transform what would otherwise seem mundane and unremarkable into an opportunity for thoughtful reflection. *We* can make the world interesting to ourselves and to others through sustained acts of attention, and we can gain access to curiosity and creativity through deliberate, thoughtful practice.

We've written this book to provide ways for you to learn how to make the world a more interesting place and how to make your interests of interest to others. For this to happen, you will need to cultivate a sense that what is unknown is exciting, and you will need to become more comfortable with uncertainty and with ambiguous outcomes. Taking pleasure in confronting the limits of one's own understanding does not come naturally to anyone: we all avoid situations where our ignorance might be exposed, our faulty reasoning brought to light, our reliance on myth, hearsay, and family lore disclosed. This shared tendency to keep what we don't know hidden is precisely why practicing being attentive, curious, and creative is essential; it's a way of confronting, engaging with, and responding to the unknown. A commitment to working at the edge of one's own understanding is, we maintain, what lies at the heart of the educational enterprise. There can be no consequential learning without such a commitment.

In this book, we focus on writing as one way to practice the encounter with the unknown but, as you'll see, we understand writing to encompass more than just typing words into a computer. In fact, we often use the word *composing* to emphasize our sense that writing is an ongoing act of making sense of the world—an act that necessarily involves working with sounds and images, perceptions and intuitions, and everything else in the realm of experience that shapes both what and how we think.

That said, we do maintain that there's an important distinction between informal personal writing and public writing about ideas. Most of us don't need help posting the events of the day to Instagram or spinning memories into anecdotes that amuse our friends because we've had years of practice talking and thinking about ourselves and the events, big and small, that have taken place in our lives. Few of us have a comparable amount of practice writing about ideas—practice that depends on cultivating the mind's connective powers. But, once you start writing about ideas, you will find that the experience can end up leading you to think new thoughts. And those new thoughts can open up new worlds for you to explore. To use writing in this way is to use it as a technology for thinking new thoughts.

If you practice the approaches to writing we present in *Habits of the Creative Mind* until they become your own habits of mind, you will have achieved the two highest goals of a liberal arts education: you will have put yourself on the path to being a lifelong learner and you will have learned how to engage with the world beyond the narrow compass of the self.

Getting started on this adventure requires three things: a desire to better understand yourself and your place in the world; access to writing materials and the internet; and a commitment to making time for the work of cultivating curiosity, creativity, and learning. *Habits of the Creative Mind* provides you with a structure and a host of activities and prompts to help you practice writing about ideas, but you have to meet the project halfway by being open to the possibility that using writing to explore your mind's connective powers can help you both to think new thoughts and to think those thoughts in new ways.

We know that skepticism is an inevitable part of the process of thinking about ideas that are strange or unfamiliar, so we expect you to be skeptical along the way. But it is up to you to keep that skepticism in check so that you don't become dismissive as soon as you find yourself being asked to think in new ways about what thinking is and about what it means to be a thoughtful person. We're not asking for a lot. If you've ever found yourself wishing that you understood the world a little better or that you had a clearer sense of how to make the world a better place, then you're as open as you need to be to give our approach to writing a try.

Practice Session One: Alice's Feet

Habits: connecting, exploring, orienting

Activities: engaging with sources, reading, researching

In this essay's opening passage, Alice is having trouble finding her feet. This fact is unlikely to make any sense if you're not familiar with *Alice in Wonderland*. So, one way to find your own feet as a reader is to learn more about Carroll's book. You might choose to go to *Wikipedia*, of course, but we're always more interested in going directly to the original source when possible. And, as it happens, you'll have no trouble finding *Alice in Wonderland* online. Read the first two chapters with care. Then consider the following questions: What does it mean for Alice to find her feet in Wonderland? What work have you had to do, as a reader, to put yourself into (to find your feet in) Carroll's story? What does "finding your feet" have to do with orienting yourself as a reader? And as a writer? Take thirty minutes to write up your definition of what "finding your feet" with a text means. Make sure to detail the steps involved in this process.

Practice Session Two: Reading Montaigne in French (Even If You've Never Studied French)

Habits: connecting, orienting, paying attention

Activities: list making, note taking, reading

The sixteenth-century French nobleman Michel de Montaigne is credited with inventing the essay, but his version of the essay has little in common with the essays typically assigned in school today. He called his writings *essais*, meaning "attempts." They were not arguments or proclamations, but personal reflections that explored what he knew and what he thought. Montaigne's short essay "How Our Mind Tangles Itself Up" appears both in its original French and in an English translation at the end of this book (pp. 268–69). First read the translation. Next, look carefully at the original essay and consider what the English translator has done to help the contemporary reader make sense of Montaigne's writing. Without knowing any French or Latin, you should be able to list at least four steps the translator has taken to increase the likelihood that the meaning of Montaigne's essay survives the journey to the present day. Spend at least twenty minutes gathering your thoughts on the differences between how Montaigne's original essay attempts to orient the reader and how the contemporary translation attempts to do the same. You might begin by looking at how both the writer and his translator use white space on the page.

On Habits

What is a habit?

If you go to the *Oxford English Dictionary* (a habit we hope you acquire over the course of working with this book), you'll find that the origins of the word *habit* can be traced back as far as the twelfth century, when it referred to fashion, clothing, and mode of dress. What one wore everyday was one's habit. (This meaning of the word survives to this day as the name for religious garb designed to signal that the wearer is a member of a given religious order.) The meaning of the word *habit* evolved over time to refer both to how one generally carried oneself in public and to the way one tended to think. As the meanings of *habit* proliferated, the word implicitly retained the possibility for change: the style of clothing you're in the habit of wearing, for example, doesn't remain constant over the course of your life. (Imagine yourself at age fifty-four wearing exactly what you're wearing now!) It's easier to change the way you choose to dress, of course, than the way you're in the habit of thinking. How can you possibly change the *way* you think?

It turns out that you can shop for help in this area too—in the self-help section of your local or online bookseller. If you do this, you're sure to come across one of the best-selling books of all time, Dale Carnegie's *How to Win Friends and Influence People*. First published in 1936, Carnegie's book offered a fourteen-week do-it-yourself course on how to succeed in business and in life more generally. Carnegie launches his project in response to an idea expressed by the psychologist William James: that each of us has mental capacities we "habitually fail to use." Always the businessman, Carnegie translated James's observation into profitable advice for general readers; he promised his program would help his readers to "discover, develop, and profit by those dormant and unused assets." These "assets" are the habits of mind that will enable his readers to become successful in business.

If you seek out Carnegie's book, you're also sure to run into Stephen Covey's *The 7 Habits of Highly Effective People*, which was first published in 1989 and regularly appears on lists of the most influential business leadership books of all time. (Like *How to Win Friends*, *7 Habits* has also sold tens of millions of copies; indeed, it, too, spawned a leadership training program that has outlived its author.) In preparation for writing his book, Covey reviewed all of the literature on success written over the previous two hundred years and discovered that after World War I there was a detrimental shift from a focus on *character* to a focus on *personality* as the foundation for success. Character, Covey says, is rooted in principles such as "integrity, humility, fidelity, temperance, courage, justice, patience, industry, simplicity, modesty, and the Golden Rule." The shift to personality emphasizes instead "public image, . . . attitudes and behaviors, [and] skills and techniques, that lubricate the processes of human interaction."

Although Covey doesn't call out Carnegie by name, he clearly has him in mind when he gives examples of the damage that has been done by making personality the foundation for success: "Some of this philosophy was expressed in inspiring and sometimes valid maxims. . . . Other parts of the personality approach were clearly manipulative, even deceptive, encouraging people to use techniques to get other people to like them, or to fake interest in the hobbies of others to get out of them what they wanted." Although Covey doesn't say that Carnegie played a key role in shifting the definition of success to personality and the arts of manipulation, his indictment of Carnegie's influence is clear. For Covey, the challenge of becoming "effective" is not best exemplified in Carnegie and his strategies for winning friends, but rather in Benjamin Franklin, who sought "to integrate certain principles and habits deep within his nature" to improve his character.

The book in your hands is about cultivating positive habits but, unlike *How to Win Friends and Influence People* or *The 7 Habits of Highly Effective People*, you won't find copies of it in the self-help section of a bookstore. Nor would you find the books by Carnegie and Covey on a shelf for books concerned with creativity. There are many reasons for this, but the most salient one is the different role writing plays in our work. When Carnegie discusses writing, he tends to mean letters, memos, and thank-you notes, and he does so to emphasize the role this kind of writing can play in winning people over to seeing things your way. (He includes a long anecdote, for example, about how Lincoln learned to stop writing critical letters to the editor after one of the targets of his criticism challenged him to a duel.) And Covey sees writing as one of many ways to "sharpen your mental saw." In both instances, the authors understand writing to be a tool—for persuasion or mental saw sharpening (whatever that is). Writing is of interest to these self-help gurus only insofar as it helps one to become either a more successful or a more effective person. We, on the other hand, are interested in writing as a technology for thinking new thoughts and our goal is to help you to learn how to use writing in this way by practicing the habits of the creative mind. We make no claim that doing so will lead either to success in business or in one's personal affairs. It might, but it's more important to us that you begin to resist falling back on fixed ideas as Carnegie and Covey do. Day in and day out, you'll practice paying attention, wondering, deliberating, learning, and questioning, always in search of a new thought or insight or understanding.

Practice Session One, Part One: Your Online Habits

Habits: orienting, paying attention, questioning

Activities: reflecting, researching, writing

One place to gain direct access to your own habits of mind is the search history on your web browser. Unless you toggled your privacy settings to do otherwise, your browser's default setting is to maintain a visible record of your web browsing history so that you can quickly re-access web pages you've visited in the past. What does your web history reveal about your habits of mind? What does your toolbar reveal? After you've reviewed your search history, write a quick profile of what the history says about your reading/viewing/listening habits. What does the profile leave out?

Your Texting/Chatting History

Repeat the previous exercise reviewing your texting/chatting history. What does this history reveal about your interests? Your friendship networks? The kinds of conversations you have? After you've reviewed this history, write a second profile of what your texting history reveals about your writing habits. What are you in the habit of discussing? What does this profile leave out or miss about your habits as a writer and a thinker?

Your Social Media Footprint

Repeat the previous exercise, this time focusing on whatever social media you use now or have used in the past. Do you tweet? Blog? Post to Instagram? Use

Facebook? Are you on listservs or mailing lists? What does your use or nonuse of social media reveal about your online habits? After you've considered your current and past use of social media, write a third profile of what your social media footprint reveals about your online habits as a reader/writer/listener/viewer. What does this profile leave out?

Practice Session One, Part Two: Your Online Habits of Mind

Habits: connecting, orienting, speculating

Activities: consolidating, diagnosing, writing

Working from the three profiles you drafted during the previous practice session, write a profile that captures the *habits of mind* evidenced by your computer use. This consolidated profile should not be a list of what you've done or what your interests are; it should be a description of *how you are in the habit of satisfying those interests*. So, for example, if your search history reveals that you regularly visit news sites, your interest in news is clear; but the work of your consolidated profile is to reveal *why* the particular set of news sites that you visit satisfies your interest. Try to keep your description neutral and objective: the goal at this point is not to assess whether the habits are good or bad; the goal is to come up with as complete a description as you can about what you are in the habit of using your mind for.

Practice Session One, Part Three: In Search of Causes

Habits: orienting, reflecting, speculating

Activities: analyzing, interpreting, revising

Now that you've completed your initial profile of your interests (as evidenced by your online activity), we'd like you to spend at least an hour writing up a portrait of how you think. We're not asking you to explain *where* your interests and opinions come from. It goes without saying that what you think has been influenced by your upbringing, your peers, your schooling, and what part of the country you live in. Instead focus on *how* your thinking is influenced by these same factors. If you're interested in news, for example, think about where you live and what kinds of media you consume. How do these factors shape your interest in politics? If you're interested in music, what experiences shaped your sense of what's good, and what's not? We are asking you to become more aware of your current habits of mind so that you can develop and expand them as you make your way down the rabbit hole.

....

Practice Session Two: Defining Technology

....

Habits: orienting, paying attention, questioning

Activities: defining, researching, writing

In our essay "On Habits," we contrast our interest in writing as "a technology for thinking new thoughts" with the more traditional view of writing as a tool for communication. What exactly is a "technology"? For this practice session, we want you to look into the history of the word. The best resource for research of this kind is the *Oxford English Dictionary*. If you can't access this online through your school library, you may be able to find a paper version of the dictionary in the library's reference section. The reason we want you to use this resource is that it tracks when words enter the language and how the meaning of a word has changed over time. In so doing, the *OED* makes clear that words acquire meaning in context, through being used by writers trying to think new thoughts.

When you've had a chance to review how the meaning of the word *technology* has changed over time, we'd like you to spend twenty minutes writing up your own definition of what the word means as we use in it *Habits of the Creative Mind*. In order to do this exercise, you will need to interpret both the definition as presented in the dictionary and the term as it is used in "On Habits." When you finish, you will have defined another of *Habits'* key terms: we defined *orient* using the *OED*; then we described how the meaning of *habit* changed over time; and now you have interpreted our use of the term *technology*. Understanding and using these terms will help you to think about writing the way we do.

On Thinking New Thoughts

Where do you go to think? Some people take a walk; others sit in a place of worship; others put in earbuds and close their eyes; others take a shower. For most of us, finding a place to think involves reducing distractions and spending time alone. For centuries, the writer alone in a book-lined study, pen in hand, has represented this fact about thinking—it's something we do alone. And further, it shows that writing itself can serve as a way to keep the demands of the outside world at bay.

Now, of course, the writer sitting at a keyboard staring into a screen is never alone. With an internet connection, the screen can instantly be directed wherever the writer chooses: breaking news stories; emails announcing flash sales; top-rated videos; real-time reports on the weather around the world; music playlists; or discussion forums to assist with self-diagnosing the rash that appeared in the mirror this morning. The possible distractions are innumerable and irresistible. While pen and paper may once have served to focus the writer's attention, keyboard and screen connect the writer to the most distracting invention humans have ever created.

The difficulty we face in finding quiet places for reflection would not have surprised the nineteenth century's most famous loner, Henry David Thoreau. However, Thoreau would have been shocked by how connected we are to a virtual world and how disconnected we have become from the real world and from ourselves. In 1845, Thoreau wanted more time to think and write than living in Concord, Massachusetts, allowed, so he took up residence in a small cabin he built for himself on the shore of Walden Pond, a little more than a mile outside of town, and lived there for just over two years. In *Walden; or Life in the Woods*, the book Thoreau wrote reflecting on his experiment living apart from society, he says that he was motivated by a desire "to live deliberately, to front only the essential facts of life, and see if I could not learn what it had to teach, and not, when I came to die, discover that I had not lived."

Being alone for Thoreau was not a deprivation; it was a choice that allowed time and space for introspection, self-reflection, discovery, and writing. In *Walden*, Thoreau maintains that the aloneness experienced by someone deep in thought is different from physical isolation or social alienation. "A man thinking or working," he writes, "is always alone, let him be where he will. Solitude is not measured by the miles of space that intervene between a man and his fellows." Thoreau compares a farmer and a serious college student, both of whom toil in states of solitude:

> The really diligent student in one of the crowded hives of Cambridge College is as solitary as a dervish in the desert. The farmer can work alone in the field or the woods all day, hoeing or chopping, and not feel lonesome, because he is employed; but when he comes home at night he cannot sit down in a room alone, at the mercy of his thoughts, but must be where he can "see the folks," and recreate, and, as he thinks, remunerate himself for his day's solitude; and hence he wonders how the student can sit alone in the house all night and most of the day without ennui and "the blues"; but he does not realize that the student, though in the house, is still at work in *his* field, and chopping in *his* woods, as the farmer in his, and in turn seeks the same recreation and society that the latter does, though it may be a more condensed form of it.

Although the farmer thinks the student alone in the study should be tormented by boredom or deeply depressed, the student is actually like the farmer alone in the fields: focused on the work to be done, moving methodically from task to task. Thoreau's point is not just that their labor is commensurate, but so too is their contentment and their need for social interaction when the day's labors have been exhausted. The difference is this: the farmer needs a field to labor; the student solitude.

Everyone who has experienced hours in front of a blank screen with its flashing cursor knows that time alone with one's thoughts can be excruciating. Thoreau was not unaware of these frustrations: "It is easier to sail many thousand miles through cold and storm and cannibals, in a government ship, with five hundred men and boys to assist one," he maintains, "than it is to explore the private sea, the Atlantic and Pacific Ocean of one's being alone." Although this assertion strikes us as an exaggeration, we agree with Thoreau's larger point that learning to be alone for long periods of time is both a lot of work and essential to the project of self-mastery.

Thoreau's argument about mastery has been subsequently confirmed by the research of the psychologist K. Anders Ericsson, who spent thirty years studying experts from all walks of life — violinists, chess players, golfers, surgeons, firefighters, and even college students. Ericsson and his many collaborators have found that those who are the very best at any given activity spend significantly more time practicing in solitude. These highly skilled people don't just log more hours practicing alone than their peers; they spend that time engaged in what Ericsson calls "deliberate practice," aspiring to acquire skills that are, at any given level of achievement, just beyond their reach. Deliberate practice isn't casual and it can't be faked. Such practice is motivated by the practitioner's desire for mastery in an activity that is larger than the self. For Thoreau, that higher goal was experiential: he wanted to find a way "to live deliberately," something he had to practice every single day while living in his cabin on Walden Pond, where his days were unstructured by the rhythms of the city. He had to push himself. If he hadn't, Thoreau would've just been some guy who sat in a cabin for two years until he got bored enough to move back to the city, an unremarkable character long since lost to the passage of time.

All successful writers engage in the deliberate practice of their craft (even Dadaists committed to "automatic writing" and the Beats, who wrote under the banner "First thought, best thought"). Some writers are at their most focused and creative just after they wake. Toni Morrison, for instance, rises and makes coffee in the early morning when the sky is still dark. She sips her coffee and watches the daylight arrive, and then she is ready to write. Other writers slip off to small cottages or shacks near their homes: this is what Russell Banks and Michael Pollan do and what Virginia Woolf, Roald Dahl, and Thoreau did before them. Most of us, of course, don't have a shack of our own, but we can still learn from the examples of generations of writers who have found that the combination of some form of solitude — a temporary release from noise, worries, and responsibilities — and deliberate practice helps us to access the creative powers of the imagination and the intellect.

Where and how writers construct the spaces of solitude that support them in their efforts to think new thoughts is entirely idiosyncratic. Thoreau found his at Walden Pond (though, famously, he fails to mention that his mother frequently brought him cooked meals). By contrast, novelist Zadie Smith credits two internet-blocking applications (one called Freedom, the other SelfControl) with "creating the time" she needed to complete her novel *NW*. And although it might seem obvious that a writer working on a book called *Quiet*, about the hidden power of introverts, would have gone off somewhere by herself, Susan Cain discovered that, in fact, she couldn't find a way to get started while sitting at her neat desk, alone in her sunlit study. To escape the isolation, Cain settled in at a neighborhood café to work among other people who were also hunched over their laptops. Why did this place become Cain's primary workplace? The café, she says,

> was social, yet its casual, come-and-go-as-you-please nature left me free from unwelcome entanglements and able to "deliberately practice" my writing. I could toggle back and forth between observer and social actor as much as I wanted. I could also control my environment. Each day I chose the location of my table—in the center of the room or along the perimeter—depending on whether I wanted to be seen as well as to see. And I had the option to leave whenever I wanted peace and quiet to edit what I'd written that day.

Cain, who treasures being alone, found the kind of solitude she needed—as well as the inspiration and the stimulation to think new thoughts—in the buzzing hive of a coffee shop. The conditions that Thoreau, Smith, and Cain created to do their best work differ in their particulars, but the authors' solutions share one important characteristic: each solution shows a writer who is conscious of and highly sensitive to the fact that there's a connection between what gets written and where the writing gets produced. To think new thoughts, each writer could not go about business as usual; to think new thoughts, each writer had to put himself or herself in a new place.

Practice Session One: A Browser of Your Own

Habits: orienting, paying attention, working deliberately

Activities: bookmarking, researching

Our working assumption is that you do the bulk of your writing on a screen and that you write in many different locations. No matter what brand of computer you are using, the software designers have made default decisions for you about what they want to be immediately available to you when you are browsing or writing. Whether you work on a screen that belongs to you or on a shared computer, you need to take the time to personalize your screen in ways that help keep you focused while you are writing.

We begin with the browser because this is your portal leading to the vast informational riches on the web and to its potential to become a massive time suck. (One popular online news source has a recurring piece entitled "Websites You Should Be Wasting Your Time On Right Now!") We want you to think about how best to organize your browser so that it minimizes distractions and reinforces your commitment to being curious and creative. Your browser should, in other words, reflect both your personal choices *and* your creative aspirations.

In order to take control of your online life as a writer, you need to choose the browser you intend to use while you are engaged in the deliberate practice of cultivating the habits of the creative mind. For most writers, this means using one browser for surfing the web and another for staying focused. Once you've chosen your writing browser (be it Safari, Firefox, Chrome, Internet Explorer, or some other platform), you will need to familiarize yourself with the way the browser allows you to control the bookmarks that appear in your personalized toolbar. All browsers work pretty much the same way: there's a button you can click on the browser that allows you to bookmark the page you are looking at; once you click that button, you are given the option of storing your bookmark on the browser toolbar or elsewhere. We're going to trust you to figure out the exact procedures for the browser you've chosen. (We recommend searching for instructional videos about your browser on YouTube.)

What bookmarks belong in a writer's browser? We have some recommendations, but what's most important is that your browser shows where you take your mind to be inspired to think new thoughts. With that caveat, here are the bookmarks that we think belong in any writer's browser's toolbar:

- Your school library and/or your local library.
- Your school's portal to research journals. (Depending on your school's resources, this may give you access to JSTOR, EBSCOhost, and/or Project MUSE, all of which archive academic sources, as well as the *Oxford English Dictionary*.)
- Google Scholar.
- Google Images.
- A range of news sources for you to read regularly. (This will help you develop the habit of being knowledgeable about how different sources report and analyze important current events.) To get started, bookmark a local newspaper, one of the leading national newspapers, and a reputable source for international news.

We also recommend you create an account on Zotero or some other cloud-based archiving program that allows you to access your stored bookmarks on any machine that has access to the internet. (Richard could not have written his last book without this amazing research tool.) Once you create a Zotero account, you can download an application that, when loaded into your browser, allows you to save a complete copy of whatever page you are viewing with a single click.

After you've populated your toolbar with these resources, the rest is up to you. You might want to add additional bookmarks for sites that:

- contain trustworthy information relevant to your current research interests;
- inspire you to be a more ambitious thinker;
- provide a public forum for discussing important questions you want to think more about; or
- feature creative work that challenges you to see the world differently.

When you're finished, the toolbar on your preferred browser should be both immediately useful to you and a standing temptation for you to devote more of your free browsing time to pursuing both your higher intellectual aspirations and your creative goals.

Note: for those writers who do not have a dedicated screen of their own to personalize, much of what we assign above can be completed in the cloud by creating a Zotero account. Once you create an account, you can begin to populate your personal library with the kinds of bookmarks we've described. Then when you are composing, you can log into your Zotero account to access your stored bookmarks. This will allow you to make the screen you are using function as if it were your own.

....

Practice Session Two:
The Personalized Word Processor
(or Not)

....

Habits: organizing, orienting, paying attention

Activities: analyzing, selecting

Personalizing your word processor is a trickier business, and if you compose using Google Docs, it is actually not a meaningful activity, since Google controls what appears in its toolbar and what doesn't. Believe it or not, we actually recommend using Google Docs over other commercially available word processing programs for this very reason.

It may seem counterintuitive that we prefer a free, stripped-down word processing program to the turbocharged versions, but the reason we do so is pretty straightforward: open any commercial word processing program and you will be immediately overwhelmed by all the options available to you. This is because these programs are designed to address every imaginable publishing possibility that might arrive in an office (though we've worked in numerous offices and have yet to meet many people who knew how to get the programs to produce documents that actually look the way they want them to). Writers don't need all these options: they need to know how to change fonts and control the margins and the easiest ways to embed charts and images. Google Docs maintains this strict simplicity.

If using Google Docs isn't feasible for you or if you would prefer that your work not automatically be stored in the cloud, we recommend that you explore the options for customizing the toolbar on the word processing program you prefer. (Here, too, you can find instructional videos on YouTube that will help you with this process.) What matters here is not which choice you make, but that you make a conscious choice designed to reduce the distractions you face while composing.

2

....

BEGINNING

....

Confronting the blank screen and the blinking cursor is, for most of us, the hardest moment in the writing process. To get that cursor moving, you need to have something to say, something of interest to others. But how do you just start off being interesting? Where do interesting thoughts come from? It's a mystery — or so it seems.

The three essays in this section discuss how to begin using *Habits of the Creative Mind* to unpack this mystery. The first essay introduces learning's central paradox: when we begin to learn something new, we simultaneously have to unlearn something familiar. A beginning is also an ending. When you unlearn formulaic approaches to writing as argument, you will be on your way to learning how to think seriously about open-ended questions.

But what can you do if you've been given a formulaic topic? In our second essay in this section, we look at how trained writers turn generic questions into opportunities to do original research. All writers who set aside formulaic writing have to become comfortable contending with moments of confusion and uncertainty. In the final essay in this section, we show you how to practice confronting what is unknown to you, so that you can become more comfortable working both with questions that may have no answers and with answers that never settle things once and for all. Getting that blinking cursor moving is always a challenge, but the reward for doing so changes when the challenge is understood to be using your writing to think thoughts that are new to you.

On Unlearning

When students enter our writing classes, they often bring with them a set of rules from high school that they rely on to define good writing. They believe every paragraph should start with a topic sentence that states the paragraph's main point. They are certain all good essays have five sections or paragraphs: an introduction that states the essay's thesis; three descriptive body paragraphs, each of which discusses a different example that supports the essay's thesis; and a conclusion that restates what has been said in the previous sections. And finally, they think no good essay ever uses the word *I*.

I — or rather we! — assume you are familiar with these rules, since they've been repeated in writing classrooms for decades. Good grades tend to be assigned to writing that follows these rules, but do these rules *really* produce good writing? Think about it: When was the last time you ran across a five-paragraph essay outside of school? Try looking for one in a news source, a magazine, a book, or even a collection of essays. You might find a modified version of one in an op-ed piece, but most of the writing you find that has any power will be organized quite differently. The five-paragraph essay, it turns out, is a very limited form, one best suited to the work of making and supporting simple claims. (For teachers uninterested in teaching writing, the five-paragraph essay has the virtue of being easy to skim, and thus easy to grade.)

In college classes, professors often expect students' writing to do a kind of work that is well beyond the reach of the five-paragraph essay: contending with complexity. You may have had a professor who asked you to develop an argument by working with a handful of original sources, each with a competing point of view; or to support a new interpretation of a text not discussed in class; or to synthesize a semester's worth of lectures into a thoughtful reflection on a multifaceted problem. When professors compose assignments like these, they assume you know how to use your writing to grapple with a genuine problem, puzzle, or question; they assume you've got something else in your writing quiver besides the formula for the five-paragraph theme.

So why don't we just give you a new set of rules? A set of rules capacious enough to provide directions for handling the range of writing tasks college students encounter—the response paper in introductory history, the seminar project in advanced economics, the seven-to-eight-page argument for a 300-level psychology or politics or anthropology class? As appealing as this solution is, it's not one that is available to us—or to you—because there's not one set of rules for generating good writing that works within any single discipline, let alone across multiple disciplines. The reason for this is not, as is often supposed, that any judgment of writing quality is inevitably arbitrary, but rather that writing quality is always a function of context. Thus, what makes for a good paper in a literature class doesn't automatically make for a good paper in a history class or an econ class; indeed, it may not even make for a good paper in a literature class taught by a different professor.

How, then, does anyone in any discipline learn how to write about questions that require complex, nuanced responses? The first step involves unlearning the rules that are at the core of the five-paragraph essay. Taking that first step may seem impossible. We can't unlearn how to walk or how to talk. These habits are so deeply ingrained that it would take a catastrophe of some kind (either psychological or physical) to unseat them. And we can't unlearn how to ride a bike or how to swim; we may forget how to over time, but when we return to these activities after a long hiatus, our challenge is not to learn how to do them as if for the first time, but to remember what's involved in keeping the bicycle upright or our body afloat and moving through the water.

Writing is unlike these other activities because each act of writing is not a straightforward repetition of what you've written before. Writing something new requires that you make choices about why you're writing, whom you're writing for, what you think, and what you want your writing to accomplish. So when we say you should unlearn what you learned about writing in school, we mean we want you to actively resist the idea that writing is governed by a set of universal rules which, if followed, will clearly communicate the writer's ideas to the reader. We can't tell you to forget what you've learned (that would have the same paradoxical effect as telling you not to think about an elephant); and we can't say you shouldn't have been taught the rules governing the five-paragraph essay because, within an educational system dominated by the industry of standardized testing, you had to be able to demonstrate that you could produce writing that follows those rules. What we are asking you to do is to question the two foundational assumptions that motivate teachers to assign five-paragraph essays: namely, that writing's central function is to generate arguments and that the very best writing does this in ways that are simple, straightforward, and immediately understandable by all.

What do we propose in place of these assumptions? That you practice the habits of mind of experienced writers. Experienced writers tend to be curious and attentive. They choose to engage deeply with sources, ideas, people, and the world they live in. They are mentally flexible, self-reflective, and open to new ways of thinking, attributes that allow them to adapt to unfamiliar circumstances and problems. And they are persistent, resisting distraction and disappointment, accepting that writing down thoughts which haven't been written before is hard work. When you commit yourself to practicing these habits—curiosity, attentiveness, openness, flexibility, reflectiveness, and persistence—you will also be committing yourself to making a habit of creativity, the practice of inventing novel and useful connections, compelling ideas, and thoughtful prose. As you delve into *Habits of the Creative Mind*, you'll see that we've designed the book to give you practice developing these habits. Working your way through the book won't lead to mastery of a formula for good writing; instead you'll develop the habits of mind that increase your sensitivity to context and that allow you to use your writing to explore the unknown. You'll be practicing using your writing to show to others and yourself how your mind—not *any* mind, not *every* mind, but *your* particular mind—works on a problem.

....

Practice Session One: An Institutional Autobiography

....

Practice: beginning, orienting, paying attention

Activity: note taking, reflecting, writing

"On Unlearning" makes a series of generalizations about the current state of secondary education and, more specifically, about what students are taught to think writing is for. But we know our description isn't true for every student in every classroom. So, for this practice session, we want you to reconstruct your personal history as a reader and as a writer in school. What were your formative experiences? Was there a teacher who helped you significantly improve your writing? A specific assignment? Were there events that discouraged you from thinking of yourself as a writer? Or as a creative person?

After you've spent time reflecting, remembering, and taking notes, we want you to write up your own "institutional autobiography," in which you document and discuss your experiences with reading and writing in school. Your autobiography should present an account of both moments of learning and moments of unlearning or frustration. Ideally, you will be able to refer directly to papers you've written in the past. (Maybe they're stored on your hard drive or in your email archive.) Your autobiography will provide a snapshot of how you evaluate yourself as a reader and a writer at the beginning of your time working with *Habits of the Creative Mind*. As you move through the book's essays and practice sessions, you can return to your autobiography to see if your sense of what reading and writing are for has changed as a result of your efforts to use writing as a technology for thinking new thoughts.

Practice Session Two: How Writers Write

Habits: beginning, exploring, paying attention

Activities: annotating, note taking, writing

At the end of *Habits of the Creative Mind*, we've included one collaboratively authored reading and four single-authored readings, one of which is, in its original form, a single paragraph long. We'd like you to choose one of these readings to explore our assertion that essays show a mind at work on a problem. If we're right about this, it means that idea-rich essays offer the reader an opportunity to learn how the essay writer's mind works. For this to happen, though, the reader has to guard against the idea that there's one way to write well, one way to make a convincing argument, one use for writing.

In the reading you've selected, annotate the essay by identifying where you see signs of the writer's curiosity, attentiveness, openness, flexibility, reflectiveness, persistence, or creativity. Also note places where the writer breaks what you thought were rules of writing. Keep track of where the writer makes surprising choices, writing in ways you thought were risky or violated the rules. Then consider how, if your mind were at work on the same problem, your essay would differ from the one you've chosen to examine. After you've annotated the essay, and after you've identified moments when the writer has made interesting or puzzling moves, draft a report on what you've learned about how the writer you've engaged with works on a problem.

....

Practice Session Three: Explore Educational Reform

....

Habits: beginning, connecting, exploring

Activities: comparing, researching, writing

Can curiosity and creativity be learned? Unlearned? Relearned? For this practice session, we'd like you to work with Danielle Allen's "What Is Education For?" (included in the Readings section, pp. 270–81), Francine Prose's "Close Reading: Learning to Write by Learning to Read" (*Atlantic*, 2006), and Ken Robinson's "Do Schools Kill Creativity?" (TED, 2006). Allen, Prose, and Robinson are all interested in educational reform. After reading the pieces by Allen and by Prose and after watching the lecture by Robinson, spend time considering how to answer these three questions: Why does each of them think education should be reformed? Where do their ideas for reform come into conflict with one another? What is your own sense of what education is or might be for? After answering these questions, write a response essay in which your goal is to convene a conversation between these thinkers and to then move the discussion forward. You're not establishing who's right and who's wrong; instead you're using the words of these thinkers to generate meaningful insight into the challenges and the possibilities of educational reform. (For an example of what this might look like, return to the essay "On Habits" and review the "conversation" we develop between the self-help books of Dale Carnegie and Stephen Covey and our own effort to move the discussion about habits in a new direction with *Habits of the Creative Mind*.)

On Letting Go of Writing-by-Formula

....

In math and science, a formula is a hard-and-fast rule or fact. The chemical formula for water, for example, is H_2O, and the algebraic formula that defines the equivalence of energy and mass is $E = mc^2$. The beauty of such formulas is that they remain true, regardless of when or where they are used. Formulas in cooking, which we usually call recipes, are sometimes more flexible. If you're making a vanilla cake and you use a little less flour than the recipe calls for, you'll still end up with a cake at the end of the process. But if you substitute baking soda for the baking powder listed in the recipe, you'll push kitchen chemistry past its point of flexibility; what comes out of the oven will look more like a pancake than a cake.

If we shift our attention to human communication, we can see how cultural formulas differ from scientific formulas. When applied to culture, the primary meaning of *formula* is "a set form of words for use in a ceremony or ritual." Most events involving human communication — purchasing something in a store, getting a child to school, quitting a job — aren't ceremonies or rituals and, thus, aren't governed by strict formulas. And even when the focus is narrowed to a specific ceremony or ritual, the cultural formula for what to say isn't universal, like a scientific formula; rather, it is context-specific and subject to change over time. Take the marriage vow: the formula for what to say depends on the country in which the ceremony is to occur, whether the vow is to be made in a secular or a religious setting, and, if the setting is religious, the denominations of the participants. In the Episcopal Church, for example, the formula for what the bride and groom vow has changed over time: prior to 1922, the bride vowed "to love, cherish, and obey" the groom; since 1922, brides and grooms have vowed "to love and to cherish" one another. As of 2012, Episcopal churches have the option of consecrating the wedding vows of same-sex couples.

At their strongest, cultural formulas can only loosely define the conventions that govern a given ritual or ceremony. How loosely? Enter a church of a different denomination or a mosque, synagogue, or ashram and the formula for creating a marriage bond changes. Find the right house of worship and you can hear the couple exchange vows they've written themselves. And if you head over to City Hall to watch a couple get married by a justice of the peace, you'll find the cultural formula pared down to its legal essentials: the presiding authority oversees an exchange of vows; there's a witness or two to affirm the vows were exchanged; and there's the signing of documents afterward.

Popular entertainment is similarly formulaic. Many of you are likely to be familiar with the formula for the horror film. ("Don't go in there!") And you may even recognize the formula for parodying horror films. ("I know only dumb people in horror movies go into places like this alone, but here I go." Screams follow.) Formulas like these, which build on audience expectations, can be picked up either by watching a bunch of popular horror films or by having someone who knows the formula tell it to you.

If the formulas that govern everything from wedding vows to movie plots are flexible, what about the formulas that govern the essay? Are they similarly flexible? We'd be surprised if you thought so, since the tendency of writing teachers from elementary school onward is to represent the recipes or templates for generating the kind of writing valued in school as hard and fast. We, on the other hand, would say that following these formulas does not produce writing that is thoughtful or compelling or reflective; it just produces writing that can be graded according to the degree to which it has followed the assigned formula. When a student is asked to demonstrate information retention, as in an essay exam, formulaic writing is an entirely appropriate mode of response. But when the goal is independent thinking, original insights, or the production of writing that others will read voluntarily, writing that follows a formula is incapable of delivering the goods.

A formula for originality is a contradiction in terms. If your writing is going to help you to think new thoughts, it will be because you are using your writing to practice curiosity, creativity, attentiveness, and engagement. The only way to produce thoughtful prose is to actually be thoughtful; the only way to produce writing that is compelling is to feel compelled by ideas, events, and issues; the only way to produce writing that is reflective is to regularly engage in acts of reflection. In all of these realms, writing is not filling in blank spaces on a form; it is the act of exploring the possible.

. . . . .

At this point in the first draft of this essay, we intended to demonstrate how we distinguish between writing that's formulaic and writing that's driven by curiosity. But we discovered that a funny thing happens when you write about writing-by-formula: every path we went down to illustrate what was wrong with formulaic writing ended up being formulaic itself. If we were teaching a class, we'd ask our students to brainstorm with us about the paths we might take after we've discussed how the meaning of *formula* changes with the context. Since we can't do that with you, our readers, we're going to ask you to join us in a thought experiment about the options available to us. We'll go through them in turn.

Path One: Show why the writing in our curiosity-driven classes is better than the writing produced under other approaches. "Piece of cake!" we say. Given that we are arguing for using writing as a technology for producing thoughts that are new to the writer, it seemed only logical that we would then go on to provide our readers with an example from one of our classes that shows what "nonformulaic" writing looks like. Going in this direction felt natural, necessary, and appropriate.

It also felt familiar. And this is why, eventually, we had to admit that it didn't work. It's not that we lack examples of writing from our classes that we feel amply demonstrate the advantages of developing the habits of the creative mind. Indeed, we have showcased our students' work in a number of other essays in this book. But when we tried to frame our argument about curiosity-driven writing, we found ourselves trapped in the solipsistic activity of arguing for the superiority of writing that we ourselves have assessed as superior.

There's another problem with moving the discussion of curiosity-driven writing to examples from our own classrooms; when it comes to making our case, we hold all the cards. We don't have to show you the writing that didn't succeed; we don't have to take you through the portfolios of students who didn't make progress over the course of the semester. We just have to find examples that prove our point. And then you, the reader, have only two options: you can either agree that we've proven what we've set out to prove or you can argue that our example isn't actually writing that explores new ideas and possibilities; it's just writing to a new formula.

So much for using examples from our classes in this context. Next!

Path Two: Show why the writing produced in classes that emphasize formulaic writing is bad. "Easy as pie!" we say. To head off in this direction, all we needed was an exemplary five-paragraph essay. After much research, though, we had to concede that there was no archive of "the universally agreed-upon greatest five-paragraph essays in history" for us to draw on. We found a sample five-paragraph theme posted on a college website that seemed promising at first, but we then discovered that the sample had been copied without attribution from an online paper mill. Even the paper mill sites themselves proved to be a poor source for exemplary five-paragraph essays: it turns out these sites don't claim that the writing they are selling is actually good; they just say it's what your professors are looking for.

Our inability to find a compelling example of the five-paragraph essay led us to see that we were arguing against a phantom. We can search for "prize-winning five-paragraph essays," but no prize winners come up. We can point to a testing industry that provides models for students to emulate with clear thesis statements, clear supporting evidence and analysis, and clear structures, but we can't find truly good examples of formulaic writing that conveys important thoughts. In fact, as we continued to drill down on this problem, we were surprised to discover that the critique of formulaic writing has a long history. Michelle Tremmel, writing in 2011, found more than 120 articles published over the past fifty years in professional journals about teaching that were "clearly against the five-paragraph theme."

Our failed search for the exemplary five-paragraph essay showed us that we had set off on the wrong task. We didn't need to develop an argument against writing by formula because that argument has already been made many times over—to, as far as we have been able to determine, very little effect. Instead, we needed to ask a different question.

Path Three: Why is it that students are taught to excel at a form of writing that isn't actually "good writing"? Our answer to this question, when it finally came, surprised us: teaching students to produce formulaic essays and arguments has never actually been about teaching students to write like good writers. It has been about teaching them to be clear and rule-abiding language users. In other words, the goal of those who teach students to follow writing formulas and our goal in teaching you how to practice the habits of the creative mind are fundamentally different.

Now what? Make a joke? We believe in the power of humor to create opportunities that reason alone can't make available. And, the truth is, we are in a funny situation: two writing teachers have given themselves the worst writing prompt ever: "make an unconventional argument against convention."

Change direction. If we really want to shift the conversation about writing from following a formula to practicing habits of mind, we need to ask some new questions: What habits of mind are being encouraged by questions that ask for the faithful reproduction of the main points in a lecture? Or by questions that ask the writer to agree or disagree with a simple explanation for a complex event? Or by an assessment system that stresses clarity over shades of meaning?

If you take some time to think about these questions and to reflect on your own experiences producing writing in school, we think your reflections are likely to support our contention that the emphasis in your education has been on habits of order, clarity, and concision more than exploration, questioning, and the joys of digression.

We want you to practice writing differently. We want you to ask difficult questions and get lost in the rabbit holes of research; we want you to know what it's like to get trapped in dead ends and to learn to write your way out of such impasses. When you make writing this way a habit, you will have learned the art of using your writing to reveal the complexity of what previously seemed straightforward, obvious, or familiar.

And so, we decided that the best way to show you the habits of experienced writers at work is to do exactly what we've done here: document just how much work goes into resisting the allure of the familiar and the easily proven.

. . . . .

How then do experienced writers, who have made a habit of being genuinely curious, avoid reproducing predictable arguments when writing about long debated topics? Certain topics seem to invite predictable writing and thinking. One of the most clichéd topics in high school and college writing curricula, for example, is gun control. Given the differences between those who favor gun control and those who favor gun rights, it seems implausible that writers on either side of this debate could introduce anything that would alter where anyone stands on this issue. Pro/con, liberal/conservative, right/wrong. There doesn't appear to be a lot of room for movement.

But there is *some* room. Let's consider the first few paragraphs of the introduction to *Reducing Gun Violence in America: Informing Policy with Evidence and Analysis*, an edited collection published soon after the mass shooting at Sandy Hook Elementary School in 2012.

> The role of guns in violence, and what should be done, are subjects of intense debate in the United States and elsewhere. But certain facts are not debatable. More than 31,000 people died from gunshot wounds in the United States in 2010. Because the victims are disproportionately young, gun violence is one of the leading causes of premature mortality in the United States. In addition to these deaths, in 2010, there were an estimated 337,960 nonfatal violent crimes committed with guns, and 73,505 persons were treated in hospital emergency departments for nonfatal gunshot wounds. The social and economic costs of gun violence in America are also enormous.
>
> Despite the huge daily impact of gun violence, most public discourse on gun policy is centered on mass shootings in public places. Such incidents are typically portrayed as random acts by severely mentally ill individuals which are impossible to predict or prevent. Those who viewed, heard, or read news stories on gun policy might conclude the following: (1) mass shootings, the mentally ill, and assault weapons are the primary concerns; (2) gun control laws disarm law-abiding citizens without affecting criminals' access to guns; (3) there is no evidence that gun control laws work; and (4) the public has no appetite for strengthening current gun laws. Yet all of the evidence in this book counters each of these misperceptions with facts to the contrary.

At first glance, the moves that Daniel W. Webster and Jon S. Vernick, coauthors of the introduction to *Reducing Gun Violence*, make here are likely to seem familiar. They establish the importance of their topic by referencing what they present as undebatable facts. Next, they discuss popular thinking about gun violence and legislation. And then they announce that their book will debunk the four major misperceptions about gun violence in turn.

This description of the way Webster and Vernick build their argument misses their most important move, though: they want to shift the context of the discussion of gun violence away from headline-grabbing mass shootings in order to focus their reader's attention on the high rate of gun violence in the United States. The research they have done documents the undeniable costs of this violence, both in lives lost and in medical expenses for the roughly one hundred thousand people injured or killed by guns in the United States every year. Webster and Vernick then point to one of the problems that limits our ability to discuss workable ways to reduce gun violence: *despite* the prevalence of gun violence in the United States, mass shootings are the only instances of gun violence that get sustained attention from the media.

What Webster and Vernick do next is further evidence of curiosity-driven minds at work on a problem: they detail the conclusions that reasonable people might make from how mass shootings are covered in the media; they *imagine* themselves in the place of such viewers and list the reasons why reducing gun violence seems impossible as a result. They haven't, in other words, produced an unsupportable "most people think" statement; they've made a connection between popular opinions and what mass media focuses on—namely, mass shootings. In making this connection, Webster and Vernick have implicitly established a relationship of causality: because most people encounter information about gun violence in the context of mass shootings, they reach certain predictable conclusions about both the means and the possibility of curbing gun violence. Webster and Vernick promise to show how these conclusions no longer hold once the context is shifted from mass shootings to gun violence in general. What is required, they argue, is a shift in our attention.

Can we imagine someone being persuaded to rethink gun violence as a result of Webster and Vernick's argument? In so doing, do we imagine someone who has thought about the issue a great deal? If this person *is* persuaded, would the change in position be consequential for the person? Does this personal change also have the potential to be consequential on a larger scale? We'd answer all of these questions in the affirmative. In fact, we'd go further and say that asking questions of this sort is a good way to start a conversation about how to distinguish writing that emerges from habits of the creative mind and writing that is done to confirm beliefs the writer already holds: the first kind of writing imagines readers who can consider multiple and conflicting ideas; the second seeks out readers who already agree.

Could a less experienced student writer produce an essay about gun control that made moves similar to those we found in the opening paragraphs of Webster and Vernick's introduction? We think so, but that writer would have to be genuinely interested in gun control as a question to be understood, rather than as an issue upon which one first takes a stand and then sets out in search of evidence supporting that stand. That student would have to want to spend time doing research that drilled down into questions about gun control, and that student would have to believe that staking out a position on gun control has consequences that extend far beyond the fulfillment of a paper assignment.

If such a student were working in a course that encouraged exploring questions rather than following a formula for putting together an argument, that student would have the chance to experience just how much is involved in understanding a complex issue in depth and what it means to use one's writing to think new thoughts. And this, finally, is why we believe that shifting the teaching of writing from formulas to habits matters. This approach encourages the creation of classroom practices that allow inexperienced writers to cultivate curiosity, to risk experiment and exploration, and to engage with the most pressing questions of our time.

....

Practice Session One: Are You Persuaded by Persuasion?

....

Habits: beginning, exploring, reflecting

Activities: analyzing, researching, writing

Using the web as your archive, find an example of a persuasive essay that has been truly influential and that *actually changes your mind* on an issue. See if you can find an example written by a professional journalist or an experienced writer from a newspaper, an important magazine, or an academic journal. Spend at least thirty minutes searching for an essay that meets these criteria.

After you've found a truly persuasive essay, or after you've put in thirty minutes looking for one, take at least twenty minutes to write about your search. What challenges did you encounter? If you found a persuasive essay, was it about a topic that previously mattered to you, or was it about something you hadn't thought much about? What did you learn about persuasive writing as your search progressed? What's the value of doing this exercise?

Practice Session Two: If It's Not a Five-Paragraph Essay, What Is It?

Habits: beginning, paying attention, speculating

Activities: analyzing, note taking, writing

Select one of the five readings included in this book, read it, and then reread its introductory paragraphs with care. Spend at least twenty minutes writing about how the writer has, or in one case the writers have, composed the introduction. How does the writer choose to launch the article? How does the writer get the reader interested in the topic at hand? How does the introduction differ from a conventional five-paragraph-essay introduction? Does it share any qualities with the introductions you learned to write in school?

Next, review the entire reading and spend at least thirty minutes taking notes about how the writer exercises curiosity; connects ideas, sources, and information in surprising ways; and keeps the reader interested from the beginning of the piece to the end. In other words, explore how the article or essay *works*.

Based on what you've discovered about how the piece you selected is put together, what would you say governed the writer's decisions about how to organize the work? Does the writer follow a set of rules or a formula that you can identify? Has the writer broken rules you were taught? Spend at least forty-five minutes writing about the relationship between the writer's curiosity and how the essay is organized.

On Confronting the Unknown

In his book *Deep Survival: Who Lives, Who Dies, and Why*, Laurence Gonzales recounts the story of seventeen-year-old Juliane Koepcke, who was seated next to her mother on a flight with ninety other passengers when the plane was struck by lightning, causing it to go into a nosedive. The next thing Koepcke recalled was being strapped into her seat, but outside the plane, hurtling earthward toward the canopy of the Peruvian jungle.

What would you think if you were in Koepcke's place at that moment? Gonzales tells us that Koepcke's mind was not filled with shrieking terror, or a hastily pulled together prayer, or feelings of regret. No, Koepcke remembered "thinking that the jungle trees below looked just like cauliflowers." She passed out while still falling and, when she regained consciousness sometime later, she was on the ground, still strapped into her seat. Her collarbone was broken. There was no sign of anyone else. She decided that the planes and helicopters she could hear flying above would never be able to see her because the trees nearly blocked out the sky, so she began to walk out of the jungle.

Central to Gonzales's thesis about resiliency is that those who survive a life-threatening crisis see the future as unmapped. Koepcke, falling two miles upside down through a storm, didn't think the obvious thought — that her life was coming to an end. Instead, she was struck by the appearance of the Peruvian forest from above. And when she came to later, having crashed through the canopy, she didn't think — or didn't only think — the obvious thought about what lay ahead for a seventeen-year-old girl without her glasses, walking alone in a jungle, barefoot, slapping the ground with her one remaining shoe to frighten off the snakes that she couldn't see well enough to avoid. She walked for eleven days while she was, as Gonzales described it, "being literally eaten alive by leeches and strange tropical insects." On the eleventh day, Koepcke found a hut and collapsed inside. The next day, as chance would have it, three hunters discovered her and got her to a doctor.

Gonzales is interested in this question: Why did Koepcke survive this crash, while "the other survivors took the same eleven days to sit down and die"? Gonzales identifies a number of reasons, besides blind luck, for Koepcke's survival. First, rather than follow rules, she improvised. Second, although she was afraid, as the other survivors surely were, she used that fear as a resource for action. And third, while better-equipped travelers succumbed to much lesser challenges, Koepcke had "an inner resource, a state of mind" that allowed her to make do with what the moment offered.

As Gonzales pursues his research further, he finds other traits that resilient people share in common: they use fear to focus their thoughts; they find humor in their predicaments; they remain positive. The list goes on, but the item that most interests us is Gonzales's admonition that to survive a crisis, one must "see the beauty" in the new situation:

> Survivors are attuned to the wonder of the world. The appreciation of beauty, the feeling of awe, opens the senses. When you see something beautiful, your pupils actually dilate. This appreciation not only relieves stress and creates strong motivation, but it allows you to take in new information more effectively.

When we first read this, we wondered: If it's possible for someone to be attuned to the beauty of the world when confronted by a situation that is *life threatening*, could writers in far less dire circumstances cultivate this attunement as a habit of mind?

Here's why this connection suggested itself to us: from our years teaching writing, we know how terrifying and humbling the confrontation with the blank screen and the flashing cursor can be—for beginning writers and experienced writers alike. This confrontation is not life threatening, of course, but it can nevertheless trigger fears: Do I have anything worth saying? Can I make myself understood? Will the struggle be worth it in the end? These questions arise because the act of writing, when used as a technology for thinking new thoughts, takes us to the edge of our own well-marked path and points us toward the uncharted realms beyond.

Ultimately, each time a writer sits down to write, he or she chooses just how far to venture into that unknown territory. To our way of thinking, the writing prompt, properly conceived, is an invitation to embark into unmapped worlds, to improvise, to find unexpected beauty in the challenges that arise when the writer ventures into the unknown. We know from experience, though, that learning to approach writing this way takes practice, and that without such practice, beginning writers reject the invitation to explore and produce writing that huddles around whatever is obvious and easiest to defend.

We have designed the practice sessions in this book to help you use your writing to bring you to the edge of your understanding, to the innumerable places where you can encounter what is unknown to you. The more you practice using your writing in this way, the further you will be able to take your explorations; you'll find yourself moving from writing about what is unknown to you to what is more generally unknown to others, and then on to what may well be unknowable. Making this journey again and again is the essence of the examined life; the writing you do along the way tracks your ongoing encounter with the complexity of human experience. The more you do it, the more you know; and the more you know, the more connections you can make as you work through your next encounter with what is unknown to you. You'll never make it to absolute knowledge, but the more you practice, the more comfortable you'll be with saying, "I don't know, but I'm sure I can figure it out."

Or so we say.

We can pose our position as a challenge: Can you make your writing trigger an inner journey that is akin to falling from a plane over the Amazon, with everything that seemed solid and certain just moments ago suddenly giving way, question leading to question, until you land on the fundamental question, "What do I know with certainty?"

We all can count on being faced with challenges of comparable magnitude over the course of our lives — by the death of those we love; the experiences of aging, disease, separation, and suffering; a crisis in faith; a betrayal of trust. Writing, properly practiced, is one way to cultivate the habits of mind found in those who are resilient in moments of crisis: openness, optimism, calm, humor, and delight in beauty.

Practice Session One: Experiencing the Unexpected

Habits: beginning, connecting, orienting
Activities: reflecting, remembering, writing

One could say that seeing the future as unmapped is something children do and that part of growing up is learning to have reasonable expectations about what the future holds. What interests Gonzales are the differences between how survivors and nonsurvivors respond once disaster strikes. When the plane you're in splits in half miles above the earth, it's reasonable to assume that your future is mapped: you are going to die. Gonzales's contention is that those who respond to disaster by suspending their sense that the future is known have, perhaps paradoxically, a better chance of surviving.

The thing is, you don't know how you're going to respond to hugely significant and unexpected events until they happen. What is the most unexpected event that has taken place in your life so far? What made it unexpected? How did you respond to this confrontation with the unknown? In the event, did you settle into the moment, or did your sense of what the future held remain constant and unshaken?

Spend thirty minutes writing a profile of how you responded to the unexpected. Feel free to discuss what you would do differently if given another chance, knowing now what you didn't know then.

Practice Session Two: Experiencing Unexpected Thoughts

Habits: beginning, connecting, reflecting
Activities: reflecting, remembering, writing

The kinds of crises that interest Gonzales have a cinematic quality to them: planes split apart in midair; a hiker is trapped, miles from anyone else, with his arm pinned by a boulder; a mountain climber dangles over the edge of a cliff, his partner unable to pull him to safety. (Indeed, the last two cases have been made into major motion pictures.) But writers rarely find themselves in predicaments of this kind; their crises tend to be internal and to center on getting to the heart of a matter, finding a way to express a fugitive truth, struggling to put a new thought into words.

What has been the most striking event in your *mental* life? A crisis of faith? An existential crisis? A realization that your way of thinking about love or friendship, truth or beauty, justice or politics, or any other of the concepts that are central to human experience was grounded in a false assumption? How did you respond to this confrontation with the unknown? What happened to your experience of time while this event unfolded? Did you find yourself living from moment to moment, or did your sense of what the future held remain clear?

Spend at least an hour writing a profile of how you responded to the most striking event in your mental life. Feel free to discuss what you would do differently if given another chance, knowing now what you didn't know then.

....

Practice Session Three: Rebecca Solnit Confronts the Unexpected

....

Habits: beginning, connecting, paying attention

Activities: analyzing, annotating, reading

In "Occupied Territory" (included in the Reading section, pp. 302–08), Rebecca Solnit begins with an unexpected event: on a nature hike, lost in her thoughts, she's suddenly confronted by a large, angry, snarling dog. In tales of survival and resiliency, it is common to stress the hardships confronted and overcome, as well as acts of courage and ingenuity. As you read Solnit's thoughts after her frightening encounter with the dog off its leash, how would you characterize her way of responding to the shock she has received? In writing up your analysis, make certain to map Solnit's mental movements across the entire essay. Where does she go after telling the story about the dog and its owner? Where is she when she ends her essay?

....

Practice Session Four: Exploring the Edge of Understanding

....

Habits: beginning, exploring, questioning

Activities: mapping, writing

How we respond to "the unknown" can take many forms. In "The Edge of Identity," included in the Readings section at the end of this book, Rachel Aviv chronicles the efforts of Hannah Upp's family and friends to make sense of her repeated disappearances. In "The Fourth State of Matter" (*New Yorker*, 1996), Jo Ann Beard is halfway through her essay describing her day in detail before she reveals that it's "November 1, 1991, the last day of the first part of my life." In "An Epidemic of Fear: How Panicked Parents Skipping Shots Endanger Us All" (*Wired*, 2009), Amy Wallace presents the anti-vaccination movement as "a challenge to traditional science that crosses party, class, and religious lines." In each instance, the writers present a case study of an encounter with the unknown and subsequent efforts to make sense of responses to that encounter. Select one of these three essays and write a piece that tracks the writer's response to her encounter with the unknown. What does the writer know at the end of her piece that she didn't know at the beginning?

3

PAYING ATTENTION

I s it possible to write without paying attention? At first the question seems absurd: How could words move from your brain to your keyboard if you weren't paying attention? Writing doesn't just happen. And yet people text while walking and even while driving, which shows that writing happens all the time without one's full attention. And of course, students can now write papers while also surfing the net and snapchatting their friends.

Funnily enough, a common response to the mistakes that happen as a result of being distracted is the command to "pay attention." You step off the curb into oncoming traffic and are pulled back to safety by a friend just before you would have been hit. "Pay attention!" You're sitting in class daydreaming when your teacher calls on you. "Pay attention!" You're in a crowd and walk directly into a stranger. "Pay attention!" In each case, the command arrives too late: it's less helpful advice than it is a stinging rebuke.

We want you to think of writing not as a way to prove you *were* paying attention but as a way *of* paying attention. To this end, we open this section with an essay that explores how drawing can be used to train the mind to focus and the eye to see. Next, we show you how you can practice using your writing to make sense of the world. And in our third essay, we look at how words take on meaning in context. When you use writing to look at *how* you look, you are practicing being engaged with and interested in the world.

On Learning to See

When Betty Edwards started teaching high school art classes in the late 1960s, she was baffled as she watched her students having trouble drawing simple, familiar objects. If they could see that the orange was *in front of* the green bottle, why did they draw the two objects *next to* each other? Why had her students' ability to express themselves verbally and to reason mathematically improved from kindergarten to high school, but their ability to draw hadn't changed much since the third grade? And when her students eventually figured out how to produce drawings that were more accurate, why did the improvement seem to take place all at once rather than gradually?

Around the time that Edwards was pondering why students who learned easily in academic classes had so much difficulty in art class, neuroscientists Roger W. Sperry and Michael Gazzaniga began publishing reports that suggested that the two sides of the human brain did different kinds of mental work. The left hemisphere, where language was typically housed, was more systematic and linear. The right hemisphere was more visual, spatial, and synthetic. Once Sperry and Gazzaniga's research got picked up by the popular press, it was reduced to a simple binary opposition: the right brain is creative and the left brain is analytical.

Edwards used this research to make sense of the difficulty her students had seeing what was right in front of them as well as the breakthroughs they experienced when they suddenly began to see differently. In Edwards's view, students were rewarded in their academic classes for being verbal and analytical thinkers; they were required, one could say, to be left-brained. But to draw well, they needed access to visual, perceptual, and synthetic thought; they needed to find a way to see with the right brain. To trigger this hemispheric shift for her students, Edwards developed exercises that quieted the verbal, analytical, and systematizing thinking rewarded elsewhere in the curriculum, so that visual, creative, and associative thinking could come to the fore. As she developed these exercises, Edwards was beginning to understand that in order to learn how to draw, her students had to stop naming what they were trying to render on the page and start seeing what was in front of them in a new way—as related lines and connected spaces without names.

If they stopped saying "hand," for example, they could learn to stop drawing the symbol for a hand (five stick fingers at the end of a stick arm) and could instead begin to see the intricate pattern that is made by a particular hand resting on the edge of a particular keyboard.

Edwards's explanation of the brain's two dominant operational modes makes a kind of immediate, intuitive sense; indeed, it makes it sound like all you really have to do to draw is learn how to toggle the switch that puts your right brain in control. The truth, though, is that the workings of the human brain are more complicated than the left-brain right-brain model suggests. More current research in neuroscience has found that neural activity in the right hemisphere is *correlated* with creative and divergent thinking and that neural activity in the left hemisphere is *correlated* with analytic and convergent thinking. So, while it is true that the right part of your brain contributes a good deal to your creative potential, it is also true that your whole brain has to work in concert for you to engage in creative work.

In *A Whole New Mind*, Daniel Pink describes attending a drawing class based on the methods developed by Edwards and learning just how difficult it is to get the hand, the eye, and the brain to work together on this new way of seeing. His first attempt at drawing a self-portrait while looking at his face in a mirror was simply terrible. The eyes, nose, and lips were clumsy cartoon versions of these basic components of the human face. His placement of these features was equally cartoonish. Pink couldn't draw what was right in front of him, the most familiar, recognizable part of himself, because his preconceptions about faces—which his teacher called "remembered symbols from childhood"—blinded him to the actual contours of the face looking back at him in the mirror. To draw better, Pink needed to stop naming, analyzing, and judging what he saw and practice seeing and sketching lines, patterns, relationships, and relationships between relationships. He had to practice finding increments of simplicity in complex patterns of lines and spaces.

We believe that the kind of seeing Edwards aims to trigger through her teaching practice is a specific instance of the kind of seeing that lies at the core of creative thinking. Indeed, Edwards herself says that "this ability to see things differently has many uses in life aside from drawing—not the least of which is creative problem solving." So, although it surely seems contradictory, we adapted a couple of Edwards's exercises meant to restrain the dominance of language to serve our own interest in having you think differently about the role of language in the creative process.

Practice Session One: Drawing a Self-Portrait

Habits: paying attention, persisting, working deliberately

Activities: analyzing, drawing, reflecting, writing

Draw a self-portrait. Start by finding a spot with a mirror and plenty of light where you can work comfortably for at least thirty minutes. Using a pencil and a blank sheet of paper, draw your face. Do your best, and don't give up before you've got all your facial features looking back at you. Take the full thirty minutes.

Next, look carefully at the features you included and their relationships to one another. Why did your portrait turn out as it did? What went right? Where did you successfully transform perception into image? What went wrong? What did you *not see* as you were drawing? How did you feel while you were completing this exercise? How did you feel when you were done? Why?

As a final step, take at least fifteen minutes to write an assessment of the act of seeing that generated your self-portrait.

Practice Session Two: The World Upside-Down

Habits: paying attention, persisting, working deliberately

Activities: drawing, reflecting, writing

For this exercise, you will use a trick of Betty Edwards's that helps you see without naming: drawing an upside-down image. We'd like you to give Edwards's exercise a try, following these instructions:

1. Gather your materials: you'll need the Egon Schiele drawing reproduced on page 48, a pencil, an eraser, and a sheet of unlined paper. Then find a quiet place where you won't be interrupted for at least thirty minutes.

2. When you're ready to begin drawing, turn off your phone, close your laptop, and take off your headphones. You should do everything you can to give this exercise your undivided attention.

3. While you are making your copy of the upside-down Schiele line drawing, try not to figure out what you are looking at (and don't turn the drawing right-side up until after you're finished). You'll do a better job if you aren't

trying to name what you are drawing. Focus instead on the lines in the drawing, the relationships between those lines, and the relationships between the lines and the paper's edge. Edwards tells her students: "When you come to parts that seem to force their names on you — the H-A-N-D-S and the F-A-C-E — try to focus on these parts just as shapes. You might even cover up with one hand or finger all but the specific line you are drawing and then uncover each adjacent line."

When you are done making your copy, we'd like you to reflect upon the *experience* of drawing an upside-down image. Begin by considering the following questions: Was it difficult to stop naming and to start seeing relationships? Are there parts of your copy that are more successful than others? What happened to your sense of time while you were working on your copy?

Spend at least thirty minutes writing about what happened *in your mind* while you worked on your line drawing. There's no right answer here. Think of your writing as a sketch of your mind at work. Learning to see begins with learning how *you* see.

Egon Schiele, Self-Portrait as St. Sebastian

Practice Session Three: The Candle Problem

Habits: paying attention, playing, working deliberately

Activities: note taking, problem solving, reflecting, writing

In the 1940s, a psychologist named Karl Duncker developed a test of problem solving that's popularly known as "the candle problem." The challenge posed to participants is to figure out how to attach a lit candle to a wall without dripping wax on the floor below. To complete the challenge, participants can use only the objects pictured here:

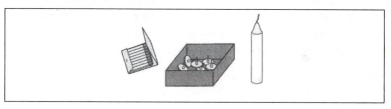

Karl Duncker Candle Problem.

Take as much time as you need to figure out how you would solve the candle problem, and then write down your solution.

Next, watch Daniel Pink's TED talk, "The Puzzle of Motivation." Pink begins talking about the candle problem and its solution at around the two-minute mark, but we want you to listen to the talk in its entirety. Take notes while you're watching, writing down anything Pink says that surprises you.

After you've listened to Pink's TED talk, we'd like you to spend forty-five minutes writing a reflective piece that considers the role *seeing* played in your response to the candle problem. Did solving the candle problem require a new way of seeing, a new way of thinking, or both? What do you think the implications of the candle problem are for learning?

Practice Session Four: Rebecca Solnit and Adam Gopnik Pay Attention

Habits: connecting, exploring, paying attention

Activities: analyzing, reading, writing

In "Life Studies: What I Learned When I Learned to Draw" (*New Yorker*, 2011), Adam Gopnik, who earned a BA and an MA in art history, details how his way of seeing art changed when he learned to draw. In "Occupied Territory," included in the Readings section (pp. 302–08), Rebecca Solnit details how her ways of thinking about time and space changed over time. As you read through both pieces, take note of passages where the writers demonstrate ways of paying attention that surprise you. What made their shifts in perspective possible? Write an essay in which you consider the roles that motive and motivation (Daniel Pink's terms from Practice Session Three) play in transformative acts of attention.

On Looking and Looking Again

....

"Pay attention!"

Walk the hallways of any elementary school, and it won't be long before you hear this exasperated command. Over time, all students learn that what their teachers mean when they say "pay attention" is "sit still and be quiet." The teachers know, of course, that there's more to paying attention than being quiet, but what that "more" turns out to be is something that can't be ordered into existence by figures of authority. So students learn early on how to get their bodies to behave in class, but getting their minds to behave is another matter.

The paradox at the beginning of the process of paying attention seems irresolvable: How does mental focus emerge out of chaos, the attentive mind out of the distracted mind? How does anyone ever learn to pay attention when the mind's preference is to drift, to wander, to surf?

Our answer is: by practice.

But how does one practice a state of mind?

The poet William Blake offers some guidance on how to think about this paradox in the opening stanza of his poem "Auguries of Innocence":

> To see a World in a Grain of Sand
> And a Heaven in a Wild Flower
> Hold Infinity in the palm of your hand
> And Eternity in an hour

On a first reading, Blake's stanza seems to offer a straightforward proposition about how to trigger a state of deep attentiveness: if you want X (to see the world in a grain of sand), then do Y (hold infinity in the palm of your hand). But if this is what it takes to pay attention, attentiveness of the kind Blake describes seems an impossibility, for how is one supposed to go about grabbing hold of infinity or experiencing "eternity in an hour"?

Perhaps we've misread the stanza. Perhaps Blake is making a statement both about what paying attention involves and what it makes possible: "To see a world in a grain of sand and heaven in a wild flower

[is to] hold infinity in the palm of your hand and eternity in an hour."
Read this way, Blake's verse is saying that if you can learn to "see a
world in a grain of sand" or "a heaven in a wild flower," then you can
gain access to realms beyond what you know and even beyond the
limits of thought—you can reach the infinite and the eternal.

From Blake's poem we could conclude that the practice of writing
poetry has trained Blake's mind to focus on the particular (a grain of
sand, a wildflower) until it leads to something much bigger (a world,
a heaven) and onward to realms beyond measure (infinity, eternity).
More generally, we can say that Blake shows us that the attentive mind
generates insights, connections, and beautiful objects and moves by
inference, analogy, and metaphor.

Does this mean that, instead of commanding a distracted student
to "pay attention," teachers should try saying, "Sit still and be a poet!"?

That command wouldn't work any better than the command to pay
attention, of course: first, even the best poet can't be a poet on command; and second, poetry is only one possible result of paying attention.

Better by far, we think, to say, "Practice looking and looking again."

A teacher we greatly admire, Ann Berthoff, developed an exercise that we've adapted here to help you experience the kind of seeing
Blake describes. To get her students to resee the natural world, Berthoff
would bring to class all manner of organic objects—a starfish, the
husk of a cactus, dried reeds, a pressed flower—and then have each
student take one of the objects home to study for a week.

For our version of this exercise, you'll need to select your own
organic object—anything from the natural world will do. You should
choose something that you can hold in your hand and that you can put
somewhere out of harm's way for a week.

We ask that, for seven straight days, you spend at least ten minutes
recording your *observations* of the object you've selected.

Here's an example of what a day's entry might look like, written by
our student Erik on day five:

> Clearly the plant is dehydrated and dying, and yet, besides
> my dismembering it of its limbs, it still has the same form
> and design as it did when I first took it home. The colors
> of the leaves have noticeably changed, but nothing else has

visibly changed as far as I can tell. Of course, the way I'm seeing this object has changed since the first day I laid my eyes upon it.

There are definitely patterns that are quite unmistakable in and on this plant. For instance, the mini-stems that connect the buds to the stem that connects back to the entire organism: there are seven of these mini-stems, and they are all about of equal length. That is interesting. If it is sunlight the buds seek, I would think that maybe one of the mini-branches would push itself considerably farther out so as to receive more energy for its own survival. But, naturally, these buds are probably not competing for energy but rather are working together for the survival and health of the entire plant.

I cannot help but draw a connection to a human body here. You can find multi-facets and numerous parts and functions of parts within a single limb of a body. In fact, you can find it in one single human cell. . . . I'm reminded of a quote from Aldous Huxley [who was quoting from William Blake]: "If the doors of perception were cleansed, everything would appear to man as it truly is, infinite." A person is not just a person with a name, a height and a weight, and a social status; each person is also composed of electricity, of a billion cells that perform who knows how many functions.

My plant here, at first glance, is just a little piece of a shrub. But if you really look at it, there is a lot going on here that makes this plant what it is. Can the physical world ever be described as infinite? Do we really actually know, in an empirical sense, of anything that is infinite? Why do we have a "word" describing something that we have never experienced? Is that evidence or a suggestion from our subconscious mind, our inner spirit, our unseen self, that there is such a thing as infinity? Is there infinity present in my little piece of shrub? I don't know, but I'm willing to bet that as more powerful microscopes are developed, there will surely be more we will be able to "see" in the physical universe around us, and this will further lend credence to the idea that, yes, with a necessary perspective, it may be possible to hold infinity in the palm of your hand. You won't know it unless you have eyes to see it, or take the time to meditate on it, and even then . . . infinity is a tough thing to swallow and ascribe to what we can perceive with our five senses. But it's not impossible.

Focusing on the plant stem, Erik makes connections to the human body, to a quote he's read in Aldous Huxley, and then back to the Blake poem we used in our writing prompt. Looking closely allows Erik to see beyond the plant back into his own mind. Thinking about how the plant is organized becomes, in this instance, a way to think about how all minds organize perceptions.

....

Practice Session One, Part One: Organic Organization

....

Habits: paying attention, persisting, working deliberately

Activities: looking, looking again, writing

Choose an organic object from the natural world, something that you can hold in your hand and that you can keep out of harm's way for a week. Then, over seven consecutive days, write for at least ten minutes each day about what you see.

> Describe how your object is put together.
>
> What questions does your object pose?
>
> What does it point to?
>
> Where did it come from?
>
> What is it a part of?

You are free to move your object, to alter it, or to interact with it in any way that furthers your effort to understand how it is put together. You can also read and do research if questions about your object come to mind. Your goal is to see how your object is organized within itself and how it is implicitly connected with other natural objects.

Write every day.

Ponder what your observations and explorations tell you about the object.

Write even if you're stuck.

If you try to sketch your object, does that help you see aspects you would otherwise miss? What if you photograph it?

Write even if you think you've said all there is to say about your object.

There's only one rule: don't anthropomorphize your object. Don't give it a human name. Don't invent a dialogue between yourself and your object. We've found that this approach only serves to obliterate the object — it displaces the act of looking and looking again.

Practice Session One, Part Two: Looking at Looking

Habits: paying attention, reflecting, speculating

Activities: analyzing, synthesizing, writing

After you've completed your seven days of writing, reread what you've written with the following questions in mind: At the end of all your looking, how would you describe the organization of your organic object? Based on what you've written, how would you describe your own way of looking? What did you see right away? What did it take you a while to see? What kinds of questions did you ask automatically? What kinds of questions emerged late in the process?

Write an essay that reflects on what this exercise of looking and looking again has helped you to recognize about seeing in general and about paying attention in particular.

Practice Session Two: Exploring Montaigne's Mind

Habits: paying attention, persisting, working deliberately

Activities: looking again, reading, refining

We've included an essay, "How Our Mind Tangles Itself Up," by Michel de Montaigne, a sixteenth-century French writer who is credited with inventing the genre of the essay as a vehicle for speculative, meditative, deliberative thought. In this practice session, we ask you to engage with Montaigne's essay for six days.

On the first day, we'd like you to read the essay once, close the book, and write a paragraph explaining how the mind tangles itself up.

On the second day, open your book and reread the essay (it's only one page long!), circling words that are unfamiliar to you. Close your book and write another paragraph, again explaining how the mind tangles itself up. (After you write this second essay, if you haven't done so already, it's a good idea to look up those unfamiliar words.)

Repeat this exercise again the third day, only this time circle the words that you think are most important and write a paragraph explaining your choices (book closed!).

Repeat this exercise again on the fourth day, only this time pay attention to the transitions from sentence to sentence. Close your book and write a paragraph about where your mind gets tangled up as you read Montaigne's essay.

Repeat again the fifth day, only this time write a paragraph about how your understanding of Montaigne's essay has changed over the course of this practice session.

Read the essay one more time on the sixth day and then, with the book open, write your own essay on untangling the tangled mind.

On Paying Attention to Words

Before we met, I had spent a lifetime devoted to Wittgenstein's idea that the inexpressible is contained — inexpressibly! — in the expressed.

This sentence is on the first page of *The Argonauts*, Maggie Nelson's genre-bending account of her evolving relationship with Harry Dodge, their decision to have a child together, and Harry's decision to have a voluntary double mastectomy. Nelson, who has published poetry, criticism, and a nonfiction book about how the cold case of her aunt's murder was solved, brings everything she has to her reflections on falling in love and building a life with someone who claims neither gender.

There are many reasons we love to teach Nelson's work. She is fearless in describing the intellectual, emotional, social, and physical challenges that arose when, in her late thirties, she moved into a non-heteronormative relationship. To make sense of how she and her family are changing, she turns to philosophers, psychoanalysts, poets, artists, feminists, queer theorists, political historians, manifesto writers, friends, acquaintances, and her own memories. Her prose is like poetry; every word counts. And, following on this, she helps us think more deeply about how words convey meaning.

Take the sentence at the top of this page. What does it mean? The meaning seems important: Nelson is telling her readers that, before she met Dodge, she "had spent a lifetime devoted" to something, but what that something is may not be clear to every reader. So, what to do? One can go find out who Wittgenstein was, but a few lines of biographical information about the early-twentieth-century Viennese language philosopher aren't likely to make the sentence's meaning any clearer. Indeed, for some readers, the sentence, "I had spent my life devoted to [Bark! Noise! Static! Buzz!]'s idea," and the sentence, "I had spent my life devoted to Wittgenstein's idea," may well remain essentially identical.

What makes the sentence difficult is not that it requires outside knowledge of Wittgenstein to be understood; it's that it asks the reader to understand the idea that "the inexpressible is contained — inexpressibly! — in the expressed." Eight words, three of them sharing the same root: express. A standard dictionary is not much use here: search and you'll find *inexpressible* is an adjective meaning — wait for it! — "that cannot be expressed." In Nelson's sentence, though, *inexpressible* is a noun — "*the* inexpressible" — not an adjective: so, perhaps it means "the set of all things that can't be expressed." You see the problem with this solution, though, don't you? How do we know what goes in this set? If something is inexpressible, can we feel it? Can we talk about it? Can we name it? Once we do any of these things, aren't we expressing what we've said was inexpressible?

To escape this loop (and loops like it), we look the key word up in a different kind of dictionary, one that allows us to see how individual words came into the English language. The *Oxford English Dictionary* does us this service, tracking individual words back to the earliest printed texts in English and then noting when and how, through use, the meaning of each word changed over time. For our purposes, the *OED* allows us to ask: When did someone writing in English first feel the need to use the word *inexpressible*? And what did it first mean?

The *OED*'s definition of *inexpressible* is more specific than what we found in our initial search: "That cannot be expressed *in words*; unutterable, unspeakable, indescribable" (our italics). The significance of the difference becomes clear once we turn our attention to the earliest example the dictionary editors found of the word's use: the *OED* tells us that John Donne, metaphysical poet and Anglican priest, first put the word into print in a 1631 sermon he delivered on Christmas Day: "Thou shalt feele the joy of his third birth in thy soul, most inexpressible this day."

This question leads us into even more research and, as we dig deeper into the context of what *inexpressible* meant to Donne, we begin to develop what we call an "interpretive definition." At this point, we're compelled to ask, how can Christ be born three times? Going back to Donne's full sermon to answer this question, we see that he relied heavily on the term *inexpressible* to convey his sense of Christian mysteries that were beyond the power of words to explain. Christ was born in heaven without a mother and then born on earth without a father; both of these births, Donne declares, are "inexpressible." And, if the listener allows it, Christ's third birth can occur, this time with neither mother nor father present, in the listener's soul. The joy the listener experiences when this happens, Donne finds, presumably after considerable effort on his part, cannot be put into words ("is most inexpressible"). Indeed, the challenge of trying to put into words the joy felt at this third birth is at its highest point (its "most inexpressible") on Christmas ("this day"), the very day Donne is delivering this sermon.

So *inexpressible* makes its first appearance in a religious context, providing Donne with a succinct way to characterize the profundity of feelings associated with the acceptance of Christ as one's savior. But when we come across the term in Nelson's prose nearly 400 years later, it is not in relation to a devotion to Christ; it's in relation to an idea of Wittgenstein's that Nelson "had spent a lifetime devoted to." The term, in other words, has traveled from the realm of the divine to the secular realm of philosophy.

As it happens, in the course of our research into this matter, we discovered that Donne used *inexpressible* in his *Devotions Upon Emergent Occasions*, which he composed in 1623 and published in 1624, a full seven years before his Christmas sermon cited above! (The second edition of the *OED* was published before the digitization of print made global searches of lexical history something anyone could do.) We found the term in Donne's "XIX Expostulation," in which Donne addresses his God and rejoices:

> O, what words but thine express the inexpressible texture and composition of thy word, in which, to one man, that argument that binds his faith to believe that to be the word of God, is the reverent simplicity of the word, and, to another, the majesty of the word.

Here Donne, Wittgenstein, and Nelson converge. Donne's first use of the term *inexpressible* occurs in a discussion of the transformative quality of God's words in the Bible, which are at once "simple" and "majestic." Nelson is not devoted to that God, but to Wittgenstein's idea about the power of language to express the inexpressible. One could say that Donne and Wittgenstein are struck by the same thing: the fact that words have the paradoxical power to express the inexpressible. The difference is that Donne credits the Christian God with the unique power to make the same words in the Bible mean different things to different readers and Wittgenstein locates this power in the structure of language itself.

· · · · ·

If you keep reading through the *OED*'s history of the uses to which *inexpressible* has been put, you'll find that its plural form, *inexpressibles*, became a euphemism for "unmentionables" (the parts of one's body considered private) in the late 1800s. Edward Gibbon, author of *The Rise and Fall of the Roman Empire*, used it in this way in a letter to Lord Sheffield on November 11, 1793, to avoid saying explicitly why he had been to a surgeon. "Have you never observed," Gibbons wrote, "through my inexpressibles, a large prominency which, as it was not at all painful and very little troublesome, I had strangely neglected for many years?" It's a strange, but telling question: in asking it, Gibbons reveals that Sheffield had occasion to see him in his undergarments and that those undergarments only partially concealed an abnormal growth, about which neither man spoke. Later in his letter, Gibbons describes surgical efforts to drain his "prominency." He never recovered from this treatment and died in the hospital on January 16, 1794.

In this instance, the inexpressibles conceal the unmentionables, placing the discussion of the area and the organs beneath the undergarments out of bounds. So, via its pluralization, inexpressible moves from the divine to the carnal; it goes from meaning "that which is too profound to be put into words" to "that which is not discussed in polite society."

· · · · ·

Nelson begins her book telling her readers that she "had spent a lifetime devoted" to the idea that the set of all things that cannot be put precisely into words is nevertheless perceptible in what does get put into words. One can easily imagine that continually confronting the fact that language cannot exactly represent what one thinks and feels would eventually extinguish any writer's desire to write. In Nelson's case, that clearly hasn't happened: we are citing a sentence she wrote that appears on the first page of her book-length reflection on her life. But, the sentence we've cited also establishes that Nelson's singular devotion to this idea about language's paradoxical powers has moved into the past tense. Something has happened that has changed

Nelson's thoughts about writing and devotion and ideas and what they are all good for, something Nelson signals by identifying the moment of change as "before we met."

As we learn on the next page of *The Argonauts*, Harry Dodge "had spent a lifetime equally devoted to the conviction that words are *not* good enough." Nelson and Dodge argue and argue over this idea, "full of fever, not malice." They are passionate in their beliefs, but part of the story of *The Argonauts* is that winning arguments doesn't necessarily pull you any closer to putting your thoughts into words; it can signal, rather, nothing more than that you've compelled the other person to stop talking or reconvinced them that words, in fact, aren't good enough and never will be.

....

Practice Session One: Tracking the Inexpressible

....

Habits: exploring, paying attention, working deliberately

Activities: defining, interpreting, researching

We'd like you to try your hand at exploring the meaning of the paradoxical word *inexpressible*. The *OED* gives us four other examples of the earliest uses of the word as a noun:

> 1667 Milton, *Paradise Lost*, viii. 113. Ere mid-day arriv'd In Eden, distance inexpressible By Numbers that have name.

> 1711 J. Addison, *Spectator*, No. 160. ¶8. I gazed with inexpressible Pleasure on these happy Islands.

> 1801 M. Edgeworth, *Prussian Vase* in *Moral Tales* III. 37. It is with inexpressible concern, that I find myself called upon . . . to be the accuser of any man.

> 1860 J. Tyndall, *Glaciers of Alps*, i. xxiii. 166. Its seclusion gives it an inexpressible charm.

The dictionary provides truncated citations; it's up to the reader to track down the original sources and then to provide the larger context. Choose one of the citations provided by the *OED* and follow the example we developed for an interpretive definition in "On Paying Attention to Words." Who is the author? What is the author writing about when the word *inexpressible* makes its appearance? Why does the author keep writing after having declared X to be inexpressible? Does your interpretive definition extend, complicate, or contradict Donne's use of the term?

Practice Session Two: Translation as Interpretation

Habits: connecting, paying attention, speculating
Activities: researching, revising, writing

What happens when ideas move from one language to another language? We'd like you to consider this question by exploring the ways that Montaigne's essay, included in the Readings section, has been translated over time. In the version we've selected, M. A. Screech translates the title to the essay, "How the Mind Tangles Itself Up." Find at least two other versions of the essay translated into English. Discuss the differences between the three versions. Is there a way to determine which is best? What would you need to know or do to be able to decide? Write up a history of the title's translation into English and make the case for which translator's decision you find to be the best.

Practice Session Three: Inexplicable versus Inexpressible

Habits: exploring, paying attention, speculating
Activities: list making, researching, writing

In "The Edge of Identity" (pp. 282–301), Rachel Aviv chronicles the case of Hannah Upp, a young woman whose experience of her own identity is discontinuous. At one point in her discussion of the concept of dissociation, Aviv generates a list of "inexplicable transformations" as recounted in newspaper stories at the turn of the twentieth century. What makes the transformations "inexplicable"? Have they become explicable over the last one hundred years? What is the relationship between the word *inexpressible* and the word *inexplicable*? Write an essay in which you discuss Aviv's relationship to the inexplicable as evidenced by her treatment of Hannah Upp's multiple disappearances.

4

QUESTIONING

"There are no bad questions": this incantation is repeated year in and year out in classrooms across the country. It represents a well-intentioned effort to establish a comfortable learning environment, but it's a hard sell since teachers and students alike know that there are not only bad questions but also whole categories of questions that are unwelcome in the classroom. There are questions most teachers dread — the intrusively personal question, the cynical question, and the do-you-mind-repeating-what-you-just-said question, to name a few; and there are questions most students dread, such as the teacher's guess-what-I'm-thinking question, the teacher's fill-in-the-blank question, and the question that exposes the student who asked it to ridicule.

Rather than make the demonstrably false assertion that there are no bad questions, we prefer to ask: What is a good question? In this section, we introduce you to two of our favorite question posers, Jad Abumrad and Robert Krulwich, the hosts of the podcast *Radiolab*. We also propose two alternatives to thesis-driven writing projects. One involves using the draft process to generate a question you genuinely want to answer. And the other involves using questions to drive your writing forward. As obvious as it may seem, it is worth saying: the only way to learn to ask good questions is to make the act of questioning a central part of your reading and writing practices.

On Asking Questions

We're devoted fans of *Radiolab*, a radio show and podcast on which the hosts, Jad Abumrad and Robert Krulwich, invite listeners to join them "on a curiosity bender." Abumrad is a composer by training and won a MacArthur Fellowship in 2011 for his work on the show, while Krulwich is a science correspondent with over three decades of broadcast experience. Working together, they make being curious about the world *sound* like an exciting adventure.

In each show, Abumrad and Krulwich assume the air of happy amateurs who delight in having seemingly simple questions open up complex realities. They typically begin with a big question — about science, the arts, medicine, philosophy, or some other aspect of human experience — and then spend an hour exploring a range of responses to the question they've posed. Their questions often express an open-minded wonder about the world: Why do we sleep? What is color? What is race? How do we assign blame? To help with their explorations, they often turn to multiple experts, but they never take what the experts say as the final word on the matter. They question, provoke, and at times openly disagree with their guests and with each other.

There's a common structure to most *Radiolab* shows: Abumrad and Krulwich move back and forth between questions, big ideas, interviews, and stories, inevitably leading their listeners to new problems and new questions, and revealing in the process that the issue they started with is more complicated than it first seemed. We admire how they move from simple wonder to complex possibilities, and we like that multiple answers, insights, and solutions are entertained along the way. We also like that *Radiolab* sounds beautiful. It's important to recognize that the creative soundscapes Abumrad and Krulwich produce are more than mere entertainment. In every episode, they demonstrate how curiosity can generate beauty as well as answers and ideas.

What we admire most about *Radiolab* is that the hosts manage to express in sound and language the whole spectrum of habits of the creative mind. You can hear Abumrad's creativity as a composer in the ways he uses sound to represent ideas that might otherwise remain too abstract for listeners to grasp. You can hear how open Abumrad and

Krulwich are to ambiguity, the unknown, and discovery as they talk their way through the implications of what they're learning. You can also hear their attention to and engagement with ideas, information, and expertise. And you can hear their reflectiveness as thoughts digress, reverse, and surprise. Most of all, you can hear their boundless curiosity at work in the shape and progress of each episode.

We'd like you to listen to two episodes of *Radiolab*—one scripted, one open-ended—so that you can hear what curiosity as a habit of mind sounds like.

....

Practice Session One, Part One: What Good Is Altruism?

....

Habits: paying attention, questioning, reflecting

Activities: listening, mapping, note taking

In "An Equation for Good," a chapter in *Radiolab*'s episode, "The Good Show," Abumrad and Krulwich consider a question that has puzzled evolutionary biologists since Charles Darwin first advanced his theory that species evolve through struggle and competition: If the "fittest" survive through tooth-and-claw rivalry, how can we explain kindness, generosity, and altruism?

1. Find a quiet place where you can listen without interruption to "An Equation for Good," which is about twenty-two minutes long. Use headphones or earbuds so you don't miss a thing.

2. Next, listen to the podcast again, this time pausing it when necessary to write down the questions Abumrad and Krulwich ask. In addition, take notes about where each question leads. What people and sources do Abumrad and Krulwich turn to for answers? What stories do they tell? Looking over your notes, do you see how their choices affect the overall shape of the show? How does a desire to create a beautiful experience also influence the shape of the show?

3. Spend at least thirty minutes creating a visual map that illustrates the development of the hosts' thinking as "An Equation for Good" unfolds. When do their ideas move in a straight line? When do their questions cause a change in direction? Do they ever take wrong turns? If so, are any

of the resulting digressions useful? By the end of "An Equation for Good," how far have Abumrad and Krulwich traveled? What do they conclude about the common assumption that *evolution* refers only to "the survival of the fittest"? (Note: You might want to experiment with making your map "move"; feel free to use presentation and/or animation software to bring your map to life.)

4. After you've created your map, pause to reflect on what you've learned. What does your map reveal about Abumrad and Krulwich's methods? Could someone else look at your map and understand what you've learned about how the show is structured? If not, how is what you've produced a map?

Practice Session One, Part Two: Is There a Secret to Success?

Habits: paying attention, questioning, reflecting

Activities: listening, mapping, note taking, writing

Next, we'd like you to listen to the *Radiolab* podcast "Secrets of Success," a conversation between Robert Krulwich and Malcolm Gladwell, author of the books *The Tipping Point, Blink,* and *Outliers.* This podcast shows how questions unfold when a curious person talks at length to a single expert, trying to understand the development and reach of the expert's ideas while also puzzling through whether to accept the expert's conclusions.

1. Find a quiet place where you can listen without interruption to the interview, which is about twenty-five minutes long. Don't forget your earbuds.

2. When you're done, listen to the podcast again, this time pausing to write down the questions and other prompts Krulwich uses to get Gladwell to explain his ideas about talent, practice, passion, and success.

3. Set aside at least thirty minutes to create a map that illustrates the unfolding conversation between Gladwell and Krulwich. When does Krulwich move the discussion in a straight line? When does he seem to change direction? Do any apparent digressions end up looping back to serve the main argument? Are there other digressions that take the conversation off track?

4. Looking back over your notes and your map, consider where you find Gladwell's responses to Krulwich's questions convincing, and where you think he leaves important questions unanswered. Imagine that you had the opportunity to ask Gladwell a few more questions regarding his argument about success. Write down three open-ended questions you would want him to answer. Then spend at least thirty minutes developing your own thoughts in response to the question you find most compelling.

Practice Session One, Part Three: Comparing Conversations

Habits: paying attention, revising, speculating

Activities: analyzing, comparing, mapping

If you've completed both parts of Practice Session One, compare your maps of the two *Radiolab* segments. What do your maps reveal about the differences between the two episodes? Is it obvious, for instance, that the first map you made represents a show that was carefully edited and the second map represents an unrehearsed dialogue? What else do the maps suggest about how the shows differ in their organization and direction? What do your maps miss about the differences between the podcasts and how might you revise your maps to account for what you missed?

Practice Session Two: What Is Education For?

Habits: paying attention, questioning, speculating

Activities: note taking, reading, remembering

Note: Before beginning this practice session, you should first complete Part One and/or Part Two of Practice Session One above.

The nonfiction writing we like best is driven by curiosity and questioning. In the Readings section (pp. 270–81), we've included a text by Danielle Allen that begins with its central question in the title: "What Is Education For?" For this session, we want you to read Allen's essay in the same way you listened to

Radiolab. Read the essay through once, underlining the questions Allen poses. Then take notes on the various answers she provides to those questions: some of the answers will draw on sources by experts; others, especially paragraphs late in essay, will explain Allen's own thoughts.

After having read and taken notes on Allen's essay, we'd like you to pose questions about your own education. Setting aside at least one hour, make a list of five or more open-ended questions about the ideas and practices that shaped your education from kindergarten through high school. Select the question you find most compelling and write an extended response that reflects on the goals and purposes of the education you've received and that then considers how those goals and purposes align with your own ideas about what education should be for.

On Writing to a Question

What's writing for? In school, the most common answer given to that question is, "To make a point." And so in school one practices having a point that can be succinctly stated in a thesis statement. "Writing is for making points" is itself an example of a succinct thesis statement. We think the requirement to *start* an essay by committing to a thesis is a good way to kill curiosity. It turns writing into a mindless fill-in-the-blank exercise: Thesis? Check. Three examples? Check. Conclusion that summarizes the previous three paragraphs? Check. This approach to writing is a machine for arguing the obvious; it does not use writing as a tool for thinking new thoughts or for developing ideas that are new to the writer.

For your writing to become a mode of learning for you, you must begin in a state of not knowing rather than committing yourself to a claim you came up with before you've done any curiosity-driven research. This is probably not a form of writing you've practiced in school, so we're going to introduce you to it by describing how Donovan Hohn began his writing project accidently, nagged by a question that just wouldn't go away.

Donovan Hohn was a high school English teacher reading a student paper when the question that eventually led him to write *Moby Duck* found him. The student paper mentioned 28,000 plastic bath toys—yellow ducks, green frogs, blue turtles, and red beavers—that began washing ashore in Alaska and Australia in the early 1990s. Curious, Hohn began to do some research online. Eventually his research took him all over the world. He learned about ocean currents, cargo ships, consumer demand for inexpensive goods, and the toxins in the Chinese factories where the ducks were made. He discovered that the toys that had been washing ashore fell from a container ship during a storm in the Pacific, after which many of them degraded and disappeared into the toxic stew of the Great Pacific garbage patch. Hohn's curiosity took him all the way from news about a flotilla of plastic ducks washing ashore in odd places to questions about the most pressing environmental concerns the world faces today.

Notice that Hohn didn't begin with a thesis that he then set out to prove. Rather, he started with a question and then threw himself into research—for years—before he knew how he would define his project's purpose. He continued working once it became clear that no single, clear answer was to be found; he assumed responsibility for making certain that the question did not remain unanswered. He just kept working away in the face of not knowing, comfortable with the practice of writing from question to question.

To help you learn from the practices used by expert writers, we've adopted a drafting strategy that throws out the idea of starting with a thesis in order to emphasize questioning as the engine of a curious and creative mind. At first our students were baffled when we suggested this approach. How, they asked us, can you begin an essay without a thesis?

We begin by assigning a reading for our students to consider. We then ask them to explore eye-catching moments in the assigned reading, such as when an author

- says something surprising or confusing;
- makes an unexpected connection;
- presents a provocative example;
- uses a familiar term in a new or peculiar way; or
- poses an idea or argument that is difficult to accept.

Then we ask them to write, but we advise them not to report what the author said and then agree or disagree with it; instead, we tell them to focus on moments in which they sense a tension between their own thoughts, knowledge, or expectations and what an author has written.

Once they've written about a passage or a series of passages, we ask them to conclude their response papers by reflecting on what they were led to wonder about over the course of their writing. Ideally, their exploration of puzzling passages has led them to a compelling question or questions, which they pose in the final sentences of their responses. These should be questions that they can't presently answer and that require more thought, reading, and research—questions they are truly curious about and *want* to answer.

Right now you might be wondering, what's the point of writing to a question you can't answer? Isn't exposing your own ignorance the exact opposite of what you should be doing in school? These are good questions!

We think there are many good reasons to use informal writing to arrive at a compelling question. When you write about confusing or interesting passages from or ideas in a text or set of texts, you are learning to use writing as a tool for thinking. And you'll see that writers discover what they think *in the act* of writing. You'll also learn to take more risks with your thinking. Ending with a question you don't know the answer to may feel uncomfortable at first—as if you're revealing a weakness. But openly confronting what you don't know is an essential part of learning to write well. Paradoxically, by writing to a question in a draft, you'll learn how to generate a truly interesting thesis. Once you've drafted a question that you're genuinely curious about, you're ready for the next step: figuring out how to respond to that question. Your response will be a thesis that's worth writing and reading about.

Practice Session One: Being Curious about Curiosity

Habits: questioning, reflecting, speculating
Activities: analyzing, note taking, reflecting

Are you a curious person? Where and when are you most curious? In school? Among your friends? At work? Elsewhere? You may not know the answers to these questions, so we'd like you to pay attention to your own curiosity for a week. Take notes every day, keeping an account of when, where, and how you pose questions, and whether you speak them out loud to others or silently to yourself.

At the end of the week, spend at least thirty minutes reviewing your notes and learning about your own curiosity. When and where were you most curious? How often did you ask questions in classes? Did you pose more questions in one class than another? Did you ask questions as you read, jotting them down in the margins or in your notes? What was your most vivid experience of curiosity-driven learning in the past week? Was it in school or elsewhere?

Practice Session Two: Working toward a Question

Habits: exploring, paying attention, questioning
Activities: engaging with sources, looking again, writing

In our essay, we describe an assignment in which students use the drafting process to write to a question. Now we want you to give it a try.

1. Begin by selecting one of the three longer essays in the Readings section. Read the essay once for understanding and then reread it.

2. As you reread the essay, look for moments in the argument that catch your attention — passages that are surprising or confusing, make an unexpected connection, present a provocative example, use a term in a new or peculiar way, or pose an idea or argument that is difficult to accept. Then write draft in which you explore three or more parts of the reading that you find interesting or baffling — places where you feel friction between the text and your own thoughts, knowledge, or expectations.

3. In the final paragraph of your draft, reflect on what you've learned about the ideas or argument in the reading you selected, and pose a question that has emerged from your work with the passages you've chosen. The primary standard for assessing the quality of the question you've generated is this: Do you genuinely want to answer it? In addition, your answer should require that you develop your own thoughts by engaging with the text you have read, and perhaps by doing additional research.

4. Having arrived at an interesting question, write an essay in which you develop a thoughtful answer to your question. Work with the reading you selected and the passages you wrote about, as well as any other passages that now seem relevant.

On Question-Driven Writing

Why write?

When posting on social media, the writer's motivation is clear: to connect with friends or to say something others will "like." As in other kinds of "unsponsored writing," such as keeping a diary or maintaining a personal blog, the central activity is giving voice to the self. This can be pleasurable; it can teach you about yourself; it can relieve stress. While there are plenty of people who never feel the desire to engage in unsponsored writing, there's not much mystery as to why some do.

What *is* mysterious is why anyone, outside of a school assignment, voluntarily writes about anything other than the self, its interests, its desires, its travails, and so on. Why write a searching analysis of a social problem, for instance, or a book-length study of voting behaviors, or a biography of someone long dead and wholly unrelated to the writer? Why do something that requires so much time and mental energy, when the odds of getting published or having your work read are so low?

Cast in these terms, the motivation to write voluntarily about something other than the self does seem mysterious. But perhaps these are not the best terms for understanding how the motivation to write emerges. So let's move from the hypothetical to the particular and consider the story of how the historian Jill Lepore set out to write a book about Benjamin Franklin and ended up writing one about Jane Franklin, his virtually unknown sister. It's obvious why a historian might want to write about Ben Franklin. He's a major figure in American history; he was an inventor, an ambassador, an educator, and a philosopher; he was one of the most famous people of his time, and he interacted with others in all walks of life. If you're a scholar of American history, writing about him sounds fun.

In "The Prodigal Daughter," Lepore describes settling into reading Franklin's papers and finding herself drawn instead to the sixty-three-year-long correspondence Ben Franklin had with his younger sister Jane. Lepore discovered that Ben Franklin wrote more letters to Jane than to anyone else. As Lepore read more and more of the letters, she became motivated to ask questions that drove her research forward. How was it possible that "no two people in their family were more alike," when "their lives could hardly have been more different"? How could Jane Franklin's character and intelligence resemble her brother's when she had little education and no formal training as a writer beyond the few lessons her brother gave her before he left home when she was only eleven. Aside from letters to family and friends, the only writing she did was to record the dates of major events in a small, handmade book she called her "Book of Ages," which Lepore describes as "four sheets of foolscap between two covers to make a little book of sixteen pages." Turn the pages of this home-made book and you'll move through a list of dates and events: Jane's birth; her marriage at age fifteen; the birth of her first child, and that child's death less than a year later; and the births and then the deaths of all but one of her twelve children over the course of her lifetime.

In contrast to her brother's life, Jane Franklin's life seemed too spare to warrant attention. And yet when Lepore told her mother what she had learned about Ben Franklin's forgotten sister, her mother said, "Write a book about her!" Lepore thought her mother was joking. How could she write a book about a phantom? Who would want to read it? It seemed like an impossible task, but when Lepore's mother's health began to fail, she returned her attention to Jane Franklin's letters "to write the only book [her] mother ever wanted [her] to write."

Lepore's personal motivation for writing a book about Jane Franklin couldn't have been stronger, but she still struggled to articulate a driving question that would transform Jane Franklin's story into a book that anyone but her mother would want to read. Not wanting to abandon Jane Franklin entirely, Lepore decided that she had enough material for a short opinion piece, "Poor Jane's Almanac," which she published in the *New York Times*. In the piece, Lepore described Jane Franklin's "Book of Ages" and the political arguments Jane had with her brother after her child-rearing days were done. Highlighting Jane Franklin's two modes of writing—the catalog of her losses and her letters to her brother—Lepore showed that Jane was born with as much potential for achievement as her famous brother, but gender, poverty, and lack of access to both education and contraception narrowed the scope of her life. "Especially for women," Lepore writes, "escaping poverty has always depended on the opportunity for an education and the ability to control the size of their families," neither of which Jane had.

Lepore was stunned by the flood of letters she received in response to "Poor Jane's Almanac." In an interview ("Out Loud: Jane Franklin's Untold American Story"), Lepore described letters from readers about how their mothers, like Jane Franklin, fought the "undertow of motherhood" to steal the time required to read, learn, and engage with the wider world. This unsolicited reader feedback helped Lepore see why her attempt to write Jane Franklin's story as a traditional biography had failed. It had been impossible for Lepore to write a compelling story about a person whose life was largely unexceptional and unknown. Readers of "Poor Jane's Almanac" weren't moved by Jane Franklin because her life had been unique; they were moved because they saw in Jane Franklin an eighteenth-century incarnation of their own twentieth-century mothers—intelligent, but thwarted.

When Lepore realized this, she found a public reason for writing at length about Jane Franklin's life: she would use Franklin's story to explore two questions: How did poverty, motherhood, and limited access to education constrain the lives of women in the eighteenth century? And why is this history of interest to twenty-first century readers? *Book of Ages: The Life and Opinions of Jane Franklin*, which was nominated for a National Book Award in 2013, is Lepore's book-length exploration of these two questions.

We know it's unlikely that you've had a writing experience like Lepore's, one where your motivation for writing shifted from a personal concern to an interest you shared with others. We say this because the motivation for virtually all of the writing students do in school comes not from the students' desire to explore an important question, but from the teachers' assignments and the students' desire for good grades. It doesn't have to be this way, though. One of the reasons we wrote *Habits of the Creative Mind* was to inspire you to practice writing as real writers do. Professional and aspiring nonfiction writers are motivated to write because they are driven by genuine questions that don't have simple answers, and they write for real readers who want to see the writer's mind at work on a problem. We want to encourage you, as apprentice writers, to practice imagining a public audience for your work. We want you to confront the challenge all practicing writers face when they are in the midst of a project: How do I make what interests me of interest to others?

Practice Session One: Bad Questions, Good Answers

Habits: connecting, questioning, speculating

Activities: analyzing, questioning, writing

As we noted in the introduction to this section, there really are bad questions. Audience matters: there are questions you can ask your friends that you wouldn't ask a stranger. And context matters: there are questions you can ask your friends in private that you wouldn't ask in public.

In her short essay, "The Mother of All Questions," Rebecca Solnit (*Harper's*, 2015) is concerned with a bad question that is regularly and predictably directed to adults like her who do not have children: "Why didn't you have kids?" Underlying the question is the suggestion that the person has failed and that she — this question is most often directed at women — is lacking, or selfish, or loveless.

Solnit prefers not to respond to this loaded question, but she shows how other bad, or wrong, questions can be turned into good questions by probing what they mean below the surface. One such question is, Are you happy? It's a bad question, in part because it's the sort of question we answer without paying attention. Solnit argues that this bad question is best answered with better questions. What is happiness? And why is it generally assumed to be one of life's most important goals?

We would like you to read "The Mother of All Questions" and then to write your own essay that turns the question, Are you happy? into better questions. In your essay, pose at least three *good* questions that challenge assumptions about the meaning of happiness and explore your own thoughts about the meaning or significance of this term.

....

Practice Session Two: Public Motives for Writing

....

Habits: questioning, speculating, working deliberately

Activities: analyzing, experimenting, reading

Public and intellectual motives for writing are often expressed as questions or as statements that take note of a puzzle or problem. Punctuation makes questions easy to identify. Statements of puzzles or problems aren't as readily recognizable, but they often take the form of sentences that use a complicating or qualifying word such as *but, however,* or *or* to point to an unexpected insight. For example, the motivating puzzle in Lepore's *Book of Ages* can be expressed by this statement: Jane Franklin's life appears to be unexceptional, *but* her life provides a valuable example of how poverty, lack of education, and motherhood severely limited what women in the eighteenth-century United States could achieve.

All the texts in the Reading section of this book are driven by the writer's desire to answer a question, grapple with a dilemma, or solve a problem.

For this practice session, we'd like you to read Rachel Aviv's essay "The Edge of Identity" (pp. 282–301). In this essay, Aviv tells a story about Hannah Upp, but her primary project extends beyond narrating the mystery that surrounds Upp. Instead, she uses Upp as a case study to think about larger questions than why this one woman periodically loses her sense of identity. Those larger questions and problems serve as the intellectual motivation for Aviv's project and make her work interesting to a general audience of readers.

But where exactly does Aviv define the puzzle that motivates her writing? After you've read Aviv's essay all the way through, see if you can identify the sentence, sentences, or paragraphs that most clearly express her project. Then experiment with restating the motive in a sentence that uses *but, or, however,* or some other complicating word. Does the statement you composed help to clarify Aviv's project for you?

....

Practice Session Three: Connecting Small Stories to Big Ideas

....

Habits: connecting, questioning, reflecting

Activities: note taking, reading, thinking

We invite you to practice a frequent motivating move in nonfiction writing: we'd like you to use a case study (a single example) to illuminate a larger issue or idea. Read Rachel Aviv's "The Edge of Identity," taking notes on how she uses her case study to bring a new idea to our attention. What is the new idea? What does she want her readers to think about this new idea by the end of her piece?

Once you have a handle on how Aviv moves from her case study of Hannah Upp to her illuminating idea, we'd like you to write up a richly detailed anecdote from your own family history. Then consider how you could use the story to shed light on an interesting cultural or social problem, puzzle, or mystery that is bigger than your particular family. In other words, define a public motive for writing. After you've selected your anecdote and before you try to make a connection to a larger idea, spend at least one hour doing research about the cultural or social issue that interests you.

After you've done sufficient research, compose an essay that links your family history to the larger issue you've researched.

5

EXPLORING

"Space, the final frontier." This phrase, heard at the opening of each episode of the original *Star Trek* television series, is accompanied by the image of the starship *Enterprise* carrying its crew off to its next adventure. The excitement offered by this kind of science fiction includes encounters with new worlds, new life forms, new forms of consciousness, and new ways of organizing societies. The adventures are imaginary, of course, but the stories themselves are ways to explore ideas and ask questions: Are there universal truths? Are there other forms of intelligent life? Is there an end to human history? Science fiction takes these big, abstract questions and creates imaginary worlds where possible answers to these questions can be explored.

We'd like you to think of the essay as a mode of writing that shares with science fiction this excitement about exploring worlds both beyond and within the self. The science fiction writer imagines spaceships to embark on these explorations; for the essayist, writing itself is the exploration vehicle. To show you what we mean by this, in the first essay in this section, we liken exploration in the internet age to Alice's trip "down the rabbit hole" and invite you to use your search engine to practice chasing ideas, thoughts, and questions wherever they may lead. In the second essay, we ask you to think about how that reading, like writing, can be creative. And in the third essay, we consider whether the choices you make about what you think are really your own choices after all.

On Going Down the Rabbit Hole

"Down the rabbit hole": it's a strange phrase, isn't it? If you've heard it before, it's possible that the first thing it calls to mind is the scene in *The Matrix* where Morpheus offers Neo two pills: "You take the blue pill—the story ends, you wake up in your bed and believe whatever you want to believe. You take the red pill—you stay in Wonderland, and I show you how deep the rabbit hole goes." In the inside-out world of *The Matrix*, reality is an illusion and what seems illusory—that time can be slowed down, that bullets can be dodged, that gravity only applies intermittently—is actually possible for those who occupy a deeper reality.

Morpheus (the name Ovid gives the god of dreams in his long poem *Metamorphoses*) refers to "Wonderland" and "the rabbit hole" on the assumption that Neo—and those watching the film—will make the connection to Lewis Carroll's *Alice's Adventures in Wonderland*. In that story, a young girl named Alice is sitting on a riverbank, bored with how the day is going, when a rabbit carrying a pocket watch rushes past her. Alice follows the rabbit, who disappears down a rabbit hole. She sticks her head in and begins to fall down the hole, and what follows is a series of adventures that has captivated generations of readers for nearly 150 years.

Think of all that happens to Alice in the few pages that make up the first chapter of her *Adventures*: when she finally hits bottom (when she sees how deep the rabbit hole goes), the rabbit is just turning a corner in another long tunnel, so she gives chase. When she turns the same corner, Alice finds herself in a long hallway with doors on both sides, all of them locked. Then she discovers a key that opens a very small door, which leads to a beautiful garden on the other side. Because she is too big to fit through the door, Alice keeps exploring the hallway. She finds a bottle with a note that says DRINK ME. Alice complies, and suddenly she's "shutting up like a telescope" until she's only ten inches tall. She wants to go into the garden but can no longer reach the key to open the small door, and so she begins to cry. She looks down, discovers another small door, opens it, and finds a small cake with the words EAT ME written on top in currants. Alice follows these instructions too, which leads to this statement at the beginning of the second chapter:

> "Curiouser and curiouser!" cried Alice (she was so much surprised, that for the moment she quite forgot how to speak good English); "now I'm opening out like the largest telescope that ever was! Good-bye, feet!" (for when she looked down at her feet they seemed to be almost out of sight, they were getting so far off).

Why is the otherworldliness at the heart of both *The Matrix* and *Alice's Adventures in Wonderland* so appealing? Why do we take such pleasure in imagining that there's the world we experience every day and that there is also, just beyond this everyday world (or just beneath it, assuming rabbit holes go down), another world where everyday laws no longer apply? One explanation for this fantasy's appeal is that life in the other extraordinary world is action-packed: once the rules that govern the ordinary are suspended, anything can happen—rabbits can talk; bodies can bend out of the way of approaching bullets; a boy with a scar on his forehead can fight off the forces of evil. But this isn't really an explanation so much as it is a description masquerading as an explanation. Why are we drawn to the extraordinary?

Ellen Dissanayake has spent nearly five decades exploring the allure of the extraordinary. Working in evolutionary aesthetics, a field she helped to invent, Dissanayake has concluded that humans are hardwired to seek out the extraordinary; it is, she says, in our nature to do so. In making her argument, Dissanayake sets out to establish that the desire to "make special" or to "artify" (she uses both terms interchangeably) serves a number of evolutionary purposes central to the survival of the species—the most significant being that acting on this desire is a response to anxiety and uncertainty. Over time, certain ways of making special become ritualized: the wedding ceremony or the walk across the graduation stage, for example, or the gift of flowers to someone who is sick. What we find most appealing in Dissanayake's thesis is the idea that art is not an end product; it's the practice of making special, which can manifest at any time—at the feast for a visiting dignitary or over coffee between friends or in the care one takes choosing which words to put on the page.

Is there an art to doing research? We think so. Most handbooks will send you out to do your research with a plan, an outline, or a map of some kind. The idea behind all this advance preparation is to protect you from getting lost while mucking about in the endless thicket of information that's out there. But that's precisely the problem with this common sense plan for research: the end results are never surprising to the reader or the writer because the whole point of this approach is to do research in which there will be no surprises!

We invite you to envision the research process not as a voyage through already mapped territory but as a trip down the rabbit hole. We want you to set for yourself the goal of generating research that is extraordinary — research that proceeds by "making special," by "artifying." We want your research to lead you to write something that rewards repeated acts of attention, research that takes you on an adventure and brings you into contact with facts and ideas that are new to you.

What does artful, special, or extraordinary research look like? Obviously, there's no formula. We have two examples for you to consider. When Rebecca Skloot was sixteen, she registered for a community college biology course to make up for having failed the course during her freshman year of high school. During the section on cell division, Skloot's teacher, Mr. Defler, told his students about HeLa cells and then wrote "Henrietta Lacks" in big letters on the blackboard. Mr. Defler went on to explain that Lacks had died of cervical cancer, that a surgeon had taken a tissue sample from her tumor, and that "HeLa cells were one of the most important things that happened to medicine in the last hundred years." Before erasing the name from the board and dismissing the class for the day, Mr. Defler added one more fact: Henrietta Lacks was a black woman.

Skloot followed Mr. Defler back to his office, asking questions: "Where was she from? Did she know how important her cells were? Did she have any children?" Mr. Defler told her that Lacks's life was a mystery. "If you're curious," he said, "go do some research, write up a little paper about what you find and I'll give you some extra credit."

Skloot couldn't find any information on Lacks beyond a parenthetical reference in her biology textbook, but she didn't forget about this mysterious woman whose cells had helped protect millions from contracting polio. Some ten years later, when Skloot was working on her undergraduate degree in biology, she took her first writing course, and the teacher began by asking the students to "write for 15 minutes about something someone forgot." Skloot wrote about how Henrietta Lacks had been forgotten by the world.

Over time, Skloot resolved to write "a biography of both the cells and the woman they came from." As her commitment to her project deepened, her research became "a decadelong adventure through scientific laboratories, hospitals, and mental institutions, with a cast of characters that would include Nobel laureates, grocery store clerks, convicted felons, and a professional con artist." She met Lacks's five adult children and their families, who knew nothing of Lacks's importance to medical research. And this raised yet more questions for Skloot about medical ethics, inheritance, and the self. If Henrietta Lacks's cells were so important to medical science and had given rise to a multibillion-dollar industry, why couldn't Lacks's children and grandchildren afford health insurance?

More than two decades after Rebecca Skloot first heard the name Henrietta Lacks, she finished her book. Putting her research skills to use once more, she tracked down the biology teacher who first told her about HeLa cells and sent him a note: "Dear Mr. Defler, here's my extra credit project. It's 22 years late, but I have a good excuse: No one knew anything about her." Thanks to Skloot's persistence and the extraordinary research she conducted, this is no longer true: *The Immortal Life of Henrietta Lacks* was published in 2010; over 1.25 million copies have since been sold; HBO made a docudrama based on the book in 2017, starring Oprah Winfrey as Deborah Lacks, one of Henrietta Lacks's daughters.

If that example of extraordinary research seems too extraordinary (after all, how many writing assignments have a due date twenty-two years in the future?), consider this example of how curiosity-driven research can make the everyday world shimmer with meaning, excerpted from an email we received from Chris Osifchin, a former student who wrote to us a year after graduating:

> I've been really getting into Richard Linklater lately, after watching *Dazed and Confused* (my favorite movie

of all time) for about the thirtieth time. I watched his movie *Slacker* and also part of *Waking Life*, and what was interesting to me was the portrayal of nothing as everything and how it is displayed in a much more explicit manner than *Dazed*.

I then saw a tweet from an awesome Website, Open Culture, directing Tweeters to the films and works of Susan Sontag. Never heard of her. Isn't it funny how connections come about? As I read more about her, and more of her pieces, I began to make a connection between Linklater's work and Sontag. The first piece of Sontag's work that I read was "Against Interpretation." I found it fascinating, and also true to a point. The best art does not try to mean anything, it just [lies] there in the glory and awe of its creation. . . .

Next, I read a NYT review of Sontag's first novel, *The Benefactor*, and was struck by how similar it seemed to *Waking Life*. The review even says, "Hippolyte also dreams numerous repetitious dreams, ponders them endlessly, and keeps encountering Frau Anders, like a guilty conscience. The intent is to present waking life as if it were a dream. And to present dreams as concrete as daily living." This is precisely what *Waking Life* is portraying. I think the depiction of dreams as reality and reality as dreams or any combination of those is not "without motive or feeling" as the reviewer says, but rather allows you to view things from a less interpretive point of view, as Sontag might [argue for].

Now, after reading this review, I decided to see if Linklater was influenced by Sontag. I literally searched on Google "Richard Linklater influenced by Susan Sontag." Interestingly enough, and why I decided to send this email to you, Sontag mentions Linklater's *Dazed and Confused* in an article on the Abu Ghraib torture incident, "Regarding the Torture of Others." In it, Sontag mentions the increasing brutality of American culture and the increasing acceptance of violence. Not only did this make me think of [*The Ballad of Abu Ghraib*] and reading it in your class, but it also made me think of a specific moment in *Waking Life* [here he provides the link to the YouTube clip of the moment he references]. "Man wants chaos. In fact, he's gotta have it. Depression, strife, riots, murder. All this dread. We're irresistibly drawn to that almost orgiastic state created out of death and destruction. It's in all of us. We revel in it!" It seems to me that this connects very well to Abu Ghraib as a whole, not just the immediate actions of the guards. Sontag's observation that "secrets of private life that, formerly, you would have given nearly anything to conceal, you now clamor to be invited on a television show to reveal" collides at the intersection of American fantasies played out on TV screens all the time and [in] the real world. It's an interesting comment on American society as a whole—who would have thought that reality TV would come back to bite America in a *war*? And with the extension of reality TV that is now, what I can't think to call anything but the "reality Web" (i.e., social media/ networks), it is becoming more prevalent than ever. Sontag puts it better than I have—"What is illustrated by these photographs is as much the culture of shamelessness as the reigning admiration for unapologetic brutality."

For our former student, the world of ideas, like the rabbit hole in *Alice in Wonderland*, is endlessly surprising and extraordinary. He begins by writing about rewatching Richard Linklater's movie *Dazed and Confused* and then, before he knows it, he's off on an entirely self-motivated search through film, philosophy, war, and media in search of artists and thinkers who can help him better understand our "culture of shamelessness" and "unapologetic brutality." With genuine curiosity and some practice doing research, you can transform the world of ideas, as Chris did, into a place for exploration, where every turn has the potential to inspire new connections and thinking itself becomes both art and play.

....

Practice Session One, Part One: Drilling Down

....

Habits: exploring, questioning, working deliberately

Activities: note taking, reading, researching

Type "Ellen Dissanayake" into the Google search engine. Press *Enter*.

Everyone who does this at the same time is likely to get very similar results. We can call this "ordinary research." If you click on the Wikipedia entry for Dissanayake, you'll find yourself on a page that provides a thumbnail sketch of the author and her work. Again, in gaining this foothold on Dissanayake's work, you'll be doing what any ordinary researcher starting out would do.

It's what you do next that matters. Choose one of Dissanayake's works that you find online and read it.

Your next task is to make your research into this researcher of the extraordinary extraordinary. (We composed that last sentence with *Alice's Adventures in Wonderland* in mind.) Set aside at least an hour for exploratory research. Begin by choosing a phrase, a quotation, a reference, or a footnote from the Dissanayake work you read and then do another Google search. Read two or more of the recommended links. Then choose a phrase, a quotation, a reference, or a footnote from the second set of works and do another Google search. Repeat. Repeat. And repeat again, until you've burrowed down to an insight or a question that you yourself find extraordinary.

We call this process, where you move from one linked source to the next, "drilling down." Spend at least thirty minutes reflecting on this process. As you drilled down in your research, beginning with your first search about Dissanayake and ending with an extraordinary insight or question, how did you distinguish between ordinary and extraordinary moments of discovery? What choices yielded genuine surprises? Begin a list of useful strategies to include in your repertoire as a curious researcher, a list you can add to as you continue to practice drilling down.

Practice Session One, Part Two:
On the Extraordinary

Habits: exploring, persisting, questioning

Activities: engaging with sources, note taking, researching

Write an essay that uses your research into the extraordinary to present a special or artful idea, insight, or question. Don't write a schoolish "report" about your research. Instead, make something special with your words; write something that rewards repeated acts of attention.

Practice Session Two, Part One:
The Rabbit Hole of Identity

Habits: exploring, speculating, working deliberately

Activities: charting, note taking, reading

Rachel Aviv's "The Edge of Identity," included in our Readings section, is centrally concerned with exploring a mystery: Where does Hannah Upp go when she disappears? Where does this exploration lead Aviv? Who does she speak with as she conducts her research? Whose work does she read? Where is she at the end of her search? Take notes while you read Aviv's article, as if you were tracking the movement of her thoughts. Then write a report about what your notes enable you to see about Aviv's writing practice.

Practice Session Two, Part Two:
The Rabbit Hole of Identity

Habits: connecting, exploring, paying attention

Activities: note taking, questioning, reading

In "What Does It Mean to Die?" (*New Yorker*, 2018), Rachel Aviv recounts the case of Jahi McMath, who suffered "brain death" after routine surgery, and her parents' ongoing rejection of the doctor's judgment that their child was dead. Read this essay and consider the following questions: Where does the exploration of McMath's life lead Aviv? Who does she speak with as she conducts her research? Who does she read? Where is she at the end of her search? As you read, take notes as if you were tracking the movement of Aviv's thoughts. When you're done, compare your notes about "What Does It Mean to Die?" to your notes about "The Edge of Identity." What do the two sets of notes together reveal about Aviv's habits of mind? Is there a method to her ways of conducting research?

Practice Session Two, Part Three: The Rabbit Hole of Identity

Habits: connecting, exploring, persisting

Activities: analyzing, researching, writing

Now that you've used your notes to speculate about Aviv's research and writing habits, do online research about her history as a writer. Don't stay on the surface; drill down. How does knowing about Aviv's career contribute to your understanding of her writing?

Write an essay in which you explore Aviv's approach to going down the rabbit hole. Your essay should include discussion of her two articles along with the best parts of your research about her writing career.

On Creative Reading

Once you've learned to read, it's easy to lose sight of just what a complicated business reading actually is. You see the letters *c-a-t*, and without effort you know that together they refer to the furry, whiskered, four-legged purring thing curled before the fire. To accomplish this seemingly simple act of translation, you had to learn a sign system (the alphabet), a host of rules governing the combination of the signs in the given system (for example, there are vowels and consonants, and they can be put together only in certain ways), and the connection between the signifier (the word that results from the orderly combination of sounds) and the signified (the object, idea, or sensation out there in the world).

Even at this most rudimentary stage, there's an inescapable arbitrariness at the heart of the reading process: Why does *c-a-t* and not some other series of letters signify that furry thing? Why *that* sound for *that* creature? And beyond the arbitrariness of the sign system, there's an even deeper mystery: How does the child watching the parent's finger point to the letters on the page ever make the leap to that moment when the sound, the letters, and the image in the picture book suddenly connect, and meaning gets made?

Solving the mystery of how and why humans developed this ability to work with sign systems is a job for evolutionary neuroscientists, and their answer, when it comes, will apply to humans in general. We're interested in a more personal issue: Once the process of reading has been routinized and internalized, why is it that different people reading the same material reach different conclusions? Or to put this another way, why is there ambiguity? Why is there misunderstanding? What happens in the movement from decoding the letters on the page or screen to creating an interpretation of what those letters, considered in context, might mean that causes one reader's mind to go in one direction and another reader's mind to go in a different direction?

The mystery of the individual response is made clear as soon as class discussion about an assigned reading begins. Where'd *that* idea come from? How'd the teacher get *that* out of *those* words? And because students can't see inside the teacher's mind, they often conclude that the connections the teacher is making are arbitrary and, beyond that, that anything other than reporting the facts is "just a matter of opinion." For many students, the mystery of how teachers—and experts, in general—read is never solved. For these students, the experience of higher-order literacy, where reading and writing become ways to create new ideas, remains out of reach.

Social bookmarking, a gift from the internet, gives us a way to make visible for others some of the previously invisible workings of the creative reader's mind. Below we walk you through an example of how using social media worked in one of our classes, and then we give you some exercises to get you started on your way. Although there are lots of social bookmarking tools to choose from, we use Diigo because it allows you to share annotated web pages so others can see both the passages you've highlighted and your inline comments. And, just like that, two previously invisible aspects of the reading process—what people read and how they respond to what they've read—become visible and available for others to consider.

So what does *creative* reading look like in practice?

Our example comes from a creative nonfiction course we taught where the central text was *On Photography*, a collection of essays by Susan Sontag, first published in 1977, that remains to this day a touchstone in discussions of how the free circulation of images changes societal norms. In the collection's second essay, "America, Seen through Photographs, Darkly," Sontag criticizes the work of Diane Arbus who, Sontag maintains, used her camera to depict all of her subjects, regardless of age or social status, as "inhabitants of a single village . . . the idiot village [of] America." We asked our students if Sontag's assessment of Arbus was fair. "How would we know?" they replied. "There aren't any photographs in the whole book, so we just have to take her word for it."

This response was truer for Sontag's readers forty years ago, since those unfamiliar with Arbus's work would have had to exert a great deal of energy and commitment over a sustained period of time to see copies of the images Sontag discusses in "America, Seen through Photographs, Darkly." At a minimum, these readers would have had to go a local library during operating hours to find out if there were any books, magazines, or newspaper articles with Arbus's photographs on the shelves in the library's collection. Contemporary readers, by contrast, need only type "Diane Arbus" into a search engine to find the specific images Sontag refers to in her piece and more: Arbus's shots of circus freaks; off-balance, oddly dressed socialites; nudists in their living rooms; a giant man towering over his tiny parents; and of course, the twin girls whose portrait inspired Stanley Kubrick's terrifying twins in *The Shining*.

Sheepishly, our students acknowledged that they could have conducted such a search. Doing so, however, would've required a kind of initiative that most people don't associate with assigned reading. The creative reader, we tell our students, not only practices filling in informational gaps so as to better understand the writer's point of view, but also seeks out answers to the questions raised by these individual acts of information gathering. All our students could find the Arbus images, but what happened next was up to each student.

After our student Alice had seen the pictures, she asked: "Well, how did people at the time react? We know Sontag didn't like Arbus's work, but did *they?*"

As so often happens in our classes, we didn't know the answer to the question our student had posed. (And in this instance, even if we had known, we wouldn't have said so.) Alice asked a good question—because finding out the answer would end up requiring some creativity on her part *and* because wondering about how others see what you're seeing always serves to highlight the fact that meaning is both a public and a private matter. So we said, "That's a Diigo moment," which is shorthand in our classes for, "See what you can find out on your own and post the results to our class's social bookmarking group."

Back in her room, Alice set off to answer her own question. She entered some search terms, cast about a bit, and then settled on a path that took her to *Athanor*, a journal published by Florida State University's Department of Art History, and an article by Laureen Trainer entitled "The Missing Photographs: An Examination of Diane Arbus's Images of Transvestites and Homosexuals from 1957 to 1965." Alice posted a link to the piece on the class Diigo site and then highlighted a passage that struck her:

> However, the reaction to [Arbus's] images was intense
> anger, an emotional response prompted by the cultural war

against sexual "deviants." Yuben Yee, the photo librarian at the [Museum of Modern Art in New York], recalls having to come early every morning to wipe the spit off of Arbus's portraits. He recalls that, "People were uncomfortable — threatened — looking at Diane's stuff." Even within the art world, Arbus was thought to be photographing subject matter that was ahead of her time. As Andy Warhol, who had seen some of Arbus's portraits, commented, "drag queens weren't even accepted in freak circles until 1967." Arbus's images were not only disturbing to her audience on an aesthetic level, but her unabashed and unapologetic views of transvestites touched a deeper nerve in the people who viewed them.

Beneath this quote, Alice wrote about the difference between a time when people spat on images of transvestites in the Museum of Modern Art (MoMA) and her own experience looking at the images a half century later, when there are prime-time television shows dedicated to drag queen competitions.

How did people respond to Arbus's work at the time? Some people spat on them! By posting the link to the source that her research had led her to, Alice made her way of answering this question visible to the rest of the class. In this instance, she also found something that was new to her teachers, new to the class, and new to her. And, in so doing, she gave us a glimpse of what was going on in her mind while she was reading. Yes, it is true that she had just uncovered a piece of information. Yes, it is true that she had not yet done anything with this information. But meaningful engagement with information can happen only *after* one has had the experience of posing an open, exploratory question.

Alice kept looking — it's a requirement in our courses. The next source she posted to Diigo would likely raise the hackles of many teachers: Wikipedia! It's an outrage!

Well, actually, it isn't. If we grant that students are going to use Wikipedia (and SparkNotes and YouTube and, and, and), we can focus on how to use these sources productively rather than insist on unenforceable prohibitions.

So, Wikipedia: Is there a beneficial way to use a collaboratively written, ever-changing encyclopedia? How could the answer to that question be anything other than yes?

Alice posted the link to Wikipedia's Arbus entry as well as excerpts from the section of that entry that specifically concern the reception of Arbus's work. She deleted material that was not of interest to her; separated past reactions from more contemporary responses; added an inline comment that directly connected the Wikipedia entry to Sontag's argument; reordered the information so as to place the introductory material in this section of the Wikipedia entry at the end of her own citation; and eliminated entirely a passage where it is observed that "Sontag's essay itself has been criticized as 'an exercise in aesthetic insensibility' and 'exemplary *for its shallowness*'" (italics added).

All of this editorial activity gives us a much richer sense of what Alice did while she was reading. Alice amassed many examples of how the subjects of Arbus's images responded to being photographed; how anonymous viewers at MoMA showed their disgust when the photographs were first displayed; and how critics — those who were Arbus's contemporaries and those who came after her — reacted to the photographs. Then she concluded her entry with the news that Arbus had photographed Sontag and her son.

Who was this last bit of information news to? Alice. The other students in the course. Her teachers. And given that Sontag herself does not reveal this fact anywhere in *On Photography*, it's safe to say that it would also be news to the vast majority of Sontag's readers, past and present.

Alice posted this fact to Diigo without comment. She thought she was done.

But the practice of creative reading is never done. In this case there was a question hanging in the air, waiting to be asked. And because the social bookmarking tool made what Alice was reading and how she was reading it visible to her classmates and to her teachers, it became possible for us to pose the question that we knew would keep the creative reading process going for Alice: What does the picture Arbus took of Sontag look like?

This question was posed in public for all the other students to see on the Diigo site, just below Alice's entry. And soon enough, Alice posted a link to the image. True, it was only a small, low-resolution image, but it was a start. Or rather, it was a continuation, an extension of a process that started with Alice asking, "How did others see Arbus?" and eventually led Alice to discover an image of Sontag and her son looking back at the photographer whom Sontag describes as "not a poet delving into her entrails to relate her own pain but a photographer venturing out into the world to *collect* images that are painful."

This is one version of what happens when the purpose of reading shifts from the acquisition of information to the exploration of an open-ended question: reading begets more reading, one passage leads to another, and the original text is read and reread in a series of changing contexts, its meaning expanding and contracting depending on the reader's creative powers. This is the essence of higher-order reading. Some explorations will be more fruitful than others, and some more valuable for the individual than for a larger community of readers, but the movement from answers to questions, from information to ideas, remains the same.

....

Practice Session One, Part One: Arbus Photographs Sontag

....

Habits: connecting, exploring, speculating

Activities: interpreting, looking, researching

The example of creative reading we've described follows from a question about an essay to an image not included in or referenced in the original essay. We first want you to find a reproduction online of Diane Arbus's photograph of Susan Sontag with her son. What light do you think Arbus's photograph of Sontag and her son sheds on Sontag's assessment of Arbus's work in "America, Seen through Photographs, Darkly"? Spend at least twenty minutes figuring out a thoughtful, compelling answer to this question. Work only with what we've provided. *Don't* seek out the rest of Sontag's essay or more information about Arbus. What does the photograph alone tell you?

Practice Session One, Part Two: Arbus Photographs Sontag

Habits: connecting, exploring, speculating
Activities: note taking, researching, writing

As we've said, the work of creative reading is never done. What information can you find online about the image of Sontag and her son? About *their* relationship? About Sontag's fuller argument in "America, Seen through Photographs, Darkly"? (Can you find the essay itself?) What can you discover about her argument in *On Photography*? Spend at least an hour researching and reading, keeping careful notes on your discoveries.

Now you're ready to work on an extended essay about how to read Arbus's images creatively. Continue the research Alice began about how viewers have responded to Arbus's photographs in the forty years since Sontag's critique, gathering information about one or more lines of response to the photographs. Then make an argument for how you think an Arbus photograph ought to be read.

Practice Session Two: Diigo and Your Reading Practices

Habits: beginning, exploring, reflecting
Activities: mapping, note taking, reading

Open your own Diigo account. Once a day for a week, we'd like you to bookmark and annotate a page you've visited on the web. The Diigo tool allows for highlighting, but in our experience most highlighting is done in place of actual reading. We want you to mark those places in your reading that raised a question of *any kind* for you. An unfamiliar word, data that seems not to compute, an interpretation that doesn't make sense, an odd sentence structure — wherever your reading is stopped, take note of it. At the end of a week, you'll be able to build a profile of your own reading practices.

Once you have made a version of your own reading practices visible for you to consider, what do you see? Set aside at least thirty minutes to write down answers to these questions: What do your annotations reveal about the kind of reader you are? What habits do you practice currently? Were there instances when your experience of reading was more pleasurable than it was at other times? More productive? More useful? Was your practice of reading markedly different on some days, or did the outcome depend more on what you were reading at the time?

Using your research and reflections on your reading practices, compose a portrait of yourself as a reader. Where are you now as a reader? Where would you like to be? What specific steps do you need to take to become a lifelong creative reader? Write an essay that analyzes the most important events in your experience as a reader up to the present moment.

On Choosing Your Own Adventure

What question do you want to make sure you've thought about before you graduate from college?

This is a question we now pose regularly to students who work with us. We like it because it has the power to get our students to forego pseudo-research projects and focuses their attention on genuine concerns they have about their lives and about the future. We stumbled on this question during a discussion of graduation requirements in a required writing class. Acknowledging that none of us had the power to change either the number or the kind of course requirements the students had to fulfill in order to graduate, we turned our attention to what was under our control: the form and the content of the writing they were doing in our course. For some of our students, the invitation to write about a vexing question of their own choosing was a welcome development. These students flocked to our offices with promising opening questions: Why am I so unlike my twin? How can I help my future patients with end-of-life issues when my pre-med education provides no training in this area? How can I tell the difference between the real and the fake me? Why am I expected to have children when I have no interest in doing so? What's the best way for me to think about God?

The majority of the projects that this first wave of students proposed explicitly concerned identity, which didn't surprise us. We believe that one of the most important functions of the humanities in a secular society is to enable self-exploration without predetermined outcomes; we think the question, "What does it mean to be human?" is one that all students, regardless of major or professional track, should have the opportunity to explore. And we don't see this as an open invitation to share angst-driven tales of personal hardship. Because the assignment is for students to work on a question they want to be sure to have thought about before graduating, fulfilling the assignment necessarily entails doing research and pursuing that research wherever it may lead. Once the students' research was underway, the students had to build a bridge from their individual concerns to others who shared those same concerns: psychologists, historians, theologians, philosophers, hospice workers, sociologists, economists, family therapists, and artists. (This list is suggestive and what we mean for it to suggest is that research into foundational questions always means reading across disciplines and specialties.) So, if the students chose questions that were genuinely important to them, we knew that, with a little help from us along the way, their research would take them, as a matter of course, to other writers who would push, challenge, extend, expand, and complicate their thinking.

Not every student had an easy time generating a question for this assignment, of course. Some were genuinely flummoxed at the prospect of researching a question that might not have an answer. Others, we learned, weren't convinced we were serious, so they came to us with fake projects (For example, are you really concerned about high school uniforms? Is this what keeps you up at night?). And still others were leery of taking on an open-ended assignment because they sensed, accurately, that pursuing a self-generated question was going to be more work than pulling together a traditional research paper that had the right number of cited sources and met the minimum page requirements. Once the students in these camps understood that we really didn't have a list of prefabricated questions for them to choose from, they joined the fray. (What other choice did they have?)

Julie's situation was different: when she met with us, she explained that she was having difficulty choosing one question out of all the ones she wanted to pursue. As we talked about how she might make her way out of this quandary, we were already focusing on the question that would have the core of Julie's research project: How do you make decisions responsibly when the outcomes can't be known in advance? Julie explained that she struggled to make decisions because she had a history of making choices she later regretted. She'd try to go with her intuition and end up acting rashly; she'd try calm reflection and she'd end up playing three-dimensional chess with herself while the moment for addressing the problem slipped away; she'd try collecting input from others and then find herself overwhelmed by too much information. When we suggested that Julie look into what others had to say about how to make decisions, she was cautiously optimistic: the project seemed "a little meta," but she'd give it a try.

We owe the title of our essay to Julie's nonlinear final project, which she was inspired to organize on the model of the Choose Your Own Adventure stories she had enjoyed as a child. (While most stories give the reader no choice but to move from beginning, to middle, to end, Choose Your Own Adventure stories have moments when the reader gets to determine where the story goes next by selecting from a list of options.) What would happen, Julie wondered, if her account of her *research* into decision making unfolded like a Choose Your Own Adventure story? And, once we'd read Julie's final project, we found ourselves wondering what would happen if all students had a chance to think about research the way Julie had—that is, as a way of choosing their own adventures through ideas instead of as one more hurdle to clear before graduation?

Here's what appeared on the homepage for Julie's final project, under the heading, "Choose Your Own Adventure!"

There are no instructions. Decide!

To read a poem, click here.
To read about ketchup, click here.
To help me choose, click here.
To find out more about why I'm doing this, click here.

There is so much we like about what Julie has done with the website she created. Her very first act as a writer is to have her readers experience the problem that is at the heart of her project: How do you make a decision when the information you have to work with is incomplete? There's a playfulness in this menu of options that captures the absurdity of some of the choices we face: a poem or ketchup, you decide! Decide what?

Julie gives her readers four different ways into her project. We chose to click on the link that promises the chance to read a poem, but the linked page doesn't deliver on that promise. Instead, Julie begins this page by discussing a model of decision making that comes from behavioral science. Then she interrupts herself to say, "You came here for a poem, but I got sidetracked. Was this a waste of time? Are you disappointed? Here's the poem you were supposed to have read." Once again, the form and function of Julie's writing come into alignment: she's compelling her readers to have the experience that she is researching. You make a decision and then things don't turn out the way you expected. What to do?

Read a poem? Julie presents a sonnet by Bernadette Mayer that ends as follows:

To make love, turn to page 121.
To die, turn to page 172.

In analyzing the poem, Julie argues that its focus is on the "unpredictable human element" in the decision-making process. "One name for [this unpredictable human element] could be human error," Julie observes. "Another could be destiny." And then she gives her readers a new list of options for where to go next in her meditation on choice.

In subsequent sections, Julie engages with psychologist Barry Schwartz, who argues that we have acquired more freedom and autonomy than we can process, with the result that we're caught in "the paradox of choice" due to too many options; the web comic *Head and Heart*, which offers readers vignettes about the ongoing struggle between the voice of reason and the voice of emotion; Malcolm Gladwell's discussion of "intermarket variability" and the discovery that there's no one single perfect version of any given food type; philosopher Ruth Chang on how to make decisions when we know that we can never have enough information to be sure our decision is "right." Throughout, Julie provides examples in which she applies the ideas under consideration to her own life; she compares the life choices that are available to her that weren't available to her mother; and she guides her readers to her closing reflection on what she has come to understand about decision making over the course of her research.

This research project was valuable for Julie because she chose to explore a question that mattered to her and then followed that question wherever it led. Any question a writer is genuinely passionate about has the potential to generate research that helps that writer think new thoughts. We know this to be true because we've seen it happen with questions as diverse (and as impossible to assign) as: What emotional obligations do I owe to my parents? Where does my consciousness go during the hours when I'm commuting? How can I be an ethical member of the tech industry when I see the negative effect that technology is having on society? The question one starts with is just a point of departure. The adventure starts when the search for answers begins. And, we've found, once you've taken yourself away on one of these adventures, you're likely to want to go on another and another. The adventures you choose to go on are the traces of your creative mind hard at work being curious about the world in all its complexity.

Practice Session One, Part One:
Possible Adventures

Habits: beginning, exploring, questioning

Activities: wondering, writing

So, what question would you like to have thought about before you graduate? (Any milestone can be used here: before you turn twenty-five, before you commit to a career, before your children enter college, etc.) The question you generate can be in any form and touch on any topic, with two exceptions: your question cannot have a yes or no answer and you can't already have the answer to your question before you begin. We provide numerous examples of questions our students have posed for this assignment in our essay: the questions that have proven to be most meaningful for our students often begin with how or why or what. They can be big questions, unmanageable questions, or hard-to-articulate questions. All that matters at this stage is that you propose a question that you feel is urgent or important, perhaps a question that has nagged at you for years.

Practice Session One, Part Two: Setting Out

Habits: beginning, exploring, questioning

Activities: looking, questioning, researching

Once you've generated your question and you've been given the green light to proceed, you're ready to begin your adventure. We find it helpful to think about the research adventure as analogous to a physical adventure into unknown territory. How will you get the lay of the land? Are there sites in this territory that everyone visits? Dominant ideas? Important figures? Inner and outer circles? Forbidden zones? The difference between a physical adventure and a mental adventure, of course, is that all the excitement takes place in the adventurer's mind; the limit of the journey is at the furthest reaches of the adventurer's curiosity.

Where do you go to find people who can help you think about your question? The search engine on your computer is a good place to start, but what search terms should you use? You can start anywhere, of course, and though we have places where we think it's better to begin than others, what's most important at this stage is that you follow the "two-clicks-down" rule. Let's say Julie started out by typing "trouble making decisions" in her search engine. Her first page of results might give her links to articles from *Psychology Today*, *Huffington Post*, *Lifehacker*, and the like. Julie's got to start somewhere, so she chooses one of the links and starts reading. She's got to keep reading until she finds something that surprises her. That might not happen with the first link; it might not happen with any of the links of the first page; but it will happen eventually. (Real adventures aren't like action-packed movies; exploring takes time and most of that time consists of looking and looking and not finding anything.)

Once Julie finds something that interests, surprises, or confuses her, it's time to apply the two-clicks-down rule: she needs to initiate a new search into whatever captured her attention. And then she needs to repeat the process of searching, reading, reviewing, and questioning until something new captures her attention. Then she initiates yet another search keeps on digging. Each time Julie clicks down, she widens her circle of reference and she opens doors that she can go through or not, as she chooses. What she doesn't do is return from her first day of adventuring with a report on what *Psychology Today* or the *Huffington Post* has to say about why decision making is difficult. Anyone could find that out by exercising the smallest effort. But Julie's assignment, and yours, is to pursue a question she wants to have thought seriously about before graduating from college. No one would say that reading the top link provided by a search engine qualifies as an example of the effort to think seriously about anything.

Do your own searches following the example of Julie's search above. Follow the two-clicks-down rule and then write individual reports about two of your searches. Where did they take you? What did you find? Where will you look next? What insights have you gained at this point in your research?

....

Practice Session One, Part Three: Finding Crosscurrents

....

Habits: exploring, playing, working deliberately

Activities: looking again, reading, researching

Once you get the hang of the two-clicks-down rule, you'll be on your way to reading widely. Even so, it is quite possible to follow this method and miss out on the opportunity to engage with important research that might touch on your question. This is because all the major search engines rank their search results with algorithms that reward popularity in one form or another. And, further, everyone who conducts research has to contend with "confirmation bias," which means being drawn to information that fits with one's preconceptions. So, to do compelling research, at some point your adventures have to take you off in a direction you didn't expect. But how to get this to happen? You can turn to different search engines: Google Scholar delivers results that are quite different from a plain vanilla search; so, too, will searches at TED, YouTube, your school library, iTunesU, *Radiolab*, the Library of Congress, and on and on. Your goal at this point is to find voices to engage with that aren't repeating what you've already discovered. You shouldn't be trying to "back up your point." Instead, you want to produce writing that enriches your reader's understanding of the complexity of your question.

You'll know you're moving in the right direction when you find new source material that causes you to qualify the insights you articulated at the end of Part Two of this practice session.

....

Practice Session One, Part Four: Putting It All Together

....

Habits: exploring, organizing, working deliberately

Activities: engaging with sources, researching, writing

When we give this assignment, we don't provide page-length or word-count requirements. And we don't say the final versions need to have X number of citations in such-and-such a format. We say instead: hand in a snapshot of your mind at work on a problem, one you've chosen to think about because of its importance to you. Show us what thinking seriously about something means to you.

How do we know that our students have succeeded? We look for evidence that the writer has taken the search to surprising, interesting, and smart sources. (We're especially pleased when students unearth original sources and primary documents.) We also look for evidence that the writer is actively engaged in a mental adventure, rather than simply going through the motions. And we want to see that the writer has tried to make every word count.

Now it's your turn to write the final draft of your adventure. Take this as an opportunity to show how your research has helped you to resee your initial question. You're not persuading some imagined reader; you're not arguing with some imagined adversary. You're documenting your mind in conversation with itself and with the sources you discovered. Finally, your essay should capture the attention of readers; stage your adventure with them in mind.

6

CONNECTING

"Connect the dots": this phrase used to appear atop the pages of activity books designed to help young children practice counting while they worked on improving their fine motor skills. A child, crayon in hand, would draw a line from numbered dot to numbered dot, and at the end of the process, if the child had followed the dots in order, then voilà, there was a picture. If not, there was a mess.

No one would argue that connecting the dots is creative. The child has simply followed the directions to reveal a design. But once we move from children connecting dots to students using their own writing to connect ideas discussed in what they've been reading, we enter a realm where creativity becomes possible. Any two ideas can be connected; any claim can be made; any argument can be put forward. Under such chaotic conditions, how does one make connections that matter?

The essays in this section will help you to resist writing formulas that limit your encounters with the infinite range of connections to be made. To encourage you to practice using your writing to develop new habits for engaging with and exploring what is unknown to you, we want you to think of writing itself as the act of making connections. Writers make connections through their linguistic choices, through the conversations they choose to join, and through how they choose to use the words provided to them by their sources. As you experiment with making connections in each of these areas, you will be engaging directly in the creative act of making meaning: the dots you connect will be your own, and the image that results will be of your own design.

On the Three Most Important Words in the English Language

How do you know you're thinking?

This is the kind of question that stops you in your tracks. First, you think, who would ask about something so obvious? And then—well, then you're left with the challenge of putting into words a central facet of your mental life.

When we begin discussing this question in class, we are soon deep in the murk. There's involuntary mental activity, which takes place in any brain-equipped creature—for example, the turtle sunning on a log is passively monitoring the surroundings, scanning for threats. There's instinct, the lightning-quick response to incoming data—the cat pounces on whatever is rustling in the bush, killing, as the common phrase puts it, without thinking. There's dreaming, and there's daydreaming, too. There's all this involuntary mental activity going on up there that we don't control. And then there's thought, which is, in contrast, mental activity over which we have some control. So while we can't unsee what our eyes behold or unhear the sounds that enter our ears, and we can't unsmell, untouch, or unfeel, we can change how we think about what our senses are reporting. And though we can't exactly *unthink* a thought we've had, we can change that thought by *rethinking* it.

We're interested in that stretch of mental activity that you can influence. For the moment, we ask that you grant us the following proposition:

Thinking is the intentional act of making connections.

This act of connecting can take place in language, sound, and images; chefs would doubtless say it takes place in taste, and perfumers in smell. We're open to the medium; what we want to focus on is the array of connections available to the thinker.

We are pretty sure that you'll have reservations about this proposition, but we need you to suspend those reservations for the time being. Don't worry; we'll qualify and complicate the proposition by and by—we promise.

Beginning writers, like beginning thinkers, tend to rely on one connector: the coordinating conjunction *and*. For the beginning writer, writing is the act of connecting like to like, with thoughts or observations linked together via the explicit or implicit use of *and*:

> The house I grew up in had a garden. It also had a garage. It had two floors. *And* an attic.

In this additive mode of composing, the beginning writer can expand the composition as much as the assignment requires. All that the writer needs to supply is more of the same:

> It had two chimneys. It had three bedrooms. *And* one bathroom.

In the hands of an experienced storyteller, this additive mode of composing can serve as the foundation for an episodic epic poem:

> After the end of the Trojan War, Odysseus heads home. On the way back, he and his men sack the city of Ismarus. And then they sail to the land of the Lotus-Eaters. After they escape, they encounter the Cyclops, Polyphemus. And then, and then, and then . . .

Similarly, in the hands of an experienced visual artist, the assumption that *and* links like to like can be exploited to create jarring juxtapositions that bring into being something entirely unexpected. When *and* is intentionally used to link like to unlike, surprising things can happen. Chinese artist Ai Weiwei is a master of making unexpected visual connections, such as when he takes a two-thousand-year-old Han dynasty vase and paints the swooping Coca Cola logo across it with red acrylic. What does the "Coca Cola Vase" mean? There's no single answer to that question. The artist connects ancient art and new art; Chinese cultural history and global capitalism; a highly valued object from the past and a mass-produced logo from the present.

Beginning writers are more likely to make simple connections via addition (A and B and C) than via qualification (A and B but not C). The machinery of the five-paragraph theme makes no room for thinking of this kind; there's just the thesis, the three supporting examples (A and B and C), and the conclusion. Qualification muddies the waters.

It's not that beginning writers have no access to the word *but*. Indeed, when we confer with beginning writers, we often find that their minds are abuzz with qualifications, exceptions, contradictions, and confusions. However, little of this mental activity makes it onto the page because our students have been told repeatedly that the goal of writing in school is clarity. They learn to equate *clarity* with *simplicity*, so they avoid presenting anything that might complicate their efforts to produce an argument that is straightforward and to the point. When this strategy of avoiding complications is rewarded, writing's function is limited to the activity of simplification, and the goal of writing in school becomes nothing more than producing "arguments" that are clear, direct, and easy to follow.

Obviously, writing has a communicative function (moving idea X from point A to point B), but this isn't writing's sole function. Writing can also serve as a technology for thinking new thoughts — that is, thoughts that are new to the writer. We believe that this use of writing, as a heuristic for venturing into the unknown, is as important as its communicative use. Indeed, it is through learning how to use writing for discovery, comprehension, and problem solving that we come to have ideas that are worth communicating.

In high school (and, alas, sometimes in college) students are told to start with a thesis and then find evidence to support their position. These instructions reduce writing to the process of reporting what fits the thesis and ignoring the rest. The problem with such writing is not that it is unclear but rather that it is, from the outset, *too* clear: it says what it's *going* to say (thesis), then it says it (three supporting examples), and then it says what it said (conclusion). Reading writing of this kind is like being plunged into the great echo chamber of nothingness.

This problem is easily solved: in our classes, we insist that our students bring the coordinating conjunction *but* into their writing. Things get messy right away, and clarity, misunderstood as simplicity, gives way to qualification and complexity. At the start, some of the qualifications are silly, and others are improbable. But the qualifications become more meaningful over time, and the prose begins to engage more productively with the complexities of lived experience. The writing thus begins to capture the shape of a mind at work on a problem.

But is the passkey for entry into critical thinking.

If you want to test out this assertion, we invite you to consider how different Abraham Lincoln's Gettysburg Address would be if it ended after the second paragraph:

> Four score and seven years ago our fathers brought forth, on this continent, a new nation, conceived in Liberty, and dedicated to the proposition that all men are created equal.
>
> Now we are engaged in a great civil war, testing whether that nation, or any nation so conceived and so dedicated, can long endure. We are met on a great battle-field of that war. We have come to dedicate a portion of that field, as a final resting place for those who here gave their lives that that nation might live. It is altogether fitting and proper that we should do this.

Lincoln speaks at the dedication of the cemetery at Gettysburg, Pennsylvania, for the Union casualties of the Battle of Gettysburg. He invokes the nation as if it were one thing, but the nation is at war with itself. Those who have gathered for the dedication of the cemetery do so to recognize the sacrifice of those who died so that the "nation might live."

If the speech ended here, it would end with the statement that recognizing the fallen is "altogether fitting and proper." Lincoln's intent is clear: it's appropriate to recognize those who have died defending the liberties of those who are still living. He's saying aloud what everyone present already knows; the point he is making is obvious to all.

But the speech *doesn't* end here. Lincoln continues:

> But, in a larger sense, we can not dedicate — we can not consecrate — we can not hallow — this ground. The brave men, living and dead, who struggled here, have consecrated it, far above our poor power to add or detract. The world will little note, nor long remember what we say here, but it can never forget what they did here.

Everything hinges on the qualification that Lincoln introduces in the third paragraph of his speech. What those who are assembled are doing is "altogether fitting and proper," *but* the living do not, in fact, have the power to do what those who fought on that land have done.

With this qualification, Lincoln is able to shift the audience's attention from an understanding of dedication as a commemorative event bounded in time to its redefinition as an open-ended activity carried out by the living in the service of a vulnerable ideal:

> It is for us the living, rather, to be dedicated here to the unfinished work which they who fought here have thus far so nobly advanced. It is rather for us to be here dedicated to the great task remaining before us — that from these honored dead we take increased devotion to that cause for which they gave the last full measure of devotion — that we here highly resolve that these dead shall not have died in vain — that this nation, under God, shall have a new birth of freedom — and that government of the people, by the people, for the people, shall not perish from the earth.

Lincoln's use of *but* at the beginning of the third paragraph of his address allows him to connect dedication as a ceremonial event to the ongoing activity of being dedicated to some higher ideal. The connection is not like to like: coming to the dedication is not the same thing as dedicating oneself to the preservation of the nation. Without the *but*, we have a speech that thanks people for coming to a battlefield; with that qualification, we have a speech that links the deaths that took place on the battlefield to a larger set of ideas, values, hopes, and aspirations.

How do you get from critical thinking to creative thinking? Here's a rubric that oversimplifies to the point of distortion:

and	Foundation for thought	Basis for black-and-white, yes/no, binary thinking
but	Foundation for critical thought	Enables qualifications, exceptions, conditions, ambiguity, uncertainty
or	Foundation for creative thought	Enables alternatives, possibilities; is future oriented

We know this table can't withstand rigorous critical examination. Indeed, we'd say the table predicts its own dismantling, since it assumes both a critical thinker who will respond to the clear-cut grid by qualifying the table's assertions and a creative thinker who will imagine other grids or other ways of modeling the relationship between coordinating conjunctions and modes of thought.

So, just like the overly simplified left-brain right-brain distinction discussed in "On Learning to See" (pp. 45–46), our table doesn't fully depict how thought happens. It's simply a heuristic device, a helpful strategy for identifying different mental operations; it's a way to get you to think about thinking as the process of making connections.

With those qualifications, we stand by this assertion:

> Consciously introducing *but* and *or* to your mental activity
> is a surefire way to generate new thinking.

It really is that simple.

Practice Session One: Visual Microstories

Habits: connecting, organizing, playing, reflecting

Activities: analyzing, selecting, writing

Find three images that are important to you. They can be pictures of you or pictures you took yourself; pictures from the internet; pictures of historical events or pictures of historical importance; pictures of art objects; even advertisements. They need not all be important in the same way.

Place the images before you. What are the implicit connections between them — A and B and C? A or B or C? A and B but not C? A or B and C? The possibilities are not infinite, but they are multiple. Spend at least five minutes jotting down notes about the implicit connections — connections that are not openly expressed but that are capable of being understood — between the images as they are laid out before you.

When you've completed your reflections, change the order of the images. What happens to the implicit connections? Repeat the exercise above with the newly ordered images.

When you've completed these two reflections about connections, take at least twenty minutes to write a reflective account of what happened to the connections when you reordered the images. Why does their order make a difference?

Practice Session Two: Connection Detection

Habits: connecting, paying attention, reflecting

Activities: analyzing, comparing, reading

We'd like you to look at Rebecca Solnit's "Occupied Territory" (pp. 302–08), which we've included in the Readings section at the end of this book. Read it through once; then return to it and mark where Solnit makes connections.

Make a list of explicit (expressed) or implicit (unexpressed) *and* connections that set information or ideas next to each other.

Then list connections that explicitly or implicitly use the word *but* to establish qualifications, exceptions, conditions, ambiguity, or uncertainty.

Next, list connections that explicitly or implicitly use the word *or* to point out alternatives or possibilities.

Finally, spend at least thirty minutes writing a reflective piece about the connections you listed in the *but* and *or* categories. Which connection is the most important? Which is the most surprising?

Practice Session Three: Whose Space Is It Anyway?

Habits: connecting, exploring, speculating

Activities: analyzing, being open to uncertainty and complexity, reading, researching

After our students compose the first draft of an essay, we often find ourselves saying something along the lines of, "Yes, you've chosen a promising topic [or made a valid observation], but the issue is more complicated than it first appears." Then we invite our students to make their thinking more complex by connecting their initial thoughts, new ideas, or information using *but* or *or* instead of *and*. These objections, qualifications, and additions can't be pulled out of thin air, however. They have to be discovered through reading, research, and thought.

Solnit's "Occupied Territory" (pp. 302–08) offers a stark account of how people in the United States — women and men, minority populations and whites, people with disabilities and people without — experience space differently. While it's easy to take a polarized position on Solnit's argument by simply agreeing or disagreeing with her, it's more interesting to use her work as a starting place for thinking more deeply about the points she raises.

Select three or four passages that confuse, surprise, disturb, or otherwise interest you, and then spend at least two hours researching the events or history Solnit discusses. As you dig down into your research, pay attention to places where you learn things that deepen or complicate your understanding of either Solnit's argument or your own thinking. In other words, look for places where you can make new connections.

Write an essay that discusses how your research has informed and altered your thinking about Solnit's argument. As you write, use the "three most important words" (and variations) to present research that adds to, qualifies, contradicts, or suggests alternatives both to Solnit's ideas *and* to your own previously held opinions.

On Joining the Conversation

The literary critic Kenneth Burke described the exchange of academic ideas as a never-ending parlor conversation. "Imagine," he wrote,

> that you enter a parlor. You come late. When you arrive, others have long preceded you, and they are engaged in a heated discussion, a discussion too heated for them to pause and tell you exactly what it is about. In fact, the discussion had already begun long before any of them got there, so that no one present is qualified to retrace for you all the steps that had gone before. You listen for a while, until you decide that you have caught the tenor of the argument; then you put in your oar. Someone answers; you answer him; another comes to your defense; another aligns himself against you, to either the embarrassment or gratification of your opponent, depending upon the quality of your ally's assistance. However, the discussion is interminable. The hour grows late, you must depart. And you do depart, with the discussion still vigorously in progress.

With this extended metaphor, Burke offers us a way to think about how to write academic arguments. Preparing to write a paper about a topic that is new to you is like entering a parlor where a "heated discussion" is already taking place. For a while, all you can do is read what others have written and try to follow the debate. Then, after a bit, you begin to figure out what's being discussed and what the different positions, conflicts, and alliances are. Eventually, after you catch the "tenor" or drift of the conversation, a moment arrives when you feel you have something to contribute to the conversation, and you "put in your oar." And so you begin writing, even though you know that you won't have the last word—that no one will ever have the last word.

Doubtless, there is much about Burke's vision of academic writing that you've already heard: to write, you need to understand what others have written about the problem or question that intrigues you, and you must be able to represent, analyze, and synthesize those views.

You also have to be interested enough in joining the conversation to develop a position of your own that responds to those sources in compelling ways. What *is* surprising about Burke's scenario is his insistence that the conversation never ends: it is "interminable." There are no decisive arguments in Burke's parlor, or even any lastingly persuasive ones; there is only the ceaseless exchange of positions.

But why, you might reasonably ask, would anyone choose to engage in a conversation without end? To answer this question, we'd like to walk you through an example of a writer working with multiple sources to explore an open-ended question. Such questions can't be answered with a yes or no, or by simply reporting facts. Open-ended questions have many possible answers; the best answers reveal hidden complexities, introduce important distinctions, delight in nuance and subtlety, place the issue at hand in a new context, deepen understanding, point to a new question or the next question. The best answers make connections that extend the discussion.

Although Burke's parlor is generally used to describe how academic arguments emerge and evolve, magazine journalists and other nonfiction writers also engage in conversations with books they've read and research they've done. In his article "An Animal's Place," for example, Michael Pollan grapples with the ideas of Peter Singer, a philosopher who argues that eating meat is unethical and that vegetarianism is a moral imperative. With the opening sentence of "An Animal's Place," Pollan wants his readers to know that he's a meat eater and that he expects to dislike Singer's ideas: "The first time I opened Peter Singer's *Animal Liberation*, I was dining alone at The Palm, trying to enjoy a rib-eye steak cooked medium-rare." Reading a treatise on vegetarianism while eating meat: classic! Pollan hasn't yet read the book, but he's been warned that Singer's argument is going to challenge him to the core. It is "one of those rare books that demands that you either defend the way you live or change it."

When Pollan opens *Animal Liberation* over a fifty-dollar steak, he blocks out the noisy restaurant and creates his own Burkean parlor. Having entered the conversation late, he tries to catch "the tenor of the argument" against being a carnivore. Pollan discovers that Singer opposes not only eating meat, but also wearing fur, using animals in experiments, and killing animals for sport. While all these practices are common in our time, Singer argues that future generations will see them as expressions of our "speciesism" and that they will be looked back on, in Pollan's words, as "a form of discrimination as indefensible as racism or anti-Semitism." As Pollan learns more about Singer's ideas, he realizes he must take seriously the question that drives *Animal Liberation*: "If possessing a higher degree of intelligence does not entitle one human to use another for his or her own ends, how can it entitle humans to exploit nonhumans for the same purpose?"

Pollan begins to do some research to learn more about Singer's many intellectual, legal, and political allies around the world. He learns that, in May 2002, German lawmakers granted animals the constitutional right to be treated with respect and dignity by the state. In addition, England has banned the farming of animals for fur and several European nations have banned confining pigs and laying hens in small crates. He notes that Singer cites the eighteenth-century philosopher Jeremy Bentham, who argued that even though animals cannot reason or speak, they are owed moral consideration because they can suffer. He reads other people who are in Singer's Burkean parlor, among them: Matthew Scully, a political conservative and former speechwriter for President George W. Bush, who wrote a best seller about routine cruelty toward animals in the United States; and Nobel Prize-winning novelist J. M. Coetzee, who declared that eating meat and purchasing goods made of leather and other animal products is "a crime of stupefying proportions," akin to Germans continuing with their normal lives in the midst of the Holocaust.

Before Pollan can join Singer in a discussion of the ethical treatment of animals, he needs to find his own allies in the ongoing conversation. He is intrigued by John Berger's essay "Why Look at Animals?" which argues that humans have become deeply confused about their relationship to other animals because they no longer make eye contact with most species. This helps Pollan to explain the paradox that even as more and more people in the United States are eager to extend rights to animals, in our factory farms "we are inflicting more suffering on more animals than at any time in history." By reading sources as varied as Scully's *Dominion* and farm trade magazines, Pollan learns that these farms, also known as confined animal feeding operations, or CAFOs, reduce animals to "production units" and subject them to a life of misery.

These sources don't make it easy for Pollan to reject Singer's argument that everyone who considers eating meat must choose between "a lifetime of suffering for a nonhuman animal and the gastronomic preference of a human being." Pollan is unhappy with the options before him. He doesn't want to refuse to pay attention to the suffering of animals in factory farms, but he also doesn't want to stop eating animals, so he brings a completely new voice into the conversation: not a philosopher or a lawyer, but a farmer. Joel Salatin, owner of Polyface Farm in Virginia, raises cattle, pigs, chickens, rabbits, turkeys, and sheep on a small farm where each species, including the one represented by the farmer himself, performs a unique role in the ecosystem. The cows graze in the pasture; afterward, the chickens come in and eat insect larvae and short grass; then the sheep take their turn and eat what the cows and chickens have left behind. Meanwhile, the pigs compost the cow manure in the barn. On Salatin's farm, the mutual interest of humans and domestic animals is recognized, even when the animals are slaughtered for meat. Each animal lives according to its natural inclinations; and when an animal is slaughtered, its death takes place in the open. After visiting Salatin's farm, Pollan concludes that slaughtering animals where nothing is hidden from sight is "a morally powerful idea." He values Salatin's decision to grant each animal a respectful death, in contrast to what happens in factory farms, where animals are "treated as a pile of protoplasm."

After having explored what others have to say about the ethics of animal agriculture, Pollan is finally ready to define his own position: "what's wrong with animal agriculture—with eating animals—is the practice, not the principle." The challenge, in Pollan's view, is less philosophical than practical: Do animals raised for meat live lives that allow them to express their natures? Do they live good lives? Pollan decides that if he limits his consumption of meat to animals that are raised humanely, then he can eat them without ethical qualms. He is so pleased with his creative solution to the problem Singer posed that he writes to the philosopher to ask him what he thinks about the morality of eating meat that comes from farms where animals live according to their nature. Singer holds to his position that it is wrong to kill an animal that "has a sense of its own existence" and has "preferences for its own future" (that is, a pig, but not a chicken), but he also admits that he would not "condemn someone who purchased meat from one of these farms."

Does this mean that Pollan has won the argument? Not really. The discussion in Burke's parlor has not ended. New voices have entered to engage with both Pollan and Singer, and new ideas have emerged about sustainability, agriculture, economics, and ethics. Curious, reflective, and open-ended thinkers continue to enter, mingle, and depart, with "the discussion still vigorously in progress."

Practice Session One, Part One: Mapping the Conversation

Habits: beginning, paying attention, working deliberately

Activities: note taking, reading, reflecting

For this practice session, we'd like you to read Michael Pollan's "An Animal's Place" and think more about how he uses sources and what it means to be "in conversation" with words on a page or screen. Read the piece with care, taking notes about where and how Pollan uses his sources to develop his own thoughts. After reading, take at least thirty minutes to consider the following questions about entering into a conversation with sources, writing down your answers in preparation for discussion: Where did Pollan engage with sources in ways that surprised you? Where did he use sources in ways that you'd like to emulate? What different kinds of conversations did Pollan engage in with his sources? Why did he choose to be in conversation with some sources more than others? What have you learned from these exercises about writing "in conversation" with sources?

Practice Session One, Part Two: "Unspeakable Conversations"

Habits: beginning, connecting, paying attention

Activities: note taking, reading, reflecting

After you've completed practice session one, we'd like you to read Harriet McBryde Johnson's "Unspeakable Conversations." Johnson is also in conversation with Peter Singer, but she is interested in Singer's controversial views on euthanasia. Read Johnson's article with care, observing the many different ways she joins in conversation with her sources. Identify sources that serve as the focus of analysis; supply background or information; provide key ideas or concepts; provide positions or arguments to grapple with; or shift the direction of the conversation.

After you've finished reading, spend at least thirty minutes making a list of the many ways Johnson uses her source material. Note that she does not explicitly identify every source of information. What would you say is the difference between an "unspeakable conversation" and an uncited one?

Practice Session One, Part Three: The Good Life

Habits: beginning, connecting, reflecting
Activities: engaging with sources, synthesizing, writing

Now that you've read both "An Animal's Place" and "Unspeakable Conversations," we'd like you to compose an essay in which you join a conversation with Pollan and Johnson about the following question: To what extent is it possible to define what makes a "good life" (or a "good death") for humans and other animals? Use Pollan's and Johnson's essays as both sources and models of how to join a conversation in writing.

Practice Session Two: Exploring "What Is Education For?"

Habits: beginning, paying attention, working deliberately
Activities: analyzing, defining, engaging with sources

The question about what education is for may be as old as human society itself. With a question so thoroughly discussed, it's hard to see how there's anything new left to be said on the matter. And yet, this is precisely the challenge that Danielle Allen sets herself in "What Is Education For?" which we've included in the Readings section at the end of this book. As you read Allen's essay, pay attention to whom she cites and how she cites them. She's creating a conversation about the value of education: What kind of conversation is it? What is its purpose?

After you've finished reading Allen's piece, write a profile that describes what kind of a conversationalist Allen is, based on your analysis of who she cites and how she cites them.

On Working with the Words of Others

If you were to ask a teacher why it's so important to provide full and accurate citation information about what sources you used in a paper and where you used those sources, you'd likely be told that citation is a service to your readers in two important ways. First, identifying your sources in a works cited list allows readers to follow up on ideas and information they encounter in your writing. And second, naming your sources, using quotation marks, and adding footnotes mark the boundaries between your work and the work of others. Both of these answers imply that citation is primarily a means for defending yourself from dubious readers—those who would doubt the quality of your research and those who would suspect you of plagiarizing.

While we acknowledge that learning the nuts and bolts of how to cite sources in academic papers is important, it's not our highest priority.[1] In our classes we emphasize that there are many ways to engage productively with the words of others. To move our students beyond the idea that citation is for "support," we provide them with this handy list of seven ways of working with the words of others to promote thinking new thoughts.[2] Our list isn't meant to be complete or definitive; it's just the first step in getting our students to pay attention to how more experienced writers work with sources.

1. A source can serve as "a primary focus of analysis."
2. It can "supply context, background, or information."
3. It can "provide key terms or concepts."
4. It can provide an "opinion or interpretation" to grapple with.
5. It can help to "establish a question or problem worth addressing."
6. It can affirm or advance claims by providing the perspective of a recognized expert.
7. It can shift the direction of the conversation.

---

[1] There are plenty of online resources to help you learn how to use various citation formats. We recommend that you begin with the "Research and Citation Resources" available at the Purdue Online Writing Lab.

[2] The first five items on this list are from Kerry Walk's handout "Five Ways to Use Sources in Academic Argument," which has been a valuable resource at the Princeton Writing Program for many years.

To help you see what it means to work with the words of others in some of the ways listed above, we're going to turn to "Battleground America: One Nation, Under the Gun," an article by Jill Lepore, a professor of early American history, that appeared in the *New Yorker* in 2012. In this piece, Lepore writes about the history of gun laws in the United States, from the drafting of the Second Amendment in 1789 to the fatal shooting of Trayvon Martin, an unarmed 17-year-old, in Sanford, Florida, in 2012.

A SOURCE CAN SERVE AS A PRIMARY FOCUS OF ANALYSIS

At the heart of Lepore's article is an argument about what the Second Amendment meant at the time it was drafted in 1789. The amendment, which serves as Lepore's primary focus of analysis, states, "A well-regulated militia being necessary to the security of a free State, the right of the people to keep and bear arms shall not be infringed." In 1789, "arms," Lepore tells her readers, were "mostly long arms that, like a smaller stockpile of pistols, could discharge only once before they had to be reloaded." Such weapons have little in common with the semiautomatic pistols and rifles that are currently the most popular types of arms in the United States. Lepore also explains what was meant by a "well-regulated militia." At the time the Constitution was being debated and ratified, people disagreed about whether the federal government would have too much power if it were allowed to support a standing army. The Second Amendment was put in place, in other words, so that the citizens of individual states would be able to form armed militias "able to repel the danger" of a federal army, should the need arise.

SOURCES CAN SUPPLY BACKGROUND INFORMATION

To explain how the interpretation of the Second Amendment changed in the mid- to late-twentieth century, Lepore turns to a speech that Malcolm X delivered in 1964, in which he declared that the amendment guaranteed "the right to own a rifle or a shotgun." This argument was soon picked up by the radical Black Panther Party for Self-Defense. Lepore then documents how, during the 1970s, the conservative National Rifle Association (NRA) adopted the argument that the amendment protected the rights of individuals to own guns. With its opposition to gun control laws and other government regulations on firearms, the NRA became a powerful force in American politics. The 1980 election of Ronald Reagan, the first president endorsed by the NRA, made the magnitude of that force even clearer. Two years later, the U.S. Senate Judiciary Subcommittee on the Constitution produced a lengthy report titled "The Right to Keep and Bear Arms." It maintained that there was "clear—and long lost—proof that the Second Amendment to our Constitution was intended as an individual right of the American citizen to keep and carry arms in a peaceful manner, for protection of himself, his family, and his freedoms." Lepore uses these sources to show how early emphasis on "a well-regulated militia" and "the people" in the Second Amendment transformed into a contemporary argument about the individual and "his freedoms."

SOURCES CAN CONTRIBUTE KEY IDEAS

Lepore doesn't stop writing once she's offered her interpretation of what the Second Amendment meant originally and how its meaning has evolved. She turns to other historians for new insights into the history of guns in the United States. She learns from Adam Winkler's book *Gunfight: The Battle over the Right to Bear Arms in America* that gun control went hand in hand with gun ownership before the late twentieth century. The shoot-out at the O.K. Corral, Lepore learns from Winkler, was actually Wyatt Earp's effort to enforce local gun control laws. Earp drew his gun on Tom McLaury because McLaury refused to follow a local (and common) ordinance that required him, on his arrival in Tombstone, Arizona, to leave his gun at the sheriff's office. By demonstrating that gun ownership and regulations coexisted for roughly two hundred years prior to Reagan's election, Winkler establishes that gun control was not understood as an infringement of sacred freedoms until the latter decades of the twentieth century.

SOURCES CAN PROVIDE POSITIONS OR ARGUMENTS TO GRAPPLE WITH

After Lepore shows that the understanding of the Second Amendment has changed, she turns her attention to the NRA's rationale for its defense of gun ownership. She is skeptical about the NRA's claim that more guns will reduce the high rate of gun deaths. She questions the logic of laws that allow for concealed carry and the argument that communities will be better off with armed citizens patrolling the streets. She is also wary of "stand-your-ground" laws, which give people the right to use lethal force to protect themselves against threats or perceived threats. Such laws, now on the books in twenty-seven states, and accepted in limited ways in ten others, expand the zone in which civilians can use deadly force for self-protection. Here, Lepore's use of sources brings her up against a reality that highlights both the importance and the limits of her argument about the original meaning of the Second Amendment. Whatever the Second Amendment meant originally, there are powerful laws in place now that emphasize the rights of individual citizens to use their guns against other citizens.

. . . . .

So, where does all this working with the words of others get Lepore in the end? It's a fair question. If you read her article in full, which we recommend, you'll see that she concludes with a story about the son of an NRA member who was sentenced to ten years in prison for firing a gun during a road-rage incident. When she tries to get the member to comment on this, she hits a brick wall. She can't get him to see her point of view — that the NRA has done more than any other organization "to weaken Americans' faith in govern-ment, or in one another." Her piece ends with a description of a school shooting and the statistic that "in an average year, roughly a hundred thousand Americans are killed or wounded with guns." In this way, Lepore shows us an essential truth about writing: it cannot force anyone to think anything. It can, however, teach the writer to develop a richer understanding of the forces on either side of an argument.

Practice Session One: Source Detective

Habits: paying attention, questioning, reflecting
Activities: analyzing, reading, writing

Journalists who write for popular magazines or newspapers typically don't provide in-text documentation of page numbers or a list of works cited. It's rare to come across a footnote in the *New Yorker, Harper's,* or the *Atlantic.* For this practice session, we'd like you to read "Battleground America," which is available through the *New Yorker* website, and review at least three pages, paying attention to where Lepore is clear about where she found words, ideas, and information from others and where she isn't. Spend at least twenty minutes making a list of where she would need to cite her sources if she had written this article for an academic class. Also note the times you were uncertain about whether she had taken material from a source.

After reviewing how and where Lepore documents her sources, spend at least forty-five minutes writing about the different citation standards of journalism and scholarly writing. Did you find evidence that caused you to trust or to doubt Lepore as a writer? Is there any way to tell whether a citation is accurate without tracking it down and checking on it yourself?

Practice Session Two: Exploring Primary Documents

Habits: connecting, exploring, paying attention
Activities: citing sources, researching, writing

We emphasized the importance of working with primary sources in our essay, "On Working with the Words of Others." We'd like you to read Jill Lepore's "Battleground America" and list as many of her primary sources as you can. Some will be obvious; others she might only refer to generally. We've already drawn your attention to several primary documents: the Constitution, the 1964 speech by Malcolm X in which he talks about the Second Amendment, and official statements from the NRA.

After you've identified as many of Lepore's primary sources as you can, select one of the documents she mentions and go find it. If you can't access the source online, try to find it in your library.

Read the document you've chosen and then spend at least thirty minutes writing about how a more detailed citation from the document could have further complicated Lepore's discussion. If the first document you track down doesn't yield a compelling example, search for other primary source material; once you've found something compelling, complete the assignment.

....

Practice Session Three: Making Connections with Sources

....

Habits: connecting, paying attention, reflecting

Activities: analyzing, note taking, reading, writing

For this practice session, we want you to pay attention to the variety of ways writers work with the words of others. Select one of the essays included in the Readings section of this volume and read it with care.

Then spend at least forty minutes observing, marking, and identifying the many different ways the writer works with sources. You might notice sources used to supply background information, to provide key ideas or concepts, to provide positions or arguments to grapple with, or to serve as the focus of analysis. Where did the writer work with sources in ways that impressed, surprised, or perhaps disappointed you? Were there moments when you felt a citation didn't do the work the writer wanted it to? Did the writer cite sources in ways that you'd like to emulate?

Spend at least an hour writing reflectively about what you've learned from this exercise on working with the words or ideas of others.

7

WORKING DELIBERATELY

How do you develop a habit? Through practice. But what is practice? When you're a kid practicing handwriting, you learn through repetition. You copy the letters of the alphabet over and over, mastering the block shapes first before perhaps moving on to cursive. With both types of writing, you practice certain physical gestures so that you can faithfully reproduce the shape of each letter. This practice requires hand-eye coordination, fine motor control in your dominant hand, and symbol recognition. Once you've practiced these activities enough, you can reproduce all the letters of the alphabet quickly, without conscious thought. Then, in a very limited sense, you know how to write.

What do you practice if you want to become a writer? Aspiring writers are often given two pieces of well-intentioned advice: "write what you know" and "write every day." While we can quibble with this kind of advice, we'd rather have you think about what habits you should be developing through practice (that is, through writing every day). What does it mean to look at the world the way a writer does? What does it mean to read like a writer? What does it mean to ask questions like a writer? What do writers practice? They practice working deliberately; they practice staying focused; they practice distinguishing fact from interpretation without underestimating the power of either one; and they explore the deep history contained in unfamiliar words, references, and ideas. They learn as they write and they let their writing take them places they didn't know existed before they sat down to work deliberately.

On Seeing as a Writer

The very reason I write is so that I might not sleepwalk through my entire life.
—ZADIE SMITH, "FAIL BETTER"

Learning how to draw, as we discussed earlier (pp. 45–48), means learning how to see without naming; this allows the visual, spatial, and synthesizing ways of thinking to guide the hand on the page. Quieting the verbal train of thought allows you to see like an artist, but what if you want to put what you see into words? How do you learn to see as a writer does?

Young children can be intensely observant and curious. They learn about the world by paying attention and asking lots of questions. Once we become adults, many of us stop observing so acutely and constantly — in part because so much of the previously mysterious world is now familiar to us. We go on mental autopilot during routine experiences. We see what we expect to see. And we keep our surprise and wonder in check because both take up time we don't think we have to spare.

To see as a writer does, you need to practice asking questions about what you see and sense. So instead of quieting the verbal activity in your mind, you need to train yourself to question what you perceive and what you assume. This questioning serves two purposes: it makes you conscious of your own perspective, and it also makes clear that other perspectives are possible. And this, ultimately, is part of what seeing as a writer involves — noticing clashes, subtle tensions, or unexpected connections between differing perspectives.

What do we mean by this? Here's an example of such a conflict, which comes from the opening of an essay by Annie Stiver, a student in one of our creative nonfiction classes:

> Recently, while standing in line for a ticket at the New Brunswick train station, I witnessed a mother nudge her

young son, who, after barely noticing his mother's prod, continued to look steadily at a man sitting half-awake on a bench in the corner of the station. After her eyes dropped and brows narrowed on her son, she clasped his shoulder and bent down to tell him that he is "not supposed to stare at bums." The boy turned his head forward at his mother's instruction, yet as I watched him I noticed his eyes were straining towards the right side of the room where this man was. Eventually, when it was his mother's turn at the ticket machine, the boy immediately turned his head to stare full-on at the man in tattered clothing on the train station bench. I figured that the boy was an infrequent visitor to New Brunswick.

This situation got me thinking about the rate at which children are encouraged not to stare even as they are curiously struck by novel experiences and when confronted with the unexpected. How did it come to be that we are taught not to stare?

A common response is that it's simply not polite to stare. But in those moments of heightened curiosity when we are told to keep our eyes from wandering on another's "business," we are, aside from being polite, affecting our own development and behavior as we repress our individual curiosities and questions about others. What happens when we stare? I would argue that staring goes beyond seeing the "other." Rather, when we stare, we are meant to think about ourselves. Watching the boy staring at the man in the station, I remembered the familiar feeling of when I was his age during unfamiliar and curious encounters with the unknown and unexpected. We're not staring because we want to know that our way of life is more comfortable and reassuring (we can consider this impolite), but sometimes we stare because we feel instinctively that our way of life is not quite right. When this happens, we want to ask, "Why aren't more of us staring?"

As writing teachers, we look at this student's sequence of observations, interpretations, and questions, and we see the habits of a creative mind at work. Let's review how her ideas unfold:

- She began with close observation.

- She asked lots of questions—and not just questions about the facts (that is, questions starting with the words *what, where,* or *who*), but also questions about cause and significance (questions starting with *how* or *why*).

  "How did it come to be that we are taught not to stare?"

  "What happens when we stare?"

  "Why aren't more of us staring?"

- She recognized a key concept—in this case, staring—and shifted her frame of reference to focus on what's going on when a child stares.

- She shifted her perspective away from the straightforward and obvious to think from a different point of view. In this case, she thought about why the child continued to look after having been told not to.

- Remembering her own childhood, she realized that a child may stare because her or his usual way of thinking has been unsettled. Staring—or merely looking thoughtfully—can lead to reflection about oneself and one's relationship to others.

Annie doesn't follow a formula for seeing as a writer. She doesn't begin by choosing an inert topic, theme, or thesis and then searching for evidence that fits into some pre-formulated mold. She asks questions about what she observes and takes those questions seriously. Is staring always impolite? Can it be evidence of curiosity? In doing so, she is seeing as a writer, which means practicing the never-ending activity of questioning what one senses or reads or thinks and then following those questions wherever they might lead.

Now we'd like you to practice looking from different perspectives at places and the people who inhabit them, with the goal of opening up new and compelling questions about what you observe and experience.

Practice Session One, Part One: Reflecting on Public Space

Habits: beginning, reflecting, working deliberately

Activities: note taking, observing, writing

Begin by selecting a familiar, common space in your community or on your campus, somewhere you've been dozens, if not hundreds, of times. Visit at a time of day when it's likely to be busy. Observe the space for at least twenty minutes. Take notes on what you perceive. Notice who uses the space and how they move through it. Move around, exploring different perspectives.

After you've spent twenty or more minutes observing, spend at least fifteen minutes writing down questions raised by your observations. How does the space signal that it's public? Is it welcoming and beautiful, or ramshackle and in need of cleaning? Is it used by a wide variety of people or by a more homogeneous group? How does the space itself shape the experiences of the people who use it? How does it encourage or enhance some activities and limit others? These questions are just to get you started; they should trigger other questions that directly relate to your observations. You might also wonder whether it is possible to have a perspective on this public place that is uniquely your own.

Write a reflective essay that develops out of your observations and a few of your most compelling questions about the place.

Practice Session One, Part Two: Reflecting on Private Space

Habits: connecting, reflecting, working deliberately

Activities: note taking, observing, writing

Next, we'd like you to do a similar exercise with a more private place, one that's indoors, known or used by few people, and rich in sensory details. (Avoid choosing your own room or any other place that's overly familiar; it takes a lot of practice to see such places in new ways.) Spend at least twenty minutes observing and taking notes and photographs. Then spend another fifteen minutes reflecting on your experience in the space and writing down questions that your observations have raised. Start with the basics: How does the place signal that it's private? What activities does the space encourage, and what activities does it discourage? Is it possible to have a perspective on this place that is uniquely your own?

Write a reflective essay that develops out of your observations and a few of the most interesting questions you asked about the place you observed. Your goal is to compose a piece that gives your readers a new way to understand this private space.

Practice Session One, Part Three: Reflecting on a Natural Space

Habits: connecting, reflecting, working deliberately

Activities: note taking, observing, writing

Repeat this exercise in a natural, uninhabited, and unlandscaped space. Once again, observe and take notes for at least twenty minutes, and then spend fifteen minutes or more developing questions that are grounded in your particular perspective. Coming up with questions about a natural space may be hard at first, but that, too, is worth pondering.

After you've gathered your notes and questions, write another reflective essay that develops out of one or more of your most interesting questions and shows your reader how to see and think about this place in a new way.

Practice Session Two: Seeing How Other Writers See

Habits: connecting, exploring, working deliberately

Activities: note taking, reading, writing

In "On Seeing as a Writer," we examined how one of our students started to observe as a writer. Now we'd like you to analyze another writer's way of paying attention to the world. Read Rebecca Solnit's "Occupied Territory" in the Readings section at the end of this book and look for passages that reveal her particular way of seeing.

After you've found several passages that reveal Solnit's perspective, spend at least thirty minutes writing about the passages you've marked. How is her way of perceiving distinctive?

On Reading as a Writer

....

In our writing classes, we have a couple of mantras about reading that we repeat throughout the semester:

- In order to learn how to write, you have to learn how to read as a writer.

- There's only one way to learn how to read well and that's by rereading.

These mantras are connected. To read as a writer means to pay close attention to the choices other writers make. This kind of reading requires attending to lots of things at once — what the writer says, how she organizes her ideas, what types of sources she works with, and how she addresses her readers. Such multifocal reading can only be accomplished by rereading. The first time reading through a challenging work, you might only be able to focus on what it says; after you know how the writer gets from point A to point B, you can attend more carefully to the choices the writer has made along the way. As your understanding of the entire piece comes together, you are in a much better position to assess what works and what doesn't and to explain the reasons for your assessments.

If you were in a psychology class and were assigned Rachel Aviv's "The Edge of Identity," your teacher would expect you to read the article as a psych student, which would entail being able to identify Aviv's thesis and to evaluate the evidence she provides to support her thesis. But if you were asked to read Aviv's article in one of our classes, we would ask you to read as a writer: we would want you to be able to discuss in detail how Aviv presents and develops her ideas. So instead of expecting you to mark Aviv's main points with a highlighter, we would want you to write in the margins (or in your reading notebook), making connections, puzzling over references, and thinking about how the details Aviv provides contribute to the overarching effect of her piece.

Aviv begins "The Edge of Identity" (in the Readings section at the end of this book) with a story about Hannah Upp, who went missing one day in New York City and then, twenty days later, was found alive and floating in the water about two miles south of the Statue of Liberty with no memory of how she got there. Aviv reports that Upp was diagnosed with "dissociative fugue, a rare condition in which people lose access to their autobiographical memory and personal memory." As writers, we're interested in what Aviv does after opening with this harrowing story. Instead of telling her readers what happens next, she pauses Upp's narrative to provide a brief history of the "dissociative fugue" diagnosis. Sigmund Freud, the famous founder of psychoanalysis, tried his hand at making sense of this experience, "but the phenomenon did not fit easily into his sweeping theory of human behavior," Aviv writes. She notes, however, that the much lesser known psychologist Pierre Janet "developed the first formal theory of dissociation in 1889," and then she quotes Janet directly: "Personal unity, identity, and initiative are not primitive characteristics of psychological life. They are incomplete results acquired with difficulty after long work, and they remain very fragile."

That's an amazing statement from a figure few readers will have heard of, but you could easily miss its significance if you weren't paying careful attention to how Aviv is working as a writer. When you read as a writer, the move that Aviv makes here, shifting from storytelling to psychoanalytic theories about identity, calls out for further investigation. Everyone has heard of Freud, but who is Janet? How might Aviv have come upon his work? After all, she tells her readers that he and his work "fell into obscurity" once Freud's theories established their early dominance over the evolving field of psychology. If you copy and paste the two sentences of Janet's that Aviv quotes into your preferred search engine, you'll get one hit: Onno van der Hart's article, "Pierre Janet, Sigmund Freud, and Dissociation of the Personality: The First Codification of a Psychodynamic Depth Psychology," which appears in *The Dissociative Mind in Psychoanalysis: Understanding and Working with Trauma*, edited by Elizabeth Howell and Sheldon Itzkowitz.

What does this discovery tell us as readers who are interested in how writing works? That Aviv is likely to have read Hart's article as part of her own effort to make sense of Upp's disappearance. In other words, confronted with Upp's baffling behavior, Aviv began to research possible explanations for it. She could have gone to an encyclopedia or a dictionary to get a definition of *dissociation*. She could have gone to the *Diagnostic and Statistical Manual of Mental Disorders* (*DSM-5*) to learn the criteria for determining whether a patient has dissociative identity disorder (DID). Indeed, we'd hazard a guess that Aviv looked at all of these resources during her research, but citing one or more of them at the opening of her piece would have signaled that the very psychological state she wants to explore as a question is actually a settled matter. Think how different her article would be if it began: "Merriam-Webster's dictionary defines *dissociation* as . . ."

When you read as a writer, you attend to *how* the writer puts her essay together, piece by piece, word by word. Such attention makes it possible to see that a full understanding of what gets said necessarily involves considering the where, the how, the who, and the when of any given act of speaking or writing. In this instance, it matters that Aviv turns to Janet near the beginning of her piece because, in citing his work, she is indicating that she thinks his ideas deserve to be rescued from "obscurity." Upp may have been diagnosed by experts who are relying on definitions of the self and of identity that are called into question by the experience of dissociation. What if the self is not stable and constant? What if identity is not innate or inherent, but rather ever-evolving and fragmentary? What if the experience of the self as unitary conceals the fact that this unified state is "fragile"? Aviv raises all of these possibilities by citing Janet and noting that his psychological model fell into obscurity while Freud's triumphed.

Reading as a writer will change how you read. You'll start noticing what and how other writers read and how their reading shapes their writing. You'll be able to finish sentences like this one: "There's a connection between the way Aviv reads the story of Upp's disappearance and the way she reads the theories that seek to explain the experience of dissociation; that connection is . . ." We're always interested in exploring connections of this kind because they help us to see that there are always other choices we could make as writers—there are always other questions we could ask, other sources we could turn to, other turns of phrase available to sharpen our insights and to move our thinking forward. When you read as a writer, your concern shifts in these ways from a focus on whether you agree with what you're reading to *what you can learn about writing itself from what you're reading.*

....

Practice Session One, Part One: Reading Rachel Aviv as a Writer

....

Habits: connecting, reflecting, working deliberately

Activities: analyzing, note taking, reading

You can use any serious text to practice reading as a writer. For this practice session, we'd like you to continue the work we've begun reading Rachel Aviv's "The Edge of Identity." Start by reading the article from beginning to end, marking key moments in Aviv's exploration of how to understand Upp's predicament. Next, read the article again, paying attention *as a writer* to how Aviv phrases and organizes her ideas, what types of sources she uses, how and where she presents major points, and how she addresses her readers. Take notes in the margins.

What's striking about how Aviv chose to approach her topic? What parts drew you in? Are there parts of the article that confuse you, or parts where you don't know enough about psychology or trauma to follow her argument? Were there any points or turns of phrase that impressed you, or sections you found yourself rereading with appreciation?

Having read Aviv's article as a writer, identify one of the significant choices Aviv made when she composed her article, and then spend at least thirty minutes writing about that choice. As you write, quote specific passages from Aviv's article to help your reader see what you find meaningful about *how* Aviv writes as well as *what* she writes.

Practice Session One, Part Two: Writing about Reading as a Writer

Habits: connecting, reflecting, working deliberately

Activities: writing

Now that you've reread Aviv's article, write an essay about how reading as a writer altered your understanding of her writing practice. It's likely that your close attention to her work enhanced your reading significantly. It's also likely that new questions or confusions arose. Again, as you write, quote specific passages from Aviv's work to show what you find meaningful about what Aviv has said and how she said it.

Practice Session Two, Part One: Choose Your Own Adventure

Habits: connecting, playing, working deliberately

Activities: choosing, note taking, reading

We claimed above that you can read any intentionally crafted work as a writer. You can put our claim to the test by choosing any of the other readings we've included in the Readings section at the end of this book and seeing if your understanding of the piece you've selected changes as your reading practice changes. Follow the steps we outline below.

Start by reading the piece you've selected from beginning to end, marking key moments. Next, read the piece again, paying attention *as a writer* to how the author phrases and organizes her ideas, what types of sources she uses, how and where she presents major points, and how she addresses her readers. Take notes in the margins.

What's striking about how the author of the piece you selected chose to approach her topic? What parts drew you in? Are there parts of the piece that confuse you, or parts where you don't know enough about one area of specialized knowledge to follow her argument? Were there any points or turns of phrase that impressed you, or sections you found yourself rereading with appreciation?

Having read as a writer the piece you selected, identify one of the significant choices the author made when she composed her piece, and then spend at least thirty minutes writing about that choice. As you write, quote specific passages from the piece you selected to help your reader see what you find meaningful about how the author writes as well as what she writes.

....

Practice Session Two, Part Two: Putting Reading as a Writer to the Test

....

Habits: connecting, reflecting, working deliberately
Activities: writing

Now that you've read as a writer the piece you've selected, write an essay about how reading as a writer altered your understanding of the author's writing practice. It's likely that your close attention to the writing enhanced your reading significantly. It's also likely that new questions or confusions arose. Again, as you write, quote specific passages from the piece to show what you find meaningful about what the author has said and how she has said it.

On Reading in Slow Motion

In the introduction to "On Reading as a Writer," we told you about two of our mantras for reading: (1) In order to learn how to write, you have to learn how to read as a writer. (2) There's only one way to learn how to read well and that's by rereading.

We have a third mantra we repeat to our students:

Read in slow motion.

When students are learning to read as writers, it's more valuable for them to read and reread a brief selection with great care than it is for them to race through a much longer text. Reading in slow motion means looking up unfamiliar terms, names, historical events, and images. We encourage our students to track down some of the author's sources and to read those sources as writers, which means exploring the connections the author has made to or between those sources. We do this because we want our students to see that whatever they're reading is connected to a much larger network of meaning.

We believe so strongly in the value of reading in slow motion that we routinely offer classes where we spend the entire semester reading, discussing, and writing about one short book—a book that engages with a complicated subject in innovative ways. We have one rule in these classes: no reading ahead. Students are invited, encouraged, and at times even required to reread what we've already read and discussed, but when they finish the five or seven or ten pages assigned for the next class, they must stop at the designated point.

We have this rule for two reasons, both equally important. First, there's only one way to learn how to read well and that is to reread. As you reread, you inevitably notice passages you skipped over the first time; you can see patterns of thought and organization; you can pick up on repeated terms, phrases, and ideas; you can see connections unfold in time; you become aware of nuances, deflections, missteps, and gems hidden in plain sight. The words on the page or on the screen don't change, but your relationship to them does once you become more and more familiar with how the writer chooses to put those words together.

Reading in slow motion forces you to engage with writing that isn't meant to be skimmed, writing that can't be reduced to a bulleted list, a meme, or a series of snappy slides, writing that gives you access to a mind at work on a problem that warrants your time and attention.

The second reason we ask students not to read ahead is that this allows us to spend a semester considering what could or might come next in the piece we're reading. By staying together—by staying on the same page, as it were—we get to see in each class session that what happens next in any given piece of writing is the result of a choice on the writer's part. That choice may be conscious or unconscious; it may appear to be mandated by reason or convention; it might come off as inspired or irrational. But in every single instance, asking "What's next, do you think?" focuses attention on the fact that whatever comes next is never inevitable. As writers, we can always choose our own paths. Always.

Most recently, we spent a semester reading Maggie Nelson's *The Argonauts* with students in a research writing course. Nelson's genre-bending book is partly a memoir and partly a meditation on her experience falling in love with a person who does not identify as either male or female. Nelson discusses ideas that most students in the class had not encountered before—for example, heteronormativity, gender fluidity, marriage equality. She cites authors, artists, and activists who were unknown to most students in the class—Ludwig Wittgenstein, D. W. Winnicott, Gertrude Stein, Catherine Opie, among others. And she describes in detail experiences most students have spent little time thinking about—getting pregnant via artificial means, being pregnant, giving birth, getting a voluntary double mastectomy. What does one do when confronted with the assignment to read material that is by turns intensely personal and openly philosophical, playful and serious, extraordinary and mundane? What does one do when confronted with writing that references so much that is unfamiliar?

When the weekly assignment is to read only five or seven or ten pages, it is possible to do a kind of reading that isn't possible when the assignment is a hundred pages: it is possible to research what is unfamiliar—be it a word, a concept, or a reference. Instead of reading for the gist or the thesis or the main points, here the focus is on the sentence, its composition, and its contents.

After we'd been practicing this way of reading for a couple of weeks, we gave the students a version of the following assignment:

> Select a word, a passage, a citation, a reference, a concept, a figure, an image, a film, a fact, or a detail from the first twenty-six pages of Maggie Nelson's *The Argonauts* and research it. Then compose an "interpretive footnote" that illuminates both what you've selected to research and what Nelson's use of that material reveals about the project of *The Argonauts*, Nelson's habits of mind, hermeneutics (!), mirthfulness, contamination [these are all key terms from early in Nelson's text that we had discussed at length in class], or anything else you deem important. Your footnote should assume a readership composed of your peers and your professor.
>
> To complete this assignment successfully, you will have to do research that drills down past the first link in a web search, past the Wikipedia entries, past what any of your peers or your professor could find with ease and without thinking. You need to read or look or watch what your first research foray has taken you to, and then you will need to keep going till you've come across material that has helped you to think something new, see something new, understand something new, ask something new, or feel something new.
>
> You'll know you're on the right track when you've written something that enriches your peers' and your professor's understanding of a question, problem, issue, or idea that is connected in some way to the constellation of concerns that flicker and wink throughout Maggie Nelson's *The Argonauts*.

To give our students a sense of what an "interpretive footnote" looks like, we posted the following passage from *The Argonauts* on the class website:

> My stepson is too old for Fallen Soldier or Bear Family now. As I write he's listening to Funky Cold Medina on his iPod—eyes closed, in his gigantic body, lying on the red couch. Nine years old.

In class we had discussed how Nelson uses these three sentences to show that her relationship with her stepson changed as he aged. Where once they played imaginary games together (Fallen Soldier and Bear Family), now he shuts her and the rest of the world out with his iPod. And we zeroed in on the fact that Nelson wants her readers to know exactly what her stepson is listening to. A footnote would lend a hand to readers unfamiliar with the reference, we all agreed. A typical footnote might take the following form: "[1]Funky Cold Medina is a hip-hop song made famous by Tone-Lōc in 1989." A slightly fuller footnote might also include the statement: "The song is about a fictional aphrodisiac." The footnote, in other words, would aim to fill an information gap with verifiable facts.

In our slow reading classes, we expect our students to track down information of this kind; that's what search engines are for. But with the interpretive footnote assignment, we expect them to go further: Nelson didn't have to tell her readers what her stepson was listening to; she could've skipped designating the tune or she could've designated a different song. So, why "Funky Cold Medina"? The goal of the interpretive footnote is to address the *why* question (which, of course, can only be done once one has learned the answer to the *what* question). Here's one version of what a 750-word interpretive footnote on the subject might look like:

> [1]"Funky Cold Medina" was released by Tone-Lōc in 1989, seventeen years prior to the birth of Nelson's stepson and twenty-six years prior to its finding its way onto her stepson's iPod. Highly popular after its original release, the song has not aged well. Leela Ginelle, writing in the March 2015 issue of *PQ Monthly*, condemns the song for having the "Worst. Verse. Ever," one she says Lōc wrote assuming "no trans people could be listening to the song, and no one who is listening would want to be with a trans woman." Over on *Yahoo! Answers* (an admittedly lame source, but one that is nevertheless useful for this discussion), those responding to the question, "Trans people: Are you offended by the lyrics to Funky Cold Medina by Tone-Lōc?" had a range of reactions: totally offended, not offended at all, only offended by the existence of homophobic and transphobic people.
>
> So, what is Funky Cold Medina and why would trans people, in particular, be more likely than anyone else to be offended by it? A summary of the lyrics follows:
>
> The narrator in the song is in a bar and, despite looking "def," is attracting no attention from "the girls," who are

more attracted to some "no-name chump." The no-name chump reveals that the secret to his attractiveness is an aphrodisiac called "Funky Cold Medina." The narrator's attempts to use the drug are recounted in the remaining verses of the song. First, he tries it on his dog, who "does the wild thing" on his leg. This isn't what he was hoping for, but now "all the poodles" in the neighborhood hang out at his house. Then he tries it at the bar with "Sheena" and takes her home only to discover, when Sheena begins to undress, "it was a big old mess," because Sheena "was a man." The narrator tries one last time, competing on the dating game show "The Love Connection," but when he wins, the Funky Cold Medina doesn't have the effect he's looking for: his date starts talking " 'bout plans for our wedding." The song ends with the narrator fleeing the scene and swearing off that Funky Cold Medina.

The argument for contemporary listeners to be offended by the song is straightforward: when the song's narrator sees Sheena's genitalia, he throws her out, declaring that he "don't fool around with no Oscar Meyer wiener" and warning his listeners that "you must be sure that the girl is pure for the Funky Cold Medina." A trans person is represented as deceitful, is mocked, and treated violently, all in the service of amusing an audience of people amused by such things. And yet, Nelson doesn't stop her stepson from listening to this song? Isn't she offended by it?

It's possible that Nelson thinks about the meaning of this verse in the context of the entire song. Taking all the song's verses into account, one gets a picture of the narrator as someone who thinks he's attractive, but isn't, who needs to drug his possible partners to get their attention, who then ends up in bed with a partner who has a penis, and finally gives up on the whole enterprise after the drug fails to cancel out his next possible partner's overwhelming desire to get married. The narrator is hapless, bumbling, and, despite his use of the aphrodisiac/date rape drug, still very much alone and unfulfilled by the end of his tale. To be sure, along the way, the narrator mocks Sheena, but the song, as a whole, is dedicated to mocking the narrator himself as clownishly unprepared for adulthood. Indeed in Lōc's video for the song, the final scene is of the narrator in street clothes pouring his batch of Funky Cold Medina into the gutter. It's daytime. Whatever fantasies the narrator had about his nightlife at the club, we're left with a final image of him dumped back into the real world.

Nelson shows us her stepson listening to this song on his iPod. But she is also showing us her decision not to stop him from doing so. I would argue that she does so knowing that there are those in her own community who would deem the song transphobic. But she knows that the straightforward reading of the song denies words their power to bend meaning and denies one access to the pleasures that come from enjoying what Nelson calls "inappropriate objects."

We chose to write about this small detail in Nelson's *The Argonauts* because we wanted to better understand what it had to do with Nelson's larger project. And this led us deeper into the conflict over how the song's lyrics are interpreted and that led us to a consideration of parenting, a subject that lies at the heart of Nelson's reflections on giving birth to a child who will be raised in a household with a parent who doesn't conform to gender norms. This is the work that is made possible by slow reading: it allows a detail to become a world all its own and the reader to dwell in and on the particular choices the writer has made to get the words on the page to do justice to the complexity of the issues under consideration.

Practice Session One: The Interpretive Footnote and *Habits of the Creative Mind*

Habits: beginning, questioning, working deliberately

Activities: note taking, researching, writing

Select a word, a passage, a citation, a reference, a concept, a fact, or a detail from any of the essays you've read up to this point in *Habits of the Creative Mind* and research it. Then compose an "interpretive footnote" that illuminates both what you've selected to research and what our use of that material reveals about the project of *Habits*, our habits of mind, or anything else about the enterprise for generating new thoughts that you deem important. Your footnote should assume a readership composed of other readers of the essays in *Habits of the Creative Mind*.

To complete this assignment successfully, you will have to do research that drills down past the first link in a web search, past the Wikipedia entries, past what any of your peers or your professor could find with ease and without thinking. You need to read or look at or watch or listen to what your first research foray has taken you to and then you will need to keep going till you've come across material that has helped you to think something new, see something new, understand something new, ask something new, or feel something new.

You'll know you're on the right track when you've written something that enriches your peers' and your professor's understanding of a question, problem, issue, or idea that is connected in some way to the larger project of *Habits of the Creative Mind*.

Practice Session Two: The Interpretive Footnote and Choose Your Own Adventure

Habits: beginning, questioning, working deliberately

Activities: interpreting, note taking, writing

Select a word, a passage, a citation, a reference, a concept, a fact, or a detail from any of the readings we've included at the end of *Habits of the Creative Mind*, or from an essay you've chosen on your own, or from an essay your teacher has provided. Compose an "interpretive footnote" that illuminates both what you've selected to work on and what the author's choice to use that material reveals about the author's project in the essay you've selected, the author's habits of mind, or anything else about the enterprise for generating new thoughts that you deem important. Your footnote should assume a readership composed of readers familiar with the essay you've selected.

To complete this assignment successfully, you will have to do research that drills down past the first link in a web search, past the Wikipedia entries, past what any of your peers or your professor could find with ease and without thinking. You need to read or look at or watch or listen to what your first research foray has taken you to and then you will need to keep going till you've come across material that has helped you to think something new, see something new, understand something new, ask something new, or feel something new.

You'll know you're on the right track when you've written something that enriches your peers' and your professor's understanding of a question, problem, issue, or idea that is connected in some way to the larger project of the essay you've selected.

Practice Session Three, Part One: The Interpretive Footnote and the Declaration of Independence

Habits: exploring, questioning, working deliberately

Activities: note taking, reading, researching

The Declaration of Independence (pp. 263–67 in the Readings section at the end of this book) is the document that led to the founding of the United States of America. The document is composed of 1,337 words, excluding the names of the fifty-six signers. The document has a few words that you might not have used in conversation (e.g., unalienable, usurpations, invariably) but, for the most part, contemporary English speakers can understand the general meaning of this historic document.

A creative mind, however, is never satisfied with a general sense. The Declaration of Independence wasn't about forming a union anywhere at any time; it was written in 1776, in response to a specific history that the writers had with England, with the king, and with Enlightenment ideas about sovereignty, nature, and human rights. For this practice session, we want you to take the approach we've outlined in our essay above and apply it to this oft-cited document. Choose a word or a phrase or a reference that seems important to you, but that you feel you don't adequately understand. (Note: When NPR tweeted out the Declaration on July 4, 2017, they were overwhelmed by responses from followers who thought that the public radio system was describing the current political state of affairs.)

When you've made your choice, we'd like you to set about doing the research necessary to generate an interpretive footnote that does justice to the complex issues raised by the term, phrase, or reference you've selected. You may want to consult the *Oxford English Dictionary* to find the late-eighteenth-century meaning of the term or phrase you selected.

To complete this assignment successfully, you will have to do research that drills down past the first link in a web search, past the Wikipedia entries, past what any of your peers or your professor could find with ease. You need to read or look at or watch or listen to what your first research foray has taken you to and then you will need to keep going until you've come across material that has helped you to think something new, see something new, understand something new, ask something new, or feel something new.

You'll know you're on the right track when you've written something that enriches your peers' and your professor's understanding of a question, problem, issue, or idea that is connected in some way to the larger project of founding the United States.

Practice Session Three, Part Two: Danielle Allen's Interpretation of the Declaration of Independence

Habits: connecting, exploring, reflecting

Activities: analyzing, comparing

We've included Danielle Allen's essay "What Is Education For?" in the Readings section at the end of this book. Allen has also written extensively about the Declaration of Independence in her book *Our Declaration: A Reading of the Declaration of Independence in Defense of Equality*. When Allen was teaching a night class about the Declaration in Chicago, she approached it as a course in slow reading: she and her students worked through the document word by word over a semester. The result was transformative for both the students and their teacher. Allen rediscovered that the Declaration made powerful arguments for equality as well as liberty, and discovered for the first time that its 1,337 words could be made accessible to general readers, not just experts.

Through your library or your teacher, get ahold of a copy of Allen's *Our Declaration* and see what she has to say about the passage that contains the word, phrase, or reference that you researched and wrote about in the first part of Practice Session Three: The Interpretive Footnote and the Declaration of Independence.

Compare your interpretive footnote to Allen's interpretation. What does Allen say that enriches your understanding of the passage? What might your interpretive footnote contribute to Allen's understanding of the passage?

8

·················

REFLECTING

···

I f we took away all of the world's reflective surfaces, how would we see ourselves? Through our many tools of self-expression: visual images, music, dance, drama, and, of course, language. In this section, we want you to explore how language can be a reflection of that which might otherwise be invisible — namely, the thoughts in your head and the emotions in your heart. Language doesn't reflect in the ways a mirror does, however. Indeed, what makes writing so challenging is that the writer has to do the work of converting those inner thoughts and feelings into words and sentences that are understandable to others.

What distinguishes humans from all other living creatures is this ability to use language to share our self-reflections. Nowhere is this clearer than in *The Miracle Worker*, which dramatizes Helen Keller's acquisition of language, despite her being deaf, mute, and blind. Can anyone, including Keller herself, represent in language a life before language? Can you make your own attempts to make sense of your life sensible to others?

On the Miracle of Language

What are words for?

We could begin by saying that words are a way to focus the mind, that words make meaning and reflection possible.

But we could also say that words can stand in the way of insight; the ceaseless chattering of the inner critic, forever generating judgments and drawing conclusions, must be silenced for new understandings to emerge.

Or we could say that words allow us to formulate ideas and, with these ideas in mind, to make contact with the world and with each other. In this formulation, words, organized by syntax, are the components of an essentially human technology. Words enable us to escape the tyranny of the present that rules all other members of the animal kingdom.

Examples abound of the sacred significance we attribute to the acquisition of language. We'll start with two of the most familiar.

Parents eagerly await the moment when their toddler moves from making burbling proto-words to clearly saying what can be counted as the child's first word. The desire to record this moment—to be present when the child points to the night sky and says "moon," or to the snow and says "milk," or to the mother and says "mama"—is the desire to be present at the everyday miracle of language acquisition.

In Genesis, once God has created the heavens and the earth, God places Adam in the garden of Eden and then, to provide Adam with companions, forms "every beast of the field and every bird of the heavens" and brings them "to the man to see what he would call them" (Genesis 2:19). In this account, the first act of the first human is the act of naming.

But when Adam is done naming all the animals that have passed before him, he is still alone, so God fashions another living creature out of Adam's rib to serve as Adam's helper. Once again, Adam's first act upon encountering this new creature is to provide a name for her. And of course, shortly thereafter, Adam and Eve are introduced to the power of language to persuade and deceive when the serpent entices Eve to disobey God's command. In the Judeo-Christian tradition, all of human history is a direct result of the first conversation recorded in the Bible.

Our purpose in calling these two very different examples to mind may seem quixotic, but here it is: for the moment, we'd like you to suspend the idea that language is either an everyday miracle or a sacred gift. We also want you to pry language loose from the clutches of communication, where it figures as a hammer that gets the job done, and of rhetoric, where it acts as a silver tongue that artfully persuades. Against these accounts of how language works, we would like instead to highlight the creative, generative, exploratory powers with which language endows us all.

In *The Miracle Worker*, surely the best-known depiction of language acquisition of the twentieth century, the playwright William Gibson dramatizes the utterly improbable story of how Helen Keller — deaf, blind, and unable to speak — escapes a life of complete social isolation. At the play's opening, Keller's parents have hired the young, inexperienced, formerly blind, and fiercely determined Anne Sullivan to help care for and control their daughter, whose violent behavior has made her all but unmanageable. One of Helen's most distressing habits occurs at mealtimes: refusing to use tableware — or unable to understand how to use it — Helen grabs whatever food is in reach with her bare hands, stuffs what she can in her mouth, and then casts about for her next handful. And when her frustration at not finding her next mouthful mounts to the boiling point, Helen throws whatever she can get her hands on — tableware, plates, her shoes — until food is once again placed in front of her.

Sullivan decides that the only way to make progress with Helen is to start over and treat her like a very large two-year-old — that is, as a child who is on the developmental threshold of acquiring language. Sullivan signs into Helen's palm all day long, spelling out the words of objects they encounter, repeating the signings over and over, just as one would do verbally while modeling speech for a toddler. Sullivan also sets about training Helen in appropriate behavior, while struggling to convince Keller's parents that their daughter needs to be punished when she behaves improperly. In the play's climactic scene, Helen, who has learned how to use tableware, regresses and throws a tantrum during the midday meal. In her thrashing about, she spills a pitcher of water, and Sullivan drags her, kicking and writhing, from the room and out to the water pump in the yard. Placing the pitcher in one of Helen's hands, Sullivan begins furiously pumping water into the pitcher, while signing the word *water* one letter at a time, over and over, into Helen's other hand.

How does someone unable to perceive the world through sight or sound grasp the idea of language? As the play tells the story, it occurs in an instant, when Helen, feeling the water from the pump splash on her one hand and the repetition of the same pattern of pressure, traced over and over by Sullivan, in her other palm, connects these two experiences. In the screenplay for the 1962 movie version of his original teleplay, Gibson provides the following instructions to the director and the camera crew for capturing this moment:

> And now the miracle happens. We have moved around close to Helen's face, and we see it change, startled, some light coming into it we have never seen there, some struggle in the depths behind it; and her lips tremble, trying to remember something the muscles around them once knew, till at last it finds its way out, painfully, a baby sound buried under the debris of years of dumbness.

Ecstatic at her sudden understanding of the word *water*, Helen signs the word in her own palm, then in Sullivan's, and then falls to the ground, slapping it with one hand and holding her other hand out for instruction. One word leads to another and then another, the irreversible course set in motion. The miracle worker, it turns out, is language itself.

Words make thought possible; they enable us to see things we've never seen and to hear things we've never heard; they even make it possible for us to travel back and forth in time. They give us the power to create and then to ponder abstractions and arguments; they give us the means to discover new ways of understanding the natural world and ourselves. But words don't do any of these things without us. The miracle of our being able to make ourselves known to each other becomes possible only with practice — practice stringing words together into sentences, questions, and paragraphs; practice accommodating the constraints of syntax and convention; practice speaking and writing ourselves into being.

....

Practice Session One, Part One: Making Yourself Understood

....

Habits: beginning, orienting, reflecting

Activities: remembering, writing

The Miracle Worker dramatizes the power that language has for Helen Keller. While it is tempting to universalize Keller's experience, we think it's a better idea to reflect on your own experiences of trying to make your innermost thoughts known to others. What medium do you feel is best for expressing your thoughts? Words? Color? Sound? Touch? Food? Movement?

Our list of possible answers may surprise you, but we want you to reflect on the full range of your expressive experience. When was the moment that you *felt* most fully that you were expressing exactly what you wanted to express in the way you wanted to express it? Write for at least thirty minutes about that moment, doing your best to render the truest representation of your experience at the time.

....

Practice Session One, Part Two: Struggling to Make Yourself Understood

....

Habits: beginning, orienting, reflecting

Activities: remembering, writing

The power of the water pump scene in *The Miracle Worker* derives in part from all the frustration, rage, and anger that precedes it: the endless hours of instruction that seem to have no payoff, the screaming, the thrown food. Without the miracle at the pump, Helen Keller might have spent the rest of her life unable to communicate her thoughts to others except through physical behavior, in particular gestures of frustration and protest.

When you reflect on your own experience, when was the moment that you felt most fully *in*capable of making yourself understood? What prevented others from understanding you? What did you do following this experience? Was there a way, at some subsequent moment, to bring about mutual understanding, or are there some experiences that simply cannot be expressed? Write for at least thirty minutes about that moment, doing your best to render the truest representation of your experience at the time.

Practice Session One, Part Three: How Language Works

Habits: connecting, reflecting, speculating
Activities: reading, writing

When you look at what you wrote in Parts One and Two of this practice session, what do you see? What precisely does putting these two examples next to each other reveal to you about how language works? About the nature of communication? About learning and inner experience? Write an essay that speculates about why some efforts to share an understanding succeed and others fail. Your goal here is neither to argue nor to prove a point — that's not the best use of the evidence of your own experience. Your goal is to use your experience to think in new ways about language, communication, learning, and expression.

Practice Session Two: The "Best-Known Description," Revised

Habits: exploring, questioning, reflecting
Activities: imagining, reading, writing

We were surprised to learn, in the feedback we received to the first edition of *Habits of the Creative Mind*, that we were wrong to assume that most, if not all, readers knew who Helen Keller was and knew the general outline of her life story. This is a problem that is relatively easily rectified: we'd like you to access a copy of the script for either the play or the 1957 teleplay of *The Miracle Worker* and read it all the way through. (You should do this even if you're already familiar with the story!)

Once you've read the script or the teleplay, we'd like you to focus on the moment when Gibson says, "the miracle happens." Gibson provides both the words the actors speak and the stage directions they are meant to follow. The audience, though, has access only to what the actors say and the gestures they make. Why, then, does Gibson choose *not* to have any of the characters say aloud that they've witnessed "a miracle"? Write an essay in which you consider this seeming paradox: in a play about language acquisition, the audience is meant to understand what has happened in the climactic scene not by what is said, but by what they see.

On Making Thought Visible

Helen Keller (Patty Duke) at the pump, with Anne Sullivan (Anne Bancroft). Still from the 1962 film version of The Miracle Worker.

In "On the Miracle of Language," we considered the most famous teaching scene of the twentieth century: Helen Keller at the pump; Anne Sullivan furiously spelling the word *water* in Helen's palm over and over; and the breakthrough moment when Helen connects the experience of water pouring over one of her palms and the signing Sullivan is doing in her other.

Our discussion focused on the representation of this moment in William Gibson's *The Miracle Worker*. Because Gibson needed to make the workings of Keller's mind visible to his audience, he has her miraculous connection occur in an instant; it's dramatic, powerful, and visually compelling. But as we've continued to think about this play and its influence on how people the world over imagine Helen Keller, we've found ourselves led to another question: Is Gibson's version of this event, composed in the late 1950s, what actually happened at the water pump on that fateful day in 1887? The most well-known representation of how language learning occurs has made us wonder about the relationship between words and ideas and about whether words or images can ever provide unmediated access to what is going on in another person's mind.

. . . . .

Can we know what actually happened at that pump?

At first, how to answer this question seems obvious: we can know what happened if we can just find out what Helen Keller herself had to say about this transformative moment. At least, this is what we thought before we began to explore the many different accounts that Keller and her teacher provided of the miracle of Keller's language acquisition. It turns out that there isn't a "true" version of what happened at the pump; rather, there are multiple versions that were put forth at different times to serve different ends.

VERSION ONE: HELEN KELLER'S *THE STORY OF MY LIFE* (1903)

The initial public version of the pump story appears in Keller's first autobiography, *The Story of My Life*, which was published in 1903, when Keller was twenty-three and had just graduated from Radcliffe College. Keller begins her description of the moment thus: Sullivan had taken her outside for a walk, which made Keller "hop and skip with pleasure." They passed someone pumping water; Sullivan placed one of Keller's hands under the water and began signing "w-a-t-e-r" into Keller's other hand, while the unnamed third person continued to pump. Already, the differences between Keller's first-person account and the account in Gibson's teleplay announce themselves: instead of being dragged to the pump in a violent tug-of-war, Keller is happily walking with her teacher; instead of two people at the pump, there are three.

Here is Keller's description of what happened next:

> I stood still, my whole attention fixed upon the motions of [Sullivan's] fingers. Suddenly I felt a misty consciousness as of something forgotten—a thrill of returning thought; and

> somehow the mystery of language was revealed to me.
> I knew then that "w-a-t-e-r" meant the wonderful cool
> something that was flowing over my hand. That living word
> awakened my soul, gave it light, hope, joy, set it free!

Notice the words and phrases that populate this description: *misty consciousness*; *mystery*; *revealed*; *living word*; *awakened*; *soul*; *light, hope, joy*; *set it free*. We hear an echo of the born-again Christian narrative "I once was lost, but now am found" in Keller's first description of how she came to language. But Keller's version curiously makes no overt reference to Christ as the source of the "living word" that has awakened her soul; indeed, to some readers, it may well seem that Keller is describing a religious conversion without the religion.

Keller continues to draw on the vocabulary of revelation in her description of what happened immediately after her momentous discovery:

> As we returned to the house every object which I touched
> seemed to quiver with life. That was because I saw every-
> thing with the strange, new sight that had come to me. On
> entering the door I remembered the doll I had broken.
> I felt my way to the hearth and picked up the pieces. I tried
> vainly to put them together. Then my eyes filled with tears;
> for I realized what I had done, and for the first time I felt
> repentance and sorrow.

In this version, the miracle worker is language; language has made it possible for blind Helen Keller to "see" and, quickly thereafter, language has led her to feel the need to repent for her earlier actions.

We would argue that, at the age of twenty-three, Keller isn't describing what actually happened when she was six; she's shaping her description to conform with what she came to learn was a compelling way to describe a profound change in one's worldview—the story of Christian conversion. Indeed, delving deeper into Keller's memoir, we learn that Keller was exposed to the work of the eighteenth-century Christian theologian Emanuel Swedenborg when she was fourteen and that she, like William Blake, William Butler Yeats, and Ralph Waldo Emerson before her, was drawn to Swedenborg's descriptions of a Christian spirituality that transcended church-based versions of the religion.

We're not the only ones to see that Keller's first autobiography offers an idealized version of her past; John Macy, who helped Keller write *The Story of My Life*, makes essentially the same observation in an appendix to the volume. There Macy states that Keller has not provided "a scientifically accurate record of her life, nor even of the important events. She cannot know in detail how she was taught, and her memory of her childhood is in some cases an idealized memory of what she has learned later from her teacher and others." There is, we would note, nothing exceptional about this: What do you remember about your life at six? How much of your memory of that time is shaped by the stories your parents or siblings tell about you? How much is shaped by photographs and family videos, which are themselves a type of idealized memory?

Perhaps we'll have more luck if we turn to the memories of those who were adults at the time Keller learned how to communicate. Anne Sullivan could, in fact, have a truer version of what happened at the pump than Keller does.

VERSION TWO: ANNE SULLIVAN'S CORRESPONDENCE (1887)

The Story of My Life also includes in its supplementary materials Anne Sullivan's account of how Keller came to learn how to communicate. In Sullivan's correspondence with her own teachers at the Perkins Institution for the Blind, she begins her description of the events of March 20, 1887 with this excited declaration: "A miracle has happened! The light of understanding has shone upon my little pupil's mind, and behold, all things are changed!" The miracle that Sullivan goes on to describe, though, is not the miracle of Keller's language acquisition: it is that "the little savage has learned her first lesson in obedience, and finds the yoke easy." Keller has learned to sit still, to be calm. She can make the signs to spell out words, but she confuses *mug* and *milk*, which shows that she "has no idea yet that everything has a name."

Two weeks later, on April 5, Sullivan reports that "something very important has happened. Helen has taken the second great step in her education. She has learned that everything has a name, and that the manual alphabet is the key to everything she wants to know." Sullivan mentions that Keller continued to have problems distinguishing *mug* and *milk*. Sullivan then describes what led her to take Keller outside to the water pump: while washing up in the morning, Keller "wanted to know the name for 'water.' When she wants to know the name of anything, she points to it and pats my hand." Sullivan signs the word, thinking nothing of it at the time, but then later decides to take Keller out to the pump house, on the hunch that Keller's learning the sign for *water* might help straighten out "the 'mug-milk' difficulty."

Note how Sullivan's correspondence stretches out the sequence of events, placing Keller's acts of learning and discovery in the stream of time. Note, too, that in Sullivan's account, Keller's immersion in the world of signing, which involves weeks of confusion and incomprehension, nevertheless leads to the generation of a question—a question asked before Keller even knows what a question is. The experience of water on the hand. The patting of the palm. In Sullivan's account, Keller is already five weeks into an immersive instructional experience when Sullivan leads her to the pump:

> The word coming so close upon the sensation of cold water rushing over her hand seemed to startle her. She dropped the mug and stood as one transfixed. A new light came into her face. She spelled "water" several times. Then she dropped on the ground and asked for its name and pointed to the pump and the trellis, and suddenly turning round she asked for my name.

For Sullivan, the story at the pump isn't about an instant in time or a revelatory moment of conversion; it's about Sullivan's commitment to weeks of dragging Keller to the threshold of language. Thus, Sullivan's version of the story culminates not in Keller's newly discovered desire to repent but in Keller's desire to learn the name of the person who brought her out of the darkness—her teacher. In the version told by Sullivan, the teacher is the miracle worker.

Given these two versions of the scene at the pump, one might reasonably conclude that we are always the heroes of our own stories: for Keller, the scene at the pump is about her spiritual encounter with an elevated state of consciousness; for Sullivan, it is affirmation of her powers as a teacher. But this conclusion is too simplistic. If we drill down further, we find that Keller's thinking about that scene at the pump continued to change over the course of her lifetime and that she came to feel trapped by the power of the story itself because it turned out to be the only story about her that others ever wanted to hear.

VERSION THREE: HELEN KELLER'S *THE WORLD I LIVE IN* (1908)

Keller voices this frustration in her second autobiography, *The World I Live In*, which was published just five years after *The Story of My Life*.

> Every book is in a sense autobiographical. But while other self-recording creatures are permitted at least to seem to change the subject, apparently nobody cares what I think of the tariff, the conservation of our natural resources, or the conflicts which revolve about the name of Dreyfus. If I offer to reform the education system of the world, my editorial friends say, "That is interesting. But will you please tell us what idea you had of goodness and beauty when you were six years old?"

In effect, the story of Helen at the pump was already on its way to being the only story from Keller's life that there was a market for, despite the fact that Keller was the first deaf and blind American to earn a college degree and was eager to share her thoughts on the virtues of socialism and other matters of global import.

Keenly aware of this conflict between her audience's expectations and her own desires, in *The World I Live In* Keller settles for weaving her thoughts about larger world affairs into the story of her life. This is evident even in the way she retells the story of the pump in her new volume:

> Before my teacher came to me, I did not know that I am. I lived in a world that was a no-world. I cannot hope to describe adequately that unconscious, yet conscious time of nothingness. I did not know that I knew aught, or that I lived or acted or desired. I had neither will nor intellect.

Notice that in this revised account, Keller grants Sullivan a central role in her transformation, but she uses language that foregrounds the transformation as one of the mind, rather than one of the soul or the spirit. Her teacher, represented here iconically rather than by name, gave Keller access to consciousness, to desire, to will, and to the intellect. Keller is still a "self-recording creature," but the self she represents herself as recording has changed; before language, she was incapable of voicing the statement that Descartes asserted is the very foundation of our being: "I think, therefore I am." She was, by her own estimation, not human.

Is this version of what happened at the pump more accurate than either of the previous two versions? Is it possible to remember what life before language was like? Or are the results of any such efforts the product not of memory but of the imagination?

VERSION FOUR: *ANNE SULLIVAN MACY: A TRIBUTE BY THE FOSTER-CHILD OF HER MIND* (1955)

More than forty years after the publication of *The World I Live In*, Keller revised her telling of the story at the pump one final time. Looking back on the version she recorded in *The Story of My Life*, Keller now sees her earliest autobiographical work as having been produced "with the carelessness of a happy, positive young girl," and she regrets that she "failed to stress sufficiently the obstacles and hardships which confronted Teacher"(now capitalized). And so it is with the explicit project of celebrating Anne Sullivan, whom Keller identifies as the foster mother of her mind, that Keller offers her third version of the events at the pump:

> Suddenly Phantom understood the meaning of the word, and her mind began to flutter tiny wings of flame. Caught up in the first joy she had felt since her illness, she reached out eagerly to Annie's ever-ready hand, begging for new words to identify whatever objects she touched. Spark after spark of meaning flew through her mind until her heart was warmed and affection was born. From the well-house there walked two enraptured beings calling each other "Helen" and "Teacher." Surely such moments of delight contain a fuller life than an eternity of darkness.

In this retelling, Phantom, a shadow being without thought, language, or happiness, is transformed into Helen once her Teacher gives her access to the link between words and meaning, after which "her heart was warmed and affection was born." So in this final version of Keller's, a story that once had strong religious overtones gets recast in terms that evoke the pleasures of romance and culminates in the creation of "two enraptured beings" who were joined to one another forever thereafter. But not really forever, because Sullivan had been dead for nearly two decades when Keller published her tribute. Does that fact make this account more true or less so than the previous ones? Are words written in grief or words that seek to repair a past injury more or less likely to express accurately what actually happened?

VERSIONS FIVE AND SIX: WILLIAM GIBSON'S *THE MIRACLE WORKER* (1957) AND *MONDAY AFTER THE MIRACLE* (1982)

Drilling down yet further, we learn that William Gibson's relationship to the story at the pump also changed over time. As a result of the wild success of *The Miracle Worker*, Gibson's version of Keller's childhood experience has reached a much wider audience than any of the versions Keller herself composed. This is so, we would argue, because of the primacy of the image over the word. To get to Keller's versions or to Sullivan's version, one must commit to the act of reading. To get to Gibson's version, one need only take a seat in the theater or sit before a screen that's broadcasting either the original teleplay, which first appeared on television in 1957, or the movie version, which premiered in 1962 and starred Anne Bancroft and Patty Duke in the roles of Sullivan and Keller. Both actors won Academy Awards for their performances. The critical and popular success of the film helped to make *The Miracle Worker* a staple of the high school stage, where it has been regularly performed for the past sixty years, cementing in the public consciousness Gibson's version of the story — that Keller acquired language in an instant, with a violent struggle leading Keller and Sullivan to the pump, followed by Keller returning to her family for a joyous embrace.

As noted above, Keller struggled throughout her adult life to find an audience for the thoughts and ideas that her miraculous triumph over adversity made possible — thoughts about women's suffrage, pacifism, religion, and world government. Ironically, Gibson himself came to feel trapped by the success of *The Miracle Worker* and by its simplified tale of how the life of a girl with multiple disabilities was transformed by the miracle of language. In 1982, twenty-five years after the original broadcast of his teleplay, Gibson published *Monday after the Miracle*, which picks up Keller's story at the time she is attending Radcliffe College and is in the process of writing *The Story of My Life* with the help of Anne Sullivan and John Macy, an English instructor. In the second act of this sequel, Sullivan, her own eyesight failing, has married Macy, but their relationship is complicated by the fact that Keller, Sullivan's constant companion, is no longer the small, vulnerable child at the pump she once was, but is now a grown woman in her mid-twenties.

In the third act, Sullivan and Macy's marriage is in the final stage of collapse, owing to Macy's alcoholism, Sullivan's inability to conceive, their money troubles, and Macy's newfound attraction to Keller. To address the household's financial problems, Sullivan and Keller first go on the lecture circuit and then, in the play's penultimate scene, announce to Macy that they are preparing to join the vaudeville circuit, because there's much more money to be made by performing for audiences that expect to be entertained than by giving lectures to the small groups of educated people interested in Keller's ideas. (Gibson alters the actual timeline of events to create this fictional conflict: Macy and Sullivan split up years before Sullivan and Keller took their show on the road.) When Keller recites her lines from the planned vaudeville act for Macy to critique, he is driven into a rage by her announcing, "My teacher has told you how a word from her hand touched the darkness of my mind. Through love, I found my soul and God and happiness." Macy responds derisively, describing Keller as Sullivan's "trained seal, mouthing platitudes. Found God and happiness, for Christ sake."

Macy then pleads with Keller to leave Sullivan and come to Italy with him: "you can do better—better than the hag-ridden life *you'll* have with her, turning into a tin showpiece. Leave her!" In the darker, more oppressive, and lonelier world Keller and Sullivan inhabit as adults, the miracle of Keller's childhood is now openly mocked, with Macy smashing a bottle of liquor on his typewriter while repeating Keller's lines: "Through love I found my soul and God and happiness." And then, just before he storms out of their lives for good, Macy says to Keller, "you've sucked us empty, angel, you've gutted [Sullivan's] life and mine, and I swear if I could—wipe out the day you were born—"

One could argue that Gibson stages this scene to free both Keller and himself from being frozen in time at the moment Keller learned her first word. If this was Gibson's goal, however, he clearly failed: the critical reception of *Monday after the Miracle* was so negative when it premiered on Broadway in 1982 that the play closed after just one week. After being remade into a schlocky "love triangle" TV movie in 1998, *Monday after the Miracle* has essentially been consigned to the dustbin of history.

Is Gibson's second version of Keller's "awakening" more true than his first version? Less true? Completely untrue? What are we to make of the fact that audiences embrace the version of Keller's life that culminates at the water pump and reject the versions of her life that follow her into adulthood?

VERSION SEVEN: ANNE SULLIVAN MACY AND HELEN KELLER ON THE VAUDEVILLE CIRCUIT (1920–1924)

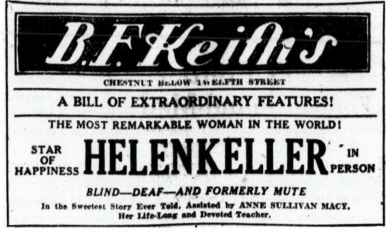

Evening Public Ledger, *June 5, 1920.*

The Granger Collection, New York

From our historical vantage point, the vision of Anne Sullivan and Helen Keller performing on the vaudeville stage alongside jugglers, acrobats, magicians, and the physically disabled is likely to seem something Gibson invented for dramatic effect. But, as we drill down further, we discover that Sullivan and Keller did indeed perform on the vaudeville stage from 1920 to 1924, and that each performance began with Sullivan first appearing on stage alone to tell the story of the pump. Then Keller would join her and, to the audience's astonishment, would actually speak the following words (demonstrating that she had learned both sign language *and* how to speak aloud):

> What I have to say is very simple. My teacher has told you how a word from her hand touched the darkness of my mind and I awoke to the gladness of life. I was dumb; now I speak. I owe this to the hands and hearts of others. Through their love I found my soul and God and happiness. Don't you see what it means? We live by each other and for each other. Alone we can do so little. Together we can do so much. Only

love can break down the walls that stand between us and our happiness. . . . I lift up my voice and thank the Lord for love and joy and the promise of life to come.

In her article "'Play[ing] Her Part Correctly': Helen Keller as Vaudevillian Freak," Susan Crutchfield argues that Keller's success on the stage was predicated on her performing the story her audience desired. Instead of explicitly stating her support for socialism, Keller recited a script that masked her politics behind a call for people to work together. In reviewing the contemporary newspaper reports on these performances, Crutchfield concludes that, "Again and again for Keller's vaudeville audience, it is her voice, her physical demonstration of her *ability* to speak rather than what she says, that generates their sense of awe."

Is Keller's vaudeville speech the truest version of the pump story, since it allows her to share a version of her thoughts about what is required to create a better world?

MAKING THOUGHT VISIBLE: A PARADOX

After considering all these versions of Keller at the pump, you're probably tempted to say that there's no way of ever knowing what happened on that fateful day when the water and the word met on Keller's palm for the first time. While that's certainly true, we're interested in the question that is raised by our journey through these many different ways of describing this pivotal moment in Keller's life: Is it ever possible to communicate to another person your own experience of thinking?

Everyone who learns how to use language experiences the miracle Keller experienced. But Keller is nearly alone in having been able to credibly claim to remember the miraculous moment when the world of experience shifted from incoherent chaos to a world of nameable objects and actions. We stipulate that this moment is both miraculous and fascinating, but we are nevertheless much more interested in the moments that follow this initial, inexplicable moment of contact — the moments that occur after the mind has matured and there are more words and experiences to work with. This is the question that we've written to ourselves as a result of meditating on the many different stories about Helen at the pump: Is it ever possible to describe a new thought coming into being, or must one compose versions of the emergence of new thought that are prepackaged to meet audience expectations? Is the writing one does about one's own thinking always a fiction? Is this true even for the version of the essay we champion in *Habits of the Creative Mind*, where the goal is to show one's mind at work on a problem?

Practice Session One: Thinking a New Thought

Habits: questioning, reflecting, speculating

Activities: choosing, remembering, writing

We'd like you to take up the questions with which we've ended our deliberations by considering your own experiences of thinking thoughts that are new to you. While at first blush it may seem that all such experiences are inevitably personal, we encourage you to consider experiences through which you came to think differently about an issue, topic, or debate, and not just experiences that made you think differently about yourself or others. We want you to choose an example that is important to you, one without which you feel your life would be diminished. Can you make it clear how you came to think this new thought?

The preceding essay gives you several examples of how to go about this task: you can provide a vivid narrative or set of narratives about the experience (as Keller does), or you can provide an evidence-driven account that proceeds via juxtaposition (as we have done). We challenge you to show your readers, to the best of your ability, not only what the new thought is, but also your own experience of that thought coming into being in your mind.

Practice Session Two: On Political Correctness

Habits: exploring, reflecting, working deliberately

Activities: defining, interpreting, researching

In the vaudeville performance put on by Keller and Sullivan, Keller would say aloud to the awestruck audience, "I am not dumb now." A century ago, it was common to refer to those who were mute as "dumb," a word that then meant both "incapable of speech" and "unintelligent." But as the example of Keller amply shows, the double meaning of this word reinforced a prejudice against those who, for whatever reason, could not speak. Nearly a century has passed since Keller performed on the vaudeville circuit, and the language used today to describe any kind of human difference, be it one of ability or sexuality or race or gender, is now much more carefully scrutinized.

Oddly, this concern for the language we use to describe those who differ from ourselves has been dubbed "political correctness." We'd like you to research the original use of the phrase "political correctness" and then explore how this phrase is used in a contemporary example of your own choosing. (We don't need to provide you with examples because the charge of political correctness is so pervasive today.) When you've collected information about the term's original meaning and your contemporary example, we'd like you to write an essay about the relationship between thought and language. Is the struggle over language necessarily a struggle over thought?

....
Practice Session Three: Choose an Example
....

Habits: reflecting, speculating, working deliberately
Activities: selecting, writing

The most common dodge we come across as writing teachers arises when a writer who, after considering a range of conflicting explanations for a given event, declares "everyone has a right to his or her own opinion." We read this statement as meaning, "I don't have a stake in this." We can imagine a reader who considers the seven different versions of the pump scene we've provided above and concludes that everyone has a right to interpret Keller's moment of language acquisition as he or she pleases. We don't think that this is a question of rights, though: by virtue of being language-using creatures, we are all hardwired to interpret. The question is not whether we have a right to interpret as we please, but whether any one interpretation is better than another. If you were writing an essay that explored the relationship between language and thought, which account of Keller's experience would you use, and why? Now write that essay, and see where your writing leads your thinking.

On the Examined Life

"The unexamined life is not worth living," Socrates declares near the end of his trial for corrupting the youth of Athens. He makes this statement after a jury has found him guilty and the trial is moving into the sentencing phase. The prosecution has called for the death penalty. Socrates, in response, has considered other possible sentences—permanent exile or being forbidden to continue to ask questions of himself and others about what it means to live a good life—and rejects them because they would make life not livable (βίος οὐ βιωτός). The most common English translation of Socrates's statement allows one to argue that he means not livable *for him*. But if we look at the sentence as it appears in Greek in Plato's *Apologia*, we find that Socrates is making a larger assertion: namely, that the unexamined life is a life not livable for "mankind" (ἀνθρώπῳ). Socrates's assertion, in other words, certainly applies to the members of the jury and, arguably, to all male citizens of Athens.

It is an open question whether Socrates was making a statement that applies to *all* humans (the literal translation of *anthropos* is "man" and, by extension, "mankind"). But, in this particular instance, he knew the jury was unlikely to be persuaded to allow him to continue teaching young men simply because he asserted that the unexamined life wasn't worth living. So, he proposed instead to pay a very small fine. His students, in an effort to save him, offered to pay a larger fine. Having heard the argument for Socrates's execution and Socrates's arguments for allowing him to go on teaching, the jury voted and sentenced Socrates to death.

For Socrates, the examined life meant something very specific—a life spent questioning one's own beliefs and the beliefs of others in an effort to find universal truths. We, too, place a high value on the examined life, but we mean something rather different by this than what Socrates meant. We see the goal of the examined life to be the understanding of one's self and one's place in the world over time and we think that writing (an activity Socrates deeply distrusted) can be a particularly vibrant resource for conducting these examinations.

To give students practice engaging with this version of the examined life, we first ask them to conduct research into questions that are genuinely of interest to them, questions for which the outcomes matter in some way. Once they've had practice doing this, we then have them consider how to make their research interesting to others. We do this because we want our students to experience complexity first-hand; we want them to confront the challenge of producing writing that triggers engaged discussion and that invites further self-reflection.

We boil all these abstractions down into an assignment we call "Be Interesting":

> Engaging with the sources you've found in your initial research, use your writing to show your mind at work on the question, problem, or mystery that has emerged from your encounter with your sources. Begin with your interests and then be interesting: use your writing to create an experience for your readers that is designed to generate interest in what you've discovered.
>
> We invite you to use any of our common readings as a model of how to move from being interested in a given question to creating writing that makes that question interesting to others.

This assignment instantly provokes animated discussions about what it means to be interested in something and whether or not there are clear signs in the writing itself that allow one to determine if a writer is genuinely invested or is just faking it. We love these discussions: if you're going to succeed in producing writing that is interesting to others, you need to spend time thinking and arguing in concrete terms about what interesting writing does. And you need to have concrete examples to consider. We look at the work of professional writers (like the pieces we've included in the Readings section of this book) and we look at work our students have produced in response to this assignment. Here, for example, is the first page of an essay by a student who wanted to make sense of an experience he'd had during the break between the fall and spring semesters.

> I had just recently come back from what I was telling people was "the best experience of my life." Over my winter break at Rutgers University, I decided to try something different and embarked on a ten-day trip sponsored by a Korean organization called the Good News Corps that eventually brought me to Monterrey, Mexico, where I participated in

the IYF (International Youth Fellowship) English Camp. The camp aimed to teach English to Mexican students of all ages over the course of three days. The whole trip only cost $300.

The memories were still fresh in my mind: the laughing, the dancing, the singing, the half-dozen girls holding me crying, thanking me for coming. Except now all these warm fuzzy feelings were being replaced with something else, something much more unsettling. I was having trouble processing what I was reading on my computer screen.

It was an article about the trip that made the front page of nytimes.com, titled "Traveling to Teach English; Getting Sermons Instead." [It was] sent to me by another student who went on the trip. The article details the account of two students who went home early in the trip while we were still in Dallas, Texas, for four days of "training" in preparation for teaching in Mexico. They felt they were victims of a scam, and were unhappy with how much of the camp centered on religion and the "Mind Lectures" of the program's leader, Ock Soo Park. This wasn't surprising, as I had met plenty of kids there who were upset for the same reasons, myself included, but most of us toughed it out for the sake of being able to go to Mexico. It was the comments section that was causing my state of disbelief.

"Evil. Creepy and Evil."

"Sounds an awful lot like the bad parts of Jonestown."

"While editorial concerns must have precluded Mr. Dwyer from calling a duck a duck, we all know these unwitting students got trapped in a recruitment session for a cult."

"Typical cult strategies."

"This sounds like the Moonie cult from years ago."

"This organization is essentially considered a cult in South Korea, known as 'Saviorists.'"

And they went on.

"This can't be right," was all I could think. Different flashes of my trip started replaying in my head. The mass baptisms in the hotel pool. The two-hour mind lectures. The lack of sleep. My moment of revelation. Could it be true? Did I willingly drink the Kool-Aid? Did I become part of a cult recruitment session for ten days?

This writer is, to our way of reading, documenting his experience (or one might say, examining his life) and he's doing so in a way that makes his examination of interest to others. We came to the conclusion that this work was indeed interesting by asking the following questions about his writing:

- Does it ask a genuine question or pose a genuine problem?
- Does it work with thought-provoking sources?
- Does it show the writer's mind at work making compelling connections?
- Is the writing used to develop ideas, arguments, or thoughts that are new to the writer?
- Does it pursue complications (perhaps by using words like *but* and *or*)?
- Is it presented in a way meant to engage smart, attentive readers?
- Does it make each word count?

Although we've provided you with only the first page of this student's essay, we think there's enough in the sample to suggest that he's off to a good start meeting the criteria we use to define interesting writing.

Our student set himself the task of figuring out whether he, an ordinary guy who is well grounded and content with his life, came close to getting brainwashed. While the writer doesn't present much research on this first page, you can definitely see his mind at work on a problem. He actively pursues complications in the shift he makes from his unsurprised response to the newspaper article about the program he'd participated in to his shock at reading the readers' comments to that same article. We don't have enough to go on at this point to comment on how he works with sources, and we can't say that every last word will count, but there's no doubt in our minds that this writer has done a great job of drawing readers into his predicament. He's on his way to moving the examination of his own life from being a dialogue with himself to being a public document others can read and reflect on.

Practice Session One, Part One:
Montaigne's Mind at Work on a Problem

Habits: paying attention, questioning, reflecting

Activities: evaluating, reading

We'd like you to practice applying the criteria for interesting writing we have offered above to the readings we've included at the end of *Habits*. Montaigne's essay (pp. 268–69) is a good one to start with: it's so short, it seems like it would have to miss the mark. (And yet, we've included it, so it's obvious that we think it's worth reading and rereading!) After you've read Montaigne's essay over as many times as it takes for you to feel you've got a good handle on what he's doing as a writer, write out brief answers to the following questions:

- Does the piece ask a genuine question or pose a genuine problem?
- Does the piece work with thought-provoking sources?
- Does the piece show the writer's mind at work making compelling connections?
- Is the writing used to develop ideas, arguments, or thoughts that are new to the writer?
- Does the piece pursue complications (perhaps by using words like *but* and *or*)?
- Is the piece presented in a way meant to engage smart, attentive readers?
- Does the piece make each word count?

When you're done, what have you learned from applying our criteria? Are there better questions to ask? (We always welcome improvements and refinements.) In making your determinations, were you a neutral judge? An engaged reader? A resistant reader? How does one assign responsibility for making writing interesting? Does the responsibility fall entirely on the writer? What share might belong to readers?

Practice Session One, Part Two: X's Mind at Work on a Problem

Habits: paying attention, questioning, reflecting

Activities: discussing, evaluating, reading

Now, repeat the activities in Part One of this practice session with one of the other four readings at the end of *Habits*. Are there questions that should be added to the criteria for longer pieces? For historical documents? Should we have different criteria for students than we have for professional writers?

Practice Session One, Part Three: Who Makes Writing Interesting?

Habits: connecting, reflecting, speculating

Activities: drafting, writing

Now that you've spent time working with our criteria and have considered ways to make the criteria better, we'd like you to reflect on the experience of assessing the writing of others. When you were practicing applying the criteria, how much responsibility did you place on the author for making the assigned writing interesting? Did applying the criteria make you see aspects of what you were reading that might otherwise have escaped your attention? If you, as a reader, play a role in making writing interesting, does that invalidate your judgments about the writing itself?

First sketch out your sense of how you went about applying the criteria. Then write an essay that reflects on what you've learned about the work of assessing the writing of others from applying our criteria. Make sure that whatever you write meets your own criteria for what makes writing interesting.

Practice Session Two, Part One: Life Examined

Habits: exploring, reflecting, speculating

Activities: brainstorming, note taking, selecting

Now it's your turn. We'd like you to tackle the "Be Interesting" assignment. First, you have to generate a question that you genuinely want to think about. This is harder than it sounds: most of us have lots of questions rumbling around in our heads produced by our annoyance with the world (i.e., why do people text and drive at the same time?) that aren't questions we actually want to do research on because we're pretty sure we already know the answer (they don't understand or care about putting the lives of others in danger). And, in these highly polarized times, there are lots of rhetorical questions about people with opposing points of view: Why do *they* think X? Because they're deranged!

For this assignment to be meaningful, you've got to choose a question that actively interests you. It can't be a simple yes or no question or a true or false question or an informational question; it also can't be a question that is exclusively about your own experience or your own memories or your own thoughts. It has to be a question that lends itself to research into something outside your own head. In our essay, we use the example of a student who begins by asking, "Was I brainwashed?" This leads him to investigate the history of the organization that sponsored his trip to Mexico and to question how one distinguishes between a cult, a scam, and an organized religion.

Generate three questions that seem plausible to you. Eliminate any that you can type into a search engine and have answered to your satisfaction with a single click. Make an argument for why each one is an interesting question to consider, according to your own criteria. Then, with those arguments in mind, ask yourself which question has the greatest likelihood of getting you to read and think about material that is new to you or to consider material that is familiar to you in new and surprising ways. Choose that question.

....

Practice Session Two, Part Two: Life Examined in Writing

....

Habits: exploring, reflecting, speculating

Activities: engaging with sources, revising, writing

With your question in hand, you're now ready to embark on the research that drives the "Be Interesting" assignment.

Engaging with the sources you've found in your initial research, use your writing to show your mind at work on the question, problem, or mystery that has emerged from your encounter with your sources. Begin with your interests and then be interesting: use your writing to create an experience for your readers that is designed to generate interest in what you've discovered.

We invite you to use any of the readings we've included at the end of this book as a model of how to move from being interested in a given question to creating writing that makes that question interesting to others.

If you come up with something really amazing, send it to us. We'd love to hear from you!

9

PERSISTING

"Genius," Thomas Alva Edison famously declared, "is one percent inspiration, ninety-nine percent perspiration." The nation's most prolific inventor is remembered for his pivotal contributions to the invention and improvement of the telegraph, the light bulb, the telephone, and the kinetoscope, a precursor to the moving picture. With that record of accomplishment, there has to be more to Edison's "genius" than his quote reveals. He was very, very smart. And he did work hard. But, like all creative people, he worked hard in a specific way: he knew to expect the creative process to be difficult in unforeseen ways; he knew that failure is always instructive; and he knew that inspiration itself comes from training the mind to think the unthinkable.

Edison is also reputed to have said, "I have not failed 10,000 times — I've discovered 10,000 ways that don't work." This less familiar quote shifts the focus from failure to solutions that do not work. In this sentence, Edison captures the essence of creative work: it is essentially connected to producing solutions that don't work and then understanding why the solutions didn't work. His purpose is not to bolster his self-esteem, but to show that the creative mind is always curious about what happens when one attempts to transform an idea into a reality.

Creative work requires that you transform your relationship to failure. Persisting in the face of failure is a job requirement for the creative mind; it is a practice without an end point. The three essays we include here will help you with that practice.

On Encountering Difficulty

In his essay "The Mind's Eye," the neurologist Oliver Sacks finds himself unexpectedly confronted with the question of free will: "To what extent are we — our experiences, our reactions — shaped, predetermined, by our brains, and to what extent do we shape our own brains?" Sacks has written himself to this question by considering a series of cases of individuals who were born with sight but then became blind. The point that Sacks wants to make in "The Mind's Eye" is deceptively simple: how one responds to becoming blind is idiosyncratic — that is, it is unique to the individual. Sacks did not always think this was the case. Initially, he accepted the prevailing idea that there was a common response to going blind: the structure of the brain made certain that the remaining senses acquired greater powers to compensate for the loss of sight. The brain's neurological response was predetermined biologically; the individual had no say in the matter.

Sacks opens his essay with a case in which sensory compensation seems like the best explanation for how the patient responded to going blind. John Hull, blind in one eye due to cataracts at seventeen, went completely blind at forty-eight, at which point he says he steadily lost access not only to his visual memories but also to what Sacks terms "the very idea of seeing." In this profound state of "deep blindness," Hull claimed that spatial references such as "here" and "there" lost meaning for him. At the same time, he became what he calls a "whole-body seer," someone whose other senses roared to life to compensate for his loss of vision and who, as a result, experienced wholly new ways of engaging with the world.

After first writing about Hull in 1991, Sacks began to hear from others whose experiences of becoming blind could not be explained in terms of sensory compensation. For example, Zoltan Torey's response to going blind was the exact opposite of Hull's: instead of embracing "deep blindness" when he lost his sight in an accident at the age of twenty-one, Torey cultivated the powers of his "inner eye," self-consciously laboring to hold on to his ability to think with and manipulate visual images. What Torey has done since going blind is almost unthinkable: he learned to multiply four-figure numbers in his head by visualizing the operations as if the calculation were written on a blackboard; he taught himself to move and manipulate three-dimensional images in his mind, breaking them apart and recombining the pieces; he even single-handedly replaced the roof gutters on his gabled home. What motivates Torey? A deep need to retain a sense of the visual.

Then there's Sabriye Tenberken, blind since twelve, who has traveled extensively in Tibet, often alone, advocating for the blind. She has cultivated a rich synesthetic inner world, one full of color and feeling, which allows her to use words to paint elaborate and fanciful descriptions of the outside world. While Torey visualizes highly detailed maps and diagrams of the real world, Tenberken delights in holding on to an inner vision that is poetic and playful.

Sacks started out looking for a neurological explanation of these varied responses to becoming blind—namely that, whereas Hull's visual cortex had atrophied completely, Torey was able to "stave off an otherwise inevitable loss of neuronal function in the visual cortex" by means of his mental gymnastics. Neurology seemed to explain this broader range of responses to going blind, but then Sacks started talking with sighted people and was surprised to find that they, too, presented widely varying capacities for visual imagination: some sighted people can hold images in their minds and manipulate them as Torey does; some, akin to Hull, cannot generate visual images or call them to mind; others can visualize in great detail only through chemical enhancement.

Where does this leave us? For Sacks, the fact that both the blind and the seeing share a spectrum of possible ways to visualize the outer world illustrates the difference between brain and mind. The power to see has a physical, neurological basis located in the brain. What happens to those impulses once the brain processes them is determined not by the brain alone but, Sacks argues, by "the higher and more personal powers of the imagination, where there is a continual struggle for concepts and form and meaning, a calling upon all the powers of the self," which we would call *the mind*. Sacks continues:

> Imagination dissolves and transforms, unifies and creates, while drawing upon the "lower" powers of memory and association. It is by such imagination, such "vision," that we create or construct our individual worlds.

Thus, at the level of the individual, one cannot predict with certainty what the neurological response to radical change will be. We see this mystery as much in Hull's embrace of deep blindness as in Torey's tending the flames of inner vision — in the interplay between the hardwiring of neurology and the software of the self. Such a mystery cannot be unraveled by science alone because the self simultaneously resides in and is created by the work of the imagination as it connects and transforms the memories and associations recorded by and stored in the brain.

To put this another way, we could say that our inner lives are both created and sustained by the imagination; and further, that in times of radical change the very survival of the self depends on imagining what was previously unimaginable — that life without sight is sensually rich, for example, or that one's blindness should be fully embraced. This observation doesn't resolve the mystery, of course, but only further sharpens it: How does one cultivate an imagination capable of such adaptation? How does one learn to live with and within new forms of embodied experience? And how does one find a way to express what is newly imagined or experienced through writing?

....

Practice Session One A, Part One: Blind Photographers

....

Habits: exploring, persisting, reflecting

Activities: looking, researching

If you are blind or visually impaired, skip this exercise and go to Practice Session One B (for blind or visually impaired students) below. If you are sighted, visit the online *Time* magazine photo gallery "Photos by Blind Photographers." The opening blurb says that the exhibit "raises extraordinary questions about the nature of sight." What do you see when you look at these photographs taken by photographers who are legally blind? How do the words that accompany each image influence what you see? Can you unsee the words and consider the images simply as photographs? Search the web for other works by these photographers and for the work of other blind photographers. Follow your curiosity.

Practice Session One A, Part Two: Blind Photographers

Habits: beginning, persisting, speculating
Activities: writing

How do blind photographers teach the sighted to see? Using examples of images you have collected through your research, write a reflective essay about what you've learned about blindness and the imagination.

Practice Session One B (for blind or visually impaired students): Seeing without Eyesight

Habits: orienting, persisting, reflecting
Activities: writing

Consider what those with sight could learn about perception from your experience. John Hull offers such a lesson when he describes the intensity of experiencing rain as a "whole-body seer":

> Rain has a way of bringing out the contours of everything; it throws a colored blanket over previously invisible things; instead of an intermittent and thus fragmented world, the steadily falling rain creates continuity of acoustic experience.... The sound on the path is quite different from the sound of the rain drumming into the lawn on the right, and this is different again from the blanketed, heavy, sodden feel of the large bush on the left. Further out, the sounds are less detailed. I can hear the rain falling on the road, and the swish of the cars that pass up and down.

Write a reflective essay that represents how you perceive your surroundings. Does your experience strike you as idiosyncratic? That is, does your individual character, temperament, or will play a role in your perception of your environment?

Practice Session Two A: Facial Recognition

Habits: exploring, paying attention, persisting

Activities: reading, testing, writing

If you are blind or visually impaired, skip this exercise and go to Practice Session Two B (for blind or visually impaired students) below.

In August 2016, the *New Yorker* published a piece by Patrick Radden Keefe that was entitled "Total Recall" in the print edition and "The Detectives Who Never Forget a Face" in the online edition. In the piece, Keefe reports on how the British police force recruits people with a gift for facial recognition to assist in the process of identifying criminals whose images have been captured by the nation's ubiquitous closed-circuit television system. We recommend Keefe's piece here because it allows us to continue a conversation Sacks initiates in "The Mind's Eye": How do we know that all sighted people do not have the same experience of the visual imagination?

When you read Keefe's piece, it's impossible not to wonder how you'd do performing the work he describes. Although Keefe provided a link to the "Cambridge Face Memory Test," at the end of his article, the link no longer works. Fortunately, other universities host similar tests online. Search for "face memory test," select a link, and sign up to see how your skills at facial recognition compare to the skills of other test takers. Before you begin, take a moment to write down your own sense of how good you are at recognizing faces. What might cause one person to be better at this than another?

Once you've completed the test, write a reflective essay about your experience. What did it show you? What did you learn by taking it? Did you make adjustments during the test in response to its increasing difficulty? Is there anything you could do to improve your score?

Practice Session Two B (for blind or visually impaired students): Recognizing People through Multiple Senses

Habits: exploring, paying attention, persisting

Activities: reading, testing, writing

Practice Session Two B begins exactly as Two A does, with a twist. In August 2016, the *New Yorker* published a piece by Patrick Radden Keefe that was entitled "Total Recall" in the print edition and "The Detectives Who Never Forget a Face" in the online edition. In the piece, Keefe reports on how the British police force recruits people with a gift for facial recognition to assist in the process of identifying criminals whose images have been captured by the nation's ubiquitous closed-circuit television system. We recommend that you read or listen to Keefe's piece because it allows us to continue a conversation that Sacks initiates in "The Mind's Eye" about the surprising ways blind or visually impaired people make sense of and interpret the world around them, including the social world.

If you are blind or visually impaired, you obviously rely on senses other than sight to identify people. Write an essay about how you recognize people. Which senses do you rely on, and which senses are more important than others? What skills and senses have you developed for identifying people that law-enforcement would find useful?

Practice Session Three: Mundane Difficulties

Habits: connecting, persisting, reflecting

Activities: selecting, writing

John Hull, Zoltan Torey, and Sabriye Tenberken help Sacks to see the power of the individual imagination in shaping how one responds to trauma. But what about ordinary, everyday problems? Does the imagination come into play when confronting a problem that is not life altering?

Choose a mundane problem that arises in the course of your day: a disagreement with a family member, difficulty finding parking, misplacing your keys. Does the resolution of this sort of problem yield evidence of the uniqueness of each individual's imagination? Or do mundane problems call for mundane solutions? Write an essay that explores multiple ways of solving an everyday problem, and consider whether your example demonstrates the powers of the human imagination.

Practice Session Four: Writing through Difficulties

Habits: connecting, persisting, reflecting

Activities: selecting, writing

Each of the four single-authored readings we've included in the Reading section at the end of this book serves as an example of a writer encountering difficulty. (We're not including the Declaration of Independence as an option for this assignment. Even though Thomas Jefferson is listed as its sole author, the document is famous for having been drafted by a committee and edited by Congress.) Choose one of these essays and, while reading it, mark the moments when the author encounters difficulty. When you're done, review the passages you've marked. Are all the difficulties of the same kind? Of the same importance? Of the same intensity?

How does the writer respond to these difficulties? Write an essay in which you examine the writer's approach to difficulty. Although you might be tempted to say that the writer's approach is simply "idiosyncratic," explore in greater detail how the writer responds to difficulty as it is experienced in the world of ideas and words.

On Learning from Failure

When we watch children building a sandcastle on a summer beach, we see creativity in action. The castle grows and becomes more elaborate as the children add moats, towers, turrets, and carefully laid rows of shells. The ongoing construction is always under threat of destruction — from the rising tide, careless passersby, impish older siblings, and frustrated members of the construction crew. But, unless disagreements and exhaustion take over, the castle builders convert whatever damage has been done into a temporary setback. They experiment to figure out how to build a better moat to stay the tide. A bucket brigade creates a pile of wetter sand. The construction project is moved up or down the beach to a better location. When children are building sandcastles, they're not afraid of failure because the stakes are low. The point is simply to have fun.

However, once we become adults, we're likely to avoid situations where the prospect of failure is high. Whether at work or school, most of us fear tackling a complex problem in front of our peers because of the possible consequences of failing: embarrassment, shame, a lower grade, a demotion. This fear of failure stifles creativity and innovation.

Not all people respond to fear of failure in the same way, though. In fact, creative people tend to have an attitude toward failure that's more like the kids on the beach than like a typical adult trying to solve a problem at work or a student trying to figure out what the teacher wants him to say. In *What the Best College Students Do*, Ken Bain argues that what sets the best students apart from the rest is their willingness to acknowledge failures, to explore them, and to learn from them. Unlike less creative people, they don't deny their mistakes or get defensive about errors.

Where does this ability to bounce back from failure come from? To answer this question, Bain points to a study that compared two groups of ten-year-olds who were each given a series of puzzles. The first eight problems required the students to make real effort, but the challenges matched the students' age and education level. The next four problems were designed to be too hard for the students to solve. Over the first eight problems, there were no differences in how the groups performed; both groups talked about the problems as they worked through them, had fun, and came up with roughly the same number of correct solutions. On the second set of problems, however, the groups' reactions differed greatly from each other. The first group got frustrated, complained, and tried to change the rules; they started to make surprisingly poor choices, shifted their focus away from the problems, and gave up. By contrast, the second group continued to encourage each other, tested different approaches, and seemed to thrive on the challenge, even though they couldn't solve the hard problems either.

What caused the divergent responses? The students were grouped by researchers based on their attitudes toward intelligence. The first group had a fixed view of intelligence and the second group believed, conversely, that with effort you could become smarter. (As shorthand, we call members of the first group the "knowers" and members of the second group the "learners.") When the knowers faced failure, they looked for an escape route, because their failures called their intelligence into question; they went into mental tailspins, reverting to strategies that might be expected from preschoolers. The learners didn't take failure personally. Because they believed they could develop intelligence, working on the problems was its own reward. Even if they never found solutions, they valued learning things along the way.

Obviously, we can't just snap our fingers and change ingrained beliefs and patterns of behavior. And we can't change the fact that in some situations, when the stakes are immediate and high, it's nearly impossible to sustain an impersonal attitude toward failure. We believe, however, that it is possible to cultivate more creative attitudes toward failure through practice. One of the most important locations for such practice is in school, working on assignments that allow time for experimentation and revision. That's why we provide practice sessions that invite you to engage with open questions that can't be answered simply with facts or by following a formula to a straightforward conclusion. We want you to use your writing to explore genuinely knotty problems, ones that challenge you to think thoughts that are new to you. Under these circumstances, it is inevitable that your initial efforts will fall short of the mark. You can see that as a failure or as an opportunity to practice new ways of working on a problem. When we learn from failure, we discover that practice never ends.

Richard likes to tell the story of what happened when he started revising his doctoral dissertation for publication. Having set the work aside for a couple of years while he was settling into his new job, he was able to return to it with fresh eyes. And after careful consideration and some additional research in the archive, he decided that there was really only one thing that needed to be changed about his dissertation, which he'd spent more than two years writing.

The thesis.

That's all. Only the frame for his argument. Only what he'd thought he'd understood about the problem.

While this may sound like an unusual experience, it's actually both common and predictable. What we put down in writing isn't destiny; it's a snapshot of a mind at work on a problem and, if that mind keeps working on the problem, then a snapshot taken at a later time will, of necessity, look different. We have a name for that difference: learning.

Practice Session One, Part One: A History of Failure

Habits: beginning, persisting, speculating

Activities: imagining, remembering, writing

As a thought experiment, look back at what kind of student you were in middle school and in high school. Then imagine what school would have been like for you if grades hadn't mattered to parents or college admissions committees. Would you have taken more risks as a writer and learner, or would you have just goofed around more?

Set aside at least forty-five minutes to reflect on the kind of school that could foster an environment in which students, including you, would be willing both to work hard and to "fail big." Write a description of the key characteristics of your imagined school. Consider whether there are classes, teachers, or majors that you think foster the kind of environment you describe.

Practice Session One, Part Two: What Education Might Entail

Habits: connecting, persisting, exploring

Activities: note taking, reading, writing

The word *failure* appears one time in Danielle Allen's "What Is Education For?" (which we've included in the Readings section at the end of this book). We'd like you to read Allen's essay, marking those places where you feel she answers the question posed in the title of her essay. When you're finished, compare the passages you've marked with what you wrote in Part One of this practice session. Is Allen's sense of education's purpose in conversation with your own experiences in school? Does her vision align with the vision you articulated?

To think these matters through, we'd like you to write an essay that considers Allen's use of "failure," a word she holds off using until the final paragraph of her essay. What would you say Allen wants us to learn from this failure?

Practice Session Two: Failing Better

Habits: connecting, persisting, speculating

Activities: reading, writing

In "Fail Better," an essay about writing, Zadie Smith identifies the cliché as a small-scale example of literary failure. She asks:

> What is a cliché except language passed down by Das Mann [the Man], used and shop-soiled by so many before you, and in no way the correct jumble of language for the intimate part of your vision you meant to express? With a cliché you have pandered to a shared understanding, you have taken a short-cut, you have represented what was pleasing and familiar rather than risked what was true and strange.

Obviously, there are occasions when settling for the pleasing, familiar, and expected is the polite thing to do (e.g., birthday cards, thank-you notes, letters of condolence), but to write an essay in this way is to fail to rise to the challenge of the form. The essayist works against cliché, both at the micro level of the sentence and at the macro level of structuring the delivery of a piece's insight, seeking new thoughts that can then be shared with writing that is productively unsettling.

We'd like you to choose one of the Readings included at the end of this volume and identify passages where the writer does (or in the case of the Declaration of Independence, the writers do) something unexpected. We are accustomed to thinking of a "failure to meet expectations" as a shortcoming, but Smith invites us to rethink such moments as instances when the writer has successfully avoided using a cliché. Spend at least forty minutes reflecting in writing about three passages you identified as instances in which the writer did something unexpected. What do these moments lead to? Is there a way to assess whether these decisions are successes or failures?

Practice Session Three: A Failure to Understand

Habits: paying attention, persisting, questioning
Activities: remembering, selecting, writing

A standard college application essay prompt asks students to write about a time when they learned from failure. Inevitably, this prompt generates essays that illustrate how the writer is a better person for having stumbled in one way or another. We want to avoid the mandatory moral message that such a prompt elicits, but we still want you to reflect on your own experience of failing to understand an important concept or idea. We want you to write, in other words, about your experience of failure in the realm of thought. What were the consequences of your failure? What did you do to try to overcome your failure to understand? What rewards, if any, followed from overcoming that failure? Write a reflective piece that captures a failure of thought and explores your response to that failure.

On Thinking Unthinkable Thoughts

"To infinity and beyond!"

If you give Buzz Lightyear's familiar rallying cry a moment's thought, you can see that what he's calling for is impossible. It's one of many jokes embedded in the *Toy Story* movies that is meant to entertain the adults in the audience: only a toy superhero would think that there is some point beyond infinity to which one could go.

We may chuckle at Buzz Lightyear's mistake, but do we really understand infinity much better than he does? If you stop and think seriously about what *infinity* means, you'll find yourself thinking that fully comprehending this concept is, by definition, impossible. And yet, while imagining the infinite may be impossible, striving to think this impossible thought has long preoccupied humankind.

The Greek philosopher Zeno used the concept of the infinite to formulate his paradox about the impossibility of movement. In order to get from point A to point B, he reasoned, you must first move half the distance. Call that halfway point C. But to move from point A to point C, you must first move half *that* distance. Call that halfway point D. And so on. Because any distance can be cut in half, the process of dividing never comes to an end — it is, by definition, infinite. If you try to think Zeno's paradox about infinite divisibility to its logical conclusion — that there are an infinite number of steps before one reaches a final destination — you will find yourself driven to conclude that motion of any kind is impossible. And yet we move.

The medieval theologian Saint Anselm defined God as "that than which a greater cannot be conceived." To have a thought equal to the divine being is thus, strictly speaking, impossible, because by definition Saint Anselm's God exceeds any conceivable thought. In this formulation, reasoning inevitably leads to an encounter with reason's limit and then to the point beyond that limit, which Anselm calls faith.

Carl Sagan, astronomer and a popularizer of science, spent much of his life trying to promote a fuller understanding of the dimensions of the cosmos. This effort, too, can be understood as an attempt to articulate a vision of the infinite. In his book, *Cosmos*, Sagan encourages readers to contemplate vastness: "We have examined the universe in space and seen that we live on a mote of dust circling a humdrum star in the remotest corner of an obscure galaxy. And if we are a speck in the immensity of space, we also occupy an instant in the expanse of ages."

As these examples are meant to show, to say that thinking the infinite is impossible is not to say that it is not worth attempting. Indeed, we would say that striving to think the infinite is an essential part of the mental training for adulthood. We believe this for many reasons, but the most important one is this: the only way to know the true limits of your thinking is to travel to the edge of your own under-standing and peer into the unknown.

Where is that limit?

How will you know when you get there?

Practice Session One, Part One: Contemplating the Infinite

Habits: orienting, persisting, speculating

Activities: thinking, writing

Find a quiet place to think about infinity. Set a timer for thirty minutes. And then close your eyes and think. If your thoughts stray, pull them back.

When the buzzer rings, write an account of your experience. What, specifically, did you do to think about the infinite? Did you have moments of success, or was your experience an uninterrupted series of failed attempts? How did you feel over the course of those thirty minutes?

Practice Session One, Part Two: Contemplating the Infinite

Habits: orienting, persisting, speculating

Activities: thinking, writing

What other thoughts seem unthinkable to you? We've focused on the infinitely big, but what about the infinitely small? What about time? The age of the Earth? The smallest fraction of a second? Are the challenges of thinking about the dimensions of infinity — as an extension of time or space — the same as those that arise when you try to think about infinity in relation to realms of human experience? That is, can you think about infinite love? Infinite forgiveness? Infinite patience? Infinite violence? Infinite cruelty?

Write an account of what you learned from this second run at infinity. If you can't think the thought, is the experience of trying a second time qualitatively different from your initial experience? What happens in your mind as you are doing this kind of thinking? What are the consequences of having tried?

Practice Session Two: Think Fast!

Habits: persisting, questioning, speculating
Activities: thinking, writing

We have a former student who interviewed for a job at a major dot-com years ago. He walked in with his résumé and transcripts documenting his superlative performance as an English major. When he took a seat, the interviewers asked him, "How many golf balls can fit in this room?" Then he was asked to say how many airplanes were in the air at that moment. And finally, he was asked to say how much concrete had been used in constructing the US interstate highway system.

Crazy questions, right? The point of the interview, though, was not to test the candidate's ability to recall information learned in the past; the point was to see how the candidate could imagine ways of solving problems that involve large numbers and several variables.

How would you answer a question of this kind? You're not in an interview situation; you have access to the internet. Choose one of the questions above — about golf balls, airplanes, or highways — and describe how you would go about formulating an answer.

Practice Session Three: The End of the World

Habits: persisting, questioning, speculating
Activities: researching, writing

There are different kinds of unthinkable thoughts. We've focused on the concept of infinity in our essay, but we could have written about the end of human civilization. In this realm, though, one could argue that there's ample evidence that segments of the entertainment industry are devoted to representing scenarios in which humans are threatened with extinction: zombies are everywhere and video games about the apocalypse abound. For those who want to believe they could survive a zombie horde or the apocalypse, there are a range of reality shows devoted to survival competitions.

We'd like you to choose one contemporary example of human civilization under threat of extinction and write an essay in which you consider your example as an effort to think the unthinkable. The example you choose can come from the realm of fiction, politics, or science. Whatever you choose, you will want to consider how the audience is being asked to think about the end of the human species.

10

ORGANIZING

Virtually every available guide to writing emphasizes the value of the outline as a way to keep your writing on track. We value outlining, too, but we don't recommend that you worry about how you're going to structure your writing until you've begun your research and have already put a lot of words on the page. When outlining takes place too early in the writing process, the outline tends to drive the research toward a predetermined conclusion. In this section, we invite you to develop a flexible approach to organizing your writing, one that can accommodate the surprising discoveries and the unexpected insights that are the fruits of curiosity-driven research.

We recommend this flexible approach because it allows revision to become a meaningful activity, one with the potential to transform what your project is and where it is going. This doesn't necessarily mean abandoning the outline, so much as it means assuming that the outline is likely to get revised as the writing project develops. It means thinking of structure as malleable rather than inevitable; it means anticipating the possibility that revision will yield unforeseen insights that require the organizing process to start over again from scratch; it means acknowledging that the failure of the original outline may well be proof that learning has occurred. The creative mind always has a plan, but that plan always includes planning on replanning.

The first two essays in this section present strategies for organizing and revising your writing. In the final piece, we change direction and look at the importance of finding places to work that help you to be a more creative and focused thinker in both the physical and the digital worlds. In both spaces, we want you to exercise control over your environment so you will be able to exert more control over your writing.

On Structure

John McPhee, a longtime staff writer for the *New Yorker*, is best known as a prolific writer of nonfiction. He's written books about subjects as diverse as the geography of the western United States (*Annals of the Former World*); efforts to contain natural destruction caused by lava, water, and mountainside debris flow (*The Control of Nature*); people who work in freight transportation (*Uncommon Carriers*); and the covert actions an American professor took to preserve dissident Soviet art (*The Ransom of Russian Art*). We hope you'll familiarize yourself with McPhee's work because "his mind," as one reviewer put it recently, "is pure curiosity: it aspires to flow into every last corner of the world, especially the places most of us overlook." But we bring McPhee to your attention here not because of his remarkable literary career, but because he may well be the best writing teacher on the planet. His former students, who collectively have published over 430 books, include David Remnick, a Pulitzer Prize winner and editor in chief of the *New Yorker*; Richard Stengel and Jim Kelly, each of whom has served as managing editor of *Time*; Eric Schlosser, author of *Fast Food Nation*; and Jennifer Weiner, best-selling novelist and contributing editor at *Mademoiselle*.

Why are McPhee's students so successful?

One reason is how McPhee trains them to think about structure. In a *New Yorker* essay simply titled "Structure," McPhee offers lessons about writing that were previously reserved for the small number of Princeton University students lucky enough to get a seat in one of his seminars. He begins his essay by describing the crisis of confidence he faced early in his career when he settled in to write a long article about the Pine Barrens of New Jersey, a region of the state that he'd been researching for eight months. "I had assembled enough material to fill a silo," he recalls, "and now I had no idea what to do with it." He spent two weeks lying on his back on a picnic table, stymied by panic, unable to see a way to organize his thoughts. Finally, he realized that an elderly native of the Pine Barrens, Fred Brown, had connections to most of the topics he wanted to discuss, so McPhee decided he could begin the essay by describing his first encounter with Brown and then connect each theme to various forays he and Brown made together. Having solved his structure problem, McPhee got off the picnic table and began to write. "Structure," he says, "has preoccupied me in every project I have undertaken since."

For four decades, McPhee has taught his students that structure should be "strong, sound, and artful" and that it is possible to "build a structure in such a way that it causes people to want to keep turning pages." As far as McPhee is concerned, "factual writing" (his preferred term for nonfiction) can be as absorbing as a good novel if the structure is right. To teach his students how to find the right structure, McPhee compares preparing to write to preparing to cook.

> The approach to structure in factual writing is like returning from a grocery store with materials you intend to cook for dinner. You set them out on the kitchen counter, and what's there is what you deal with, and all you deal with. If something is red and globular, you don't call it a tomato if it's a bell pepper.

In other words, to plan the structure of a piece of writing, you have to gather all the pieces of your research and lay them out so you can see them at a glance. And as you figure out the structure, you can only work with the facts in front of you.

Before he had a computer, McPhee would type all of his notes, study them, and separate the pages into piles about different topics so that all his facts were literally in front of him. Then, he would distill the piles into several dozen index cards. On each card he would write two or three code words that indicated to him a part of the story he wanted to tell. The codes might refer to a location (UNY for upstate New York) or to an event or anecdote ("Upset Rapid"). His office furniture at the time included "a standard sheet of plywood—thirty-two square feet—on two sawhorses." He would scatter his index cards face up on the plywood, anchoring a few pieces and moving the others around until he figured out how to organize the work in ways that were both strong and artful.

Rebecca Skloot, author of *The Immortal Life of Henrietta Lacks*, regularly uses McPhee's essay "Travels in Georgia" to teach structure to her writing students. She shows them that, if you map the narrative of "Travels in Georgia," you can see that it spirals in time: McPhee begins in the middle of the story, goes forward briefly, and then loops backward in time. By the middle of the essay, McPhee has brought his account back to where it started, and from that point on, he moves the narrative steadily forward in time. Skloot explains that McPhee calls this "the lowercase *e* structure," and she promises that once you recognize it, you'll see it everywhere—in movies, novels, and *New Yorker* articles.

Like McPhee, Skloot has a story about grappling for a long time with a writing task. In her case, though, she had to figure out how to organize ten years of research into a readable nonfiction book. She struggled because her research covered multiple time periods and followed three different narratives: the story of Henrietta Lacks, an African American woman who developed cervical cancer and died at the age of thirty-one in 1951; the story of Lacks's cancer cells, which were cultured without Lacks's consent and continue to be used to this day in medical research; and the story of Lacks's family, especially her daughter Deborah, who did not know for much of her life that her mother's cells were alive in medical labs all over the world.

Skloot's breakthrough in organizing her research into a readable book came when she was watching *Hurricane* (1999), a movie about the boxer Hurricane Carter, who was falsely convicted of a triple homicide in 1966. Skloot saw that the film braided three different narratives together: the story of Carter's conviction; the story of Carter's twenty years in prison; and the story of how a Brooklyn teen and three Canadian activists successfully lobbied to have Carter's case reopened. She wrote notes about the film's scenes on colored-coded index cards—one color for each of the three storylines—and laid them out on her bed according to where the scenes occurred in the film. Then she placed the colored index cards for the three strands of her own book on top of the cards for *Hurricane*. She saw that the film jumped more quickly between the threads of the narrative than her book manuscript did, and that the rapidity of those jumps helped sustain the momentum of each line of the intertwined narrative. When Skloot finally realized how to weave together the pieces of her own narrative, she photographed the rows of colored index cards for posterity.

Rebecca Skloot

Rebecca Skloot's notecards for The Immortal Life of Henrietta Lacks *arranged on her bed.*

For Skloot to structure her ten years of research as a braided narrative, she had to throw a lot of material away, just as McPhee did when he was sorting through the silo of material he'd collected for his article on the New Jersey Pine Barrens. But neither Skloot nor McPhee thought that time spent collecting unused research was wasted. McPhee's former student Eric Schlosser recalled how McPhee taught him that deciding what *not* to include is a crucial and often unrecognized step in defining structure. McPhee told him, "Your writing should be like an iceberg." What ends up on the printed page is just the tip of the iceberg, while beneath the surface is all the research, reading, and writing that the writer did to generate the final product. The reader may not be able to see that work, but it's there — the hidden substructure of the writer's visible work.

Practice Session One, Part One: Structure after the Fact

Habits: connecting, organizing, playing

Activities: planning, revising, working with note cards

In school, the operating assumption is often that there is one structure with which students should work: introduction, body, conclusion. Note that this approach *begins* by prescribing an organizing structure, no matter what the subject or project is, whereas the examples from McPhee and Skloot referenced in our essay above show structure emerging *after* the research process is finished or well underway. We've highlighted these examples because we think that the best time for you to make decisions about structure is *after* you've formulated the question you want to answer, the problem or puzzle you want to solve, or the idea you want to explore, and *after* you've taken time to do substantial research. Once you've gathered your materials, then you can experiment with how to organize it for your readers.

For this practice session, we are assuming you are well into a longer writing project. (We highly recommend both the "Be Interesting" assignment discussed in "On the Examined Life" [Chapter 8] and "the question you want to have thought about before graduating from college" assignment discussed in "On Choosing Your Own Adventure" [Chapter 5] as launching points for longer projects.) Get a set of index cards and make a card for every section of your project — those you've already written and those you are planning to write in order to finish the project. Set the cards out on a flat surface and then organize them so that they represent the structure you think best suits your project. When you've mapped out a structure you think works, step back and think carefully about what you see.

If you see a path that moves the reader through the development of your project, ask the following questions to think in finer detail about its organization.

- What shape is the path? Is it straight and simple because you're writing a descriptive essay ("there's this and that and the other thing")? Given the assignment or your ambitions, is this structure sufficient?
- Does the path of your project take interesting turns? Is there a step that takes your thoughts in a new direction? Are there turns that might pivot on a qualifying word or phrase such as *but, however,* or *on the other hand*?
- Does the path turn more than once? Does it double back on itself? Does it have a "lowercase e structure"? Does it braid three or more strands together?
- Is there a fork in the path? Is there a moment where you entertain multiple options?
- Are there gaps? Does the path abruptly change direction or miss a step between a given section and the one that follows?

- Are there pieces or ideas that don't fit anywhere? Does it make sense to include such material as a digression that eventually leads back to the main path? Would a digression contribute to the essay's overall project?
- Is there a dead end, a place where the path hits a brick wall or goes off a cliff? If so, can you use this dead end to rethink how you've addressed your essay's question or problem?

Take a picture of the structure you've created with your index cards, embed that picture in a document, and then write a report about what you've learned from looking at the organization of your project in this way. You may want to number key places in your diagram to help your reader follow your observations.

Practice Session One, Part Two: Playing with Alternatives

Habits: connecting, organizing, playing

Activities: planning, revising, working with note cards

Once you've completed your report on what your index cards have revealed about the structure of your project and saved a photograph of your project, gather all your index cards and shuffle them.

We'd like you to rearrange your cards in two alternate paths, making sure to photograph each one, so that you'll be in a position to compare all three. What happens if you put the end at the beginning? What if you start with a question you know you can't answer? Are there sections that can be cut? Does the structure feel organic to the material or imposed from elsewhere? What do the new plans enable you to see about the original plan?

When you've tried out at least two alternate organizational schemes, embed the images of your reorganized cards and write up a report that compares the virtues of each organizational possibility. Then explain how you made up your mind about which one to follow.

Practice Session Two, Part One: Two Paths through an Essay

Habits: organizing, orienting, paying attention

Activities: mapping, note taking, reading

Choose one of the five pieces included in the Readings section at the end of *Habits*. To complete this session, you'll need to read the piece at least twice. The first time through you will be working to follow the writer's path. Focus on understanding the argument, key ideas, and use of sources. Also take notes in the margins when you feel lost or confused. When you're done, create a map of the reading, from beginning to end. Refer to the guidelines for mapping from Practice Session One, Part One above.

Next, reread the text you've chosen, paying close attention to the challenges you face as a reader. Focus on the passages that caused you difficulty the first time through. Then, we want you to draw a second map. This one, though, should map places where you struggled as a reader. Are there places where the way the essay is organized contributed to or caused your confusion? Does your second map reveal elements in the essay's organization that you only recognized after a second reading or a third reading?

Practice Session Two, Part Two: Habits of Organization

Habits: organizing, orienting, paying attention

Activities: note taking, reading, writing

Go through all the papers you've written recently and select at least three of them to serve as the foundation for this practice session. Then make a map or sketch of how each paper is organized. Once you're done, step back and think about the relationship between the maps or sketches you just generated for this exercise and the ones you generated for Part One of Practice Session Two. Your own essays will probably be shorter than the reading you worked with in Part One, but what other differences are there between the way your own writing is organized and how the reading you chose for Part One is organized? Write an essay that uses the maps of your own writing and the maps you made in Part One as material for speculating about the relationship between the organizational decisions a writer makes and the thoughts the writer has.

On Revising

Every practice session in *Habits of the Creative Mind* is implicitly connected to revision. We've repeatedly encouraged you to look and look again. (Another name for the act of reseeing is "revision.") We showed you how being curious requires that you peer around corners, disappear down rabbit holes, and explore the unknown in order to replace old assumptions or confusions with new knowledge and understanding. We showed you that creative habits of mind include being able to reflect on (that is, to resee) how you express yourself and even how you think. In a multitude of ways, reseeing and revising are fundamental practices for writers.

So why include a separate essay on revision? Two reasons, really. First, people who take writing seriously know that writing *is* revising. Indeed, the claim that "there is no such thing as good writing, only good rewriting" is so widely acknowledged by writers that it has been variously attributed to Robert Graves, Louis Brandeis, Isaac Bashevis Singer, William Zinsser, and Roald Dahl. Second, we know that revision is not a single stage in the writing process but a range of practices that occur *throughout* the writing process. This distinction is worth driving home, we've found, because many students mistake copyediting (fixing grammatical errors, unclear sentences, and typos prior to submitting the final draft) for revision. We're interested in revision that generates new thoughts.

As writers, we know that rethinking, reseeing, and rewriting can happen at any time during the writing process. In fact, before we drafted the opening paragraphs of *this* essay, we composed two different preliminary outlines and two different introductions. When we determined that neither of those versions worked, we scrapped them and started over. This example isn't an anomaly; writers regularly spiral back to rethink what they've done, entirely abandoning earlier work and beginning all over again. Moments of revision can occur as soon as you've written your first word; they can occur just when you think you're writing your final sentence; and they can occur anywhere between those two points.

If revision isn't correcting grammatical mistakes and isn't a single step in a linear process, then what is it? We'd like to help you resee revision by describing a variety of ways to return to the writing you've already completed with the goal of improving it. You won't use all of these practices every time you rewrite, but you're quite likely to use more than one as you rework what you've written.

RESTRUCTURING

Often first drafts make sense to the writer, but the logic behind what has been written isn't yet clear enough for a reader to follow. This can be caused by gaps in the research or argument; lack of attention to what readers need to know and when they need to know it; too much information or too many ideas about one topic and not enough about another; or the lack of good transitions. These problems can be addressed through revision that focuses on structure.

To help our students make this important change in perspective, we have them produce a "post-draft outline," which gives them a way to distinguish between what they think they wrote and what they actually put down on paper.

The process for making a post-draft outline is straightforward: sequentially number every paragraph in your draft, and then, on a separate piece of paper, write a one-sentence statement about the main idea or point in each paragraph. When you're done, you'll be able to see the structure of your draft as a whole, which you can then use in a variety of ways to help assess the quality of the experience you've created for your reader.

Your outline gives you a snapshot of the path your draft has taken. To evaluate whether your argument is strong, consider the following questions:

- Is the path a straight line? Does it proceed by a series of *and* connections (that is, there's this and this and this)?
- Does the path turn? Is there a paragraph that qualifies what has gone before or takes the conversation in a new direction? Are there sentences or paragraphs that pivot — or could pivot — on a qualifying word or phrase such as *but*, *however*, or *although*?
- Does the path turn more than once? Does it double back on itself?

- Is there a fork in the path? Is there a moment when more than one option is entertained?

- Is there a paragraph that pivots on words or phrases such as *or, perhaps,* or *what if* that introduce more than one possible outcome or position?

- Are there gaps? Does the path abruptly change direction or miss a step between paragraphs?

- Are there digressions, places where there's a loop off the path that eventually returns to the main path? If the answer is yes, does each digression contribute to the essay's overall project? If the answer is no, does it make more sense to cut the digression or to reorganize the paper to help make the digression's significance clear?

- Is there a dead end, a place where the path hits a brick wall or goes off a cliff, never to return? Is this according to plan? If not, your post-draft outline has helped you to see a place where you've got important work to do.

After you have mapped and analyzed the path you took in your draft, you can begin to sketch plans for a structural revision. It is not at all unusual for this work to involve moving whole sets of paragraphs, deleting sections, and doing new research. Structural revision also requires spending time thinking about what you've left out of your draft. Are there places in the draft where you ignored ideas or information that would have complicated the journey? Or places where you went where you were expected to go instead of where your thinking was pointing you? What can you do now to introduce ideas and information that would make your essay more interesting?

By using the post-draft outline in this way, you'll be serving as your own editor: you'll assess both what your draft is and what it might become through a structural reorganization.

The history of F. Scott Fitzgerald's *The Great Gatsby* provides an example of what a difference structural revisions can make. Fitzgerald sent the manuscript of his novel to his editor, Maxwell Perkins, who immediately saw that it was brilliant but flawed. First of all, the character of Gatsby was too physically vague. "The reader's eyes can never quite focus upon him, his outlines are dim," he wrote to Fitzgerald. "Now everything about Gatsby is more or less a mystery . . . , and this may be somewhat of an artistic intention, but I think it is mistaken." Fitzgerald's reply indicates that defining Gatsby's character was something he hadn't been able to accomplish in the first draft: "*I myself didn't know what Gatsby looked like or was engaged in* & you felt it." Perkins's second complaint about Fitzgerald's presentation of Gatsby was that the character's whole history—his apprenticeship on Dan Cody's yacht, his time in the army, his romance with Daisy, and his past as an "Oxford man"—all tumbled out in one long monologue toward the end of the novel.

What to do? Perkins suggested that Fitzgerald reorganize the *whole* novel: "you can't avoid the biography altogether. I thought you might find ways to let the truth of some of his claims like 'Oxford' and his army career come out bit by bit in the course of actual narrative." Fitzgerald followed this advice, weaving bits of Gatsby's past more gracefully into earlier chapters. The result? *The Great Gatsby*, first published in 1925, has now sold over twenty-five million copies and routinely appears in lists of great American novels.

Notice that Perkins's advice about revising *Gatsby* focused on creating a better experience for the reader. Notice, too, that Fitzgerald couldn't see what *The Great Gatsby* needed until he got the feedback that made it possible for him to view the novel through the eyes of another.

RETHINKING

As essayists and academic writers, when we contemplate a new project, we spend a lot of time reading, exploring, researching, learning, and thinking before we begin a formal draft. And yet, after composing the first pages or even the entire first draft, we may still find our work unsatisfactory because, in the process of writing about our chosen topic, we have begun to question our original position. Rethinking motivates us to revise globally—to rework our ideas rather than tinker away at surface corrections.

What's the difference between rethinking and tinkering? It's difficult to point to a published example of the former because rethinking typically occurs before publication and thus remains hidden from readers. As it happens, though, we do have access to Thomas Jefferson's "original Rough draught" of the Declaration of Independence, which includes the following statement: "We hold these truths to be sacred & undeniable; that all men are created equal & independent, that from that equal creation they derive rights inherent & inalienable, among which are the preservation of life, & liberty, & the pursuit of happiness."

You'll notice that this sentence differs from the version you've encountered in your American history courses. Jefferson wrote of "sacred and undeniable" truths, but the Declaration that was signed by representatives of the thirteen colonies declares these truths to be "self-evident." There is no conclusive evidence to establish who introduced this particular change: some argue that it was Ben Franklin, others that it was Jefferson. For our purposes here, though, who authored the change is less important than the significance of the change. The writers are composing a document that argues for the creation of a new nation. Every single word matters and the final product has to be something that all the representatives can sign off on, signaling their agreement.

So, why "self-evident" truths instead of "sacred and undeniable" truths? This is not a matter of one version "sounding better" than the other; the claim being made about the truths is changed by the revision. A sacred truth is, by definition, a truth that is affiliated with a divine being; a self-evident truth is available to everyone and its source is reason alone. The framers of the Declaration were laying the groundwork for rejecting the very idea of a king endowed with divine rights and they were doing so by listing their grievances against the king. The first "self-evident" truth that "all men are created equal" is not, in fact, self-evident to Royalists who believe in the divine right of kings. In declaring this truth to be self-evident, the signatories of the Declaration of Independence are doing away with the very idea of a superior breed or caste of humans; they are, in effect, rejecting the very idea of government by royalty. Once they've signed off on this statement, it's fair to say that war with England is inevitable. The war, however, can't be construed as a religious war, where believers in one set of "sacred and undeniable" truths battle believers in another set of "sacred and undeniable truths." It's a war in which one side is fighting for truths that they deem to be obvious to any reasonable person, regardless of religious faith, truths they would have described as universal. To the men of reason who composed the Declaration, the British are refusing to acknowledge what is self-evident. They are, in sum, being unreasonable.

When you're writing for school, you have the opportunity to complicate or alter what you were thinking before you started writing. This can be triggered by attending closely to your word choice, as above; and it can also be triggered by clearly expressing truths that seem self-evident to you but nevertheless need to be explained to others, also as above. This is the lesson we'd like you to take from this example: in order to begin the process of rethinking what you've written, you need to be open to questioning everything, even your own certainties.

LETTING GO

Cutting sentences and paragraphs, or cutting everything and starting over from scratch: Has there ever been a writer who enjoys this part of the writing process? No. But the difference between beginning writers and experienced writers is that experienced writers are familiar with the blank screen; they know that the blinking cursor can be set in motion once again and that there are always more words out there somewhere. Beginning writers, without much practice starting over, tend to fear the blank screen and to see deleted work as wasted time rather than as an unavoidable part of letting the mind work on a problem.

To encourage our students to see letting go as a habit of creative minds, we tell a story about going to hear Nobel Prize–winning writer Toni Morrison read from a work in progress. Morrison approached the lectern, paused, and then told the audience that the year before she'd completed well over a hundred pages of the novel's manuscript, but that she stood before us that night to read from the forty or so pages she had left. What had happened? Revision happened. Morrison had set out in one direction and then had to spend a year peeling off pages and pages of what she'd written until she found work that met her standards.

The Morrison anecdote can be read as an extension of the quote we opened this essay with: "there is no such thing as good writing, only good rewriting," and all good rewriting involves letting go. We hear this idea repeated in Colette's definition of an author: "Put down everything that comes into your head and then you're a writer. But an author is one who can judge his own stuff's worth, without pity, and destroy most of it." Novelist Anne Lamott makes this point about letting go in perhaps its bluntest form in her popular book *Bird by Bird*, where she asserts that all good writers write "shitty first drafts," drafts that they know will be thrown away. "This," she says, "is how they end up with good second drafts and terrific third drafts."

While Lamott's specific recommendations may not apply to all writing or to all writers, we believe there's real value in her advice to view draft after draft as practice, as work that may never see the light of day but that is valuable nonetheless. If you give yourself sufficient time to use writing to help yourself think, knowing that you are going to get rid of most of it before anyone else sees it, then maybe, as Lamott writes, you'll find "something in the very last line of the very last paragraph on page six that you just love, that is so beautiful or wild that you now know what you're supposed to be writing about, more or less, or in what direction you might go—but there was no way to get to this without first getting through the first five and a half pages."

TAKING A BREAK

The best way to see your writing with fresh eyes is to set aside your draft—for a day if that's all you have, or for longer if possible. When you pick it up again, you'll be able to see more clearly what's working and what's not. The point is to give yourself time to reenergize, so that you don't resort to tinkering on the edges of your writing when you really need to be rethinking and restructuring your first draft.

Prolific writer Neil Gaiman explains that taking a break also allows you to return to your work as a reader, instead of as its writer. Once a draft is done, he advises, "put it away until you can read it with new eyes. . . . Put it in a drawer and write other things. When you're ready, pick it up and read it as if you've never read it before. If there are things you aren't satisfied with as a reader, go in and fix them as a writer: that's revision." By "fix them as a writer," he means rethinking, restructuring, letting go of what's not working, getting feedback, writing again, polishing—doing whatever it takes to move the writing forward.

Practice Session One: Getting Feedback

Habits: organizing, reflecting, working deliberately

Activities: getting feedback, revising, writing

Most writers don't publish until after they've gotten feedback from friends, colleagues, and editors. When you're looking for feedback that will help you revise, a teacher we admire, Kerry Walk, recommends writing a cover letter that you attach to your draft. The cover letter should identify:

- the main question or problem your writing seeks to address;
- the idea or point you feel you've made most successfully;
- the idea or point you feel you need help with;
- the number one concern about your paper that you'd like your reader to identify;
- any questions you have about how or where to start your revision.

The advantage of a cover letter of this kind is that it gives your reader a clear sense of how you see your draft and where you think it needs work. Your reader need not agree with your assessment, but the letter gives your reader a way to gauge his or her response to what you've written and to adjust that response accordingly.

For this Practice Session, we expect that you are in the process of revising a draft. Compose a cover letter to accompany your draft and share the letter with a reader you trust. Ask the reader to respond to your cover letter in writing or in person.

After you've received your reader's feedback, figure out what kind of revision the feedback suggests is most necessary: Should you try rethinking, restructuring, letting go, or a combination of strategies? Then revise.

Practice Session Two: Addition through Subtraction

Habits: organizing, persisting, working deliberately
Activities: editing, evaluating, revising

Take a final draft you wrote recently and see if you can cut it by at least 25 percent without losing the main argument or ideas. After you've cut your original piece by a quarter, compare the original version to the shorter, revised one. What's better about the more concise version? What's better about the longer one?

Then try cutting the shortened version by 25 percent again. What happens to your argument or ideas this time?

Practice Session Three: Revising the Declaration of Independence

Habits: connecting, organizing, working deliberately
Activities: outlining, reading, writing

In our essay above, we discussed the difference between an early draft of the Declaration of Independence and the final draft that was signed by the representatives of the thirteen colonies. We'd like you to produce a post-draft outline for the final draft of the Declaration. (We've included the Declaration in the Readings section at the end of this book.) Then write a paper that discusses the rationale for the way it is organized.

You will find that it is easier to write a one-sentence gloss for some of the paragraphs than it is for others. The second paragraph, in particular, will really challenge you. In your paper, make sure to comment on the challenges involved in determining how the Declaration is organized. Is the rationale for its structure "self-evident"?

On Getting Your Act Together

I. IN PHYSICAL SPACE

Do you have a ritual for getting yourself into the right frame of mind for writing? Do you organize your day so it's clear when you're going to be writing? Do you have a place you can go where you can improve the chances of good ideas coming to you? For those cultivating habits of the creative mind, the answer to each of these questions is yes. We love learning about the rituals of experienced writers. For example, we have a friend who lights a candle at an appointed moment to signal to himself that it's time to focus, then writes for the time he's allotted himself, and blows the candle out when he's done.

How should you go about discovering or creating your own best conditions for writing? This is a question that Virginia Woolf gave a lot of thought in the early twentieth century. In fact she wrote a book about it, *A Room of One's Own* (1929), in which she famously declared, "A woman must have money and a room of her own if she is to write fiction." Today the requirements for writing are somewhat different. If Woolf were to publish *A Room of One's Own* today, she might declare that "a woman must have money and a laptop of her own, as well as broadband access, if she is to write fiction."

The web enables the person sitting at the keyboard to connect with readers around the world, to access virtual archives richer than any actual archive past writers had access to, and to use research tools that make it possible to chase an idea wherever it might lead. But as transformative as internet access is, we would argue that it hasn't eliminated the need that writers of any gender have for solitary time and quiet spaces to do the work of writing and revising. Indeed, because collaborating, getting feedback, and socializing can now all be done virtually, carving out a place of our own where we can work without intrusion or distraction is significantly harder than it was in Woolf's time. And even if we find a private place to work, there's always another text message, Instagram post, or breaking news story to pull us away from our writing and toss us into the digital sea.

The Granger Collection, NY

Virginia Woolf

Nearly one hundred years ago, Woolf's writing room contained a desk, a chair, books, and a lamp, but not, of course, a computer, a television, or speakers. What about a phone? During Woolf's most prolific writing years, when she lived at 52 Tavistock Square in London, she *did* have a telephone in the house — the number printed on her stationery is "Museum 2621" — but we think it's unlikely the phone was in her writing room. After all, it's not a "room of one's own" if anyone can, on a whim, dial past the closed door and interrupt the writer at her desk.

What does your typical workspace look like? How many distractions are within sight, earshot, or reach when you write?

Our students often insist that their digital devices don't distract them from getting their writing done; many also declare that they work best when they are multitasking. However, in study after study neuroscientists consistently find that people who make such claims don't really know their own minds. The habits of multitasking are so ingrained that we don't recognize when we are distracted; it has become a normal state of being. Or to put this another way, we are so accustomed to being distracted that we no longer know what it means to be focused, to dwell in our thoughts, to think deeply about matters that don't lend themselves to the five-paragraph theme or a snarky tweet.

Writing about ideas has always been a complex task, but those who wish to write well now face the additional challenge of developing the self-discipline to manage the endless flow of digital information and entertainment that competes for our attention. Making a room of one's own for writing today involves not only shutting the door or finding a quiet corner, but also blocking one's access to the internet, at least for a time, to create the conditions for attention and focus. If you don't figure out how to do this for yourself, you will never produce writing of lasting value.

. . . . .

We want to stress that when Woolf advised her readers that they should have a room of their own for writing, she didn't mean that they should retreat from the world. Woolf, in fact, had a very full social life. When she wrote *A Room of One's Own*, she had a home in Bloomsbury, where she lived among relatives and friends — painters, novelists, philosophers, and critics — now known as the Bloomsbury Group. The name "Bloomsbury" might suggest a remote village in the English countryside among green meadows and blossoming gardens, but Bloomsbury is actually a district in central London. Woolf's writing room was in the midst of a lively city.

As part of her writing ritual, Woolf would wander for hours through the London streets, observing and storing away details of daily life. In her essay "Street Haunting: A London Adventure," Woolf describes the people, sights, and scenes she encountered on a journey to purchase the essential tool of her craft, a pencil. Reflecting on all she'd seen and done on her way to the stationer's shop, Woolf closes her essay thus:

> Walking home through the desolation one could tell oneself the story of the dwarf, of the blind men, of the party in the Mayfair mansion, of the quarrel in the stationer's shop. Into each of these lives one could penetrate a little way, far enough to give oneself the illusion that one is not tethered to a single mind but can put on briefly for a few minutes

the bodies and minds of others. One could become a washerwoman, a publican, a street singer. And what greater delight and wonder can there be than to leave the straight lines of personality and deviate into those footpaths that lead beneath brambles and thick tree trunks into the heart of the forest where live those wild beasts, our fellow men?

As this passage makes clear, when Woolf ventured out of the room of her own, she took with her a way of seeing and thinking about the world that she had cultivated and nurtured in private. Her time away from the hustle and bustle of the city didn't deaden her to the pleasures of the company of friends or of the anonymous encounters that accompany movement through a day of errands; indeed, it sharpened her experience of the everyday.

· · · · ·

What do our reflections on public encounters, private rooms, and digital distractions mean for you as a writer?

An essential part of a writer's work is to choose good places to work. Writers need places where they can compose without intrusions, but they also need engagement with the world and with others. They need a computer and internet access, but they also need to develop the discipline to ward off the distractions that come with being online. So when you write, withdraw when you need to; at other times, dive into the fray. Keep in mind, too, that your life as a writer needs to have more dimensions than your screen. The internet can connect you to information and ideas that you know how to search for, but it can also disconnect you from the less predictable and less containable world around you. To write, you need not only a room of your own, but a community of your own—one that jostles, disrupts, adds to, and opens new vistas for your thinking.

II. IN DIGITAL SPACE

The word *curate* has an interesting etymological history. According to the *Oxford English Dictionary*, *curate* entered the English language in the mid-fourteenth century as a noun signifying someone "entrusted with the cure of souls: a spiritual pastor." This nominal form of the word is linked to earlier adjectival forms in medieval Latin (*curatus*) and Italian (*curato*) and to the French noun *curé*, all of which denoted "having a cure or charge."

Some six hundred years later, *curate* made its first appearance as a verb in an English dictionary. And notice what happens to the meaning of the word when it moves from being used as a noun or an adjective to being used as a transitive verb: "to act as curator of (a museum, exhibits, etc.); to look after and preserve." So, for a very long time, a curate was a religious occupation; in the twentieth century, it became a secular activity.

Self-curation does not yet appear in the *Oxford English Dictionary* or *Merriam-Webster* or the *Cambridge Dictionary*. Nevertheless, if you search the web for the term (with the hyphen), you'll find that this as-yet-unofficial word is currently in circulation and that it is used most frequently to refer to the conscious management of one's digital profile. Fancifully, we might define *self-curation* thus: "to act as curator of one's own online life; to look after and preserve an archive of one's digital existence."

In the age of paper, self-curation was a largely private affair. One kept a journal and saved letters, perhaps, or collected shells or stamps or firearms or first editions or autographs or whatever. Now that we live in the age of the screen, self-curation is a largely public affair: there is the self or the selves that an individual maintains via social media; the blogging self; the photo- or video-posting self; the reviewing self. These are selves over which a person has some measure of control. And then there is the self as represented by others—via social media, via the news, via public documents—over which a person has little or no control.

What do you know about yourself as currently represented on the web? Is that the version of yourself you would voluntarily give others access to? There's a practical reason for making this distinction: once anything associated with your name, your face, or your work appears on the web, it is potentially available to others forever. Were you identified doing a keg stand on a friend's Facebook page? Did you post a comment on a local news site railing against something you now support? How have you conducted yourself in digital space, where no one has a "room of one's own" and everything you've done online—the sites you've visited, the terms you've searched, the videos you've watched—can, potentially, be converted into publicly available information?

While there are good practical reasons to self-curate, we're more interested in the creative benefits that come with self-curation. If you take control of your online presence, you have the opportunity to represent yourself as a multifaceted individual with a range of interests. By self-curating as a writer, you make it that much easier for potential readers to find your work. And by making your work public, you create the opportunity to have the kind of readers all writers want—those who choose to read your work.

....

Practice Session One, Part One: A Physical Place of Your Own

....

Habits: exploring, organizing, persisting
Activities: mapmaking, researching

Explore your town or campus, looking for places where you could write. Look at libraries, cafés, and places that are quiet. Then, look for places that are bustling with activity and creativity, such as popular gathering or performance spaces. Make a map of places for each of the following elements of a writer's work: encountering the creative work of others; meeting and talking with interesting people; doing research; reading; composing; revising; and editing. Is there one place that accommodates all of these activities?

....

Practice Session One, Part Two: A Quiet Place of Your Own

....

Habits: exploring, organizing, persisting
Activities: experimenting, researching, writing

Find or create a quiet space where you can reliably work for long stretches of uninterrupted time. Some people can find a place for solitude within their home; others choose to write in a library or a café where they are surrounded by other people who are also working intently. Ideally, this should be a place where you can write every day.

Spend a week writing in a few promising places. Practice composing where there are minimal auditory distractions. If you use earbuds, select a "white noise" app rather than a personal playlist. Experiment with creating the conditions that allow you to spend time alone with your own thoughts. Consider what you can do to make your chosen place even more conducive to composing: find a seat cushion, buy earplugs, move your desk nearer to a window. Also practice writing at different times of the day. Try strategies for extending your focused researching and writing time, perhaps by setting timers so that you spend at least thirty minutes writing before you take a five-minute break to stretch, walk, or check text messages. See if you can gradually extend the time between breaks.

After a week, write a reflective essay about what you've learned about the places and practices that best suit your creative work.

....

Practice Session Two, Part One: The Uncurated Self
....

Habits: beginning, exploring, organizing

Activities: researching, writing

What happens when you do a Google search of your name? Do you get different results if you use Dogpile? Twitter? Facebook? Pinterest? Instagram? Your high school's home page? Do a thorough search and document all the information about you that is publicly available on the web. Then create a file of all that you find. Your final dossier should include images where appropriate.

Spend at least twenty minutes writing about the results of your research: What does the uncurated version of yourself, as represented on the web, look like?

Practice Session Two, Part Two: The Curated Self

Habits: connecting, organizing, speculating
Activities: sketching, web designing, writing

What would you like people who search for you online to find? What would best represent you as a thinker? A writer? A creative person? An artist? If you were to design a self-curated website, what would it include?

Spend at least forty-five minutes sketching by hand or using graphics tools on your word processing platform to show what such a site would look like. Another option is to actually create a self-curated website. Regardless of which option you choose, you'll need to decide what tabs you would like to appear in your home page's navigation bar. Are you a writer who works in more than one genre? Have you made videos? Taken striking photographs? Started a graphic novel? Are you involved in other projects or activities that you could represent on your website?

Design a website that represents you as someone whose creativity expresses itself in production rather than consumption; one method is to restrict your lists of favorite books, musicians, and artists to the "About" tab on your site.

Practice Session Three, Part One: The Uncurated Creative Mind

Habits: exploring, organizing, paying attention
Activities: researching, writing

What happens when you do a Google search of a contemporary visual artist or writer you admire? Do you get different results if you use Dogpile? Twitter? Facebook? Pinterest? Instagram? Spend at least thirty minutes doing a thorough search and document all the information about the artist or writer you've chosen that is publicly available on the web. (Don't choose a celebrity, an athlete, or a politician; these figures always bring gossip, scandals, and excitable fans in their wake.) Then spend an additional twenty minutes writing about the results of your search. What impression is created by the uncurated version of the writer's or artist's self?

Practice Session Three, Part Two: The Curated Creative Mind

Habits: connecting, exploring, organizing

Activities: researching, writing

Seek out the official website or websites for the contemporary visual artist or writer you selected to research. Then take at least forty-five minutes to write an essay on the difference between the official, curated self and the version of that self that emerged during your open-ended search. Drawing on your research, discuss what the artist or writer you've chosen to study might do on his or her self-curated site to engage with whatever additional unauthorized material you've discovered circulating outside the site.

Practice Session Four, Part One: Social Media and Headline News

Habits: organizing, paying attention, questioning

Activities: charting, note taking, researching

It is now common journalistic practice to head straight to the web in the immediate aftermath of a tragedy to see what social media can tell us about the possible victims or the possible perpetrators in the unfolding event. This practice has tended to have catastrophic results, as the pressure to be first on the scene with news has created a fertile ground for jumping to unfounded conclusions. This happened, for instance, after the tragedy at Sandy Hook Elementary School and after the Boston Marathon bombing. In both cases, an innocent person was linked to the atrocity and was then quickly "convicted" online on the basis of material that was later revealed to be erroneous.

Choose a recent event that has been in the headlines and spend at least forty-five minutes investigating what role social media has played in both the coverage and the interpretation of the event. Why do some responses to the event get picked up, shared, and repeated, while others are ignored? Take extensive notes, tracking key moments in the coverage of the chosen event. When you're done with your research, create a timeline that represents what you've learned about the role social media played in shaping popular understandings of the event.

········

Practice Session Four, Part Two: Curating Headline News

········

Habits: organizing, reflecting, working deliberately

Activities: analyzing, selecting, web designing, writing

If you were to curate a website dedicated to the event you selected, what would you include? Write an essay about the relationship of social media and the event you've chosen to research. Your piece should include your design for a website that would provide a richer understanding both of the event and of its coverage.

11

SPECULATING

In college classes, *writing* and *arguing* are often treated as synonyms. To be assigned a paper is to be assigned the task of presenting an evidence-based argument. But where do arguments come from? Are they first formulated in the writer's brain and then moved from there to the screen, like a box on a conveyor belt? Or do arguments come into being through the act of writing? As writers and teachers, we know the best arguments don't emerge all at once; they develop over time — while one reads, thinks, reflects, drafts, revises, reconsiders, and even restarts. And we know, as well, that silencing the initial urge to argue opens up the possibility for curiosity-driven writing.

To encourage you to let your point of view develop over time, we've chosen to use the word *speculating* instead of *arguing* to describe the kind of thinking we want you to do in your essays. Why speculate? Because the word evokes thinking that is open and imaginative. In this section we invite you to speculate in a variety of ways. First, we consider writing as an intellectual journey. Then we examine alternatives to the kind of conventional arguments and predictable debates you may have learned to write in school. We show how thoughtful writers seek new perspectives and make imaginative leaps. Finally, we consider complexity as an achievement in academic writing.

On Argument as Journey

What do you think teachers mean when they ask you to write an argument? Many of our students begin with the premise that writing an argument is like participating in a debate: they pick a side (their thesis); they gather evidence to support the side they've chosen (their proof); and they write to show that they are right and the other side is wrong (their conclusion). Winning the debate and getting a good grade are the goals—not thoughtfulness, not discovery, not learning.

There are contexts within which producing writing that adheres to this premise is entirely appropriate: a legal brief, for example, or a letter of complaint. And if you listen to pundits on cable news, follow congressional debates, or read the comment sections of online news sources, you'll see that such oppositional argumentation has become the norm in contemporary culture. We think this is unfortunate, but we recognize that, in these venues, pushing ideas to their extremes, stirring up the emotions of one's allies and enemies, and scoring points with a pithy phrase or sound bite is the goal, not the reasoned exchange of ideas.

We know that practicing argument as debate produces writing that isn't persuasive or compelling or interesting to read, so in our classes we ask our students to think of essay writing as a speculative journey. What's the difference? When you write speculatively, you begin not with a predetermined destination (your thesis), but with the goal of answering a question or solving a problem; you consider different routes to get to this goal; you do research and rethink your plan; you learn more and more; you write, make mistakes, and head off in new and unanticipated directions; you make discoveries. When you write speculative drafts, you are more likely to wander at the outset than to travel in a straight line from your introduction to your conclusion. As you revise, you will come to see a clearer purpose and path, but at the same time you will remain open to exploring detours. Along the way, as you figure out how you want to answer your central question or solve your problem, your destination will appear on the horizon. When the writing is finally done, the essay will take your readers on a journey to new ideas and this journey will be your argument.

We'd like to walk you through an extended example of argument as journey by looking at Elizabeth Kolbert's *Field Notes from a Catastrophe*, a book about global climate change. Kolbert faced an enormous challenge when she took on this topic. When she published her book in 2006, the consensus in the scientific community was clear: global warming was real and it was caused by human activity — especially our reliance on burning carbon-based fuels such as coal, oil, wood, and natural gas for energy. But outside the scientific community, politicians, business leaders, and science skeptics refused to accept that global warming was an empirically verifiable threat to the future of life on the planet. Given that the National Academy of Sciences has issued increasingly dire warnings about impending environmental disaster since 1979, what could Kolbert — or any writer, for that matter — possibly say to get the doubters and the indifferent to take the science seriously? Was there anything new she could contribute?

One of Kolbert's innovations was figuring out how to tell the story of climate change in a way that would draw readers in. She surmised that many people were reluctant to acknowledge and act on evidence of impending disaster because some of the most obvious signs were in places far away from their everyday lives. In preparation for writing *Field Notes*, Kolbert set out on a literal journey — visiting places such as Alaska, Iceland, Greenland, and Costa Rica — where she witnessed transformations in the global environment on a scale most readers would not be able to imagine. How could she get her readers to appreciate what these transformations predicted about the near future?

To address this challenge, Kolbert chose to open her book with a description of the Alaskan village of Shishmaref, which is located on an island off the coast of the Seward Peninsula, where native villagers used to be able to drive snowmobiles across twenty miles of ice to hunt seals. When Kolbert visited the village, though, the ice around the island had become so soft that it could no longer support the weight of the snowmobiles. And the village, once twenty miles from the sea, had become so vulnerable to storm surges that the residents had decided to give up their way of life and relocate. Farther inland, near Fairbanks, Kolbert saw the effects of global warming in melting permafrost. Areas of ground that had been frozen since the beginning of the last glacial cycle were threatened by thaw. And where the permafrost had been disturbed by the construction of buildings or roads, the land was especially vulnerable to warming; in some neighborhoods, building foundations were degrading and houses were collapsing. The story of the remote island of Shishmaref whose residents could no longer hunt with snowmobiles may not raise concerns for city dwellers, but the image of more conventional homes, like those in Fairbanks, crumbling as the ground softens, makes clear that there's no place to go where one can escape the effects of global warming. Thus begins the reader's journey.

Having gotten her readers to attend to disruptions in the lives of people in distant lands, Kolbert faces her next challenge: how can she hold their attention once she's working with scientific information that points to the calamities that lie ahead if humans don't dramatically reduce their reliance on fossil fuels? She does this by providing her readers not with a scientific treatise or an environmentalist's polemic, but with a travelogue that provides a series of accessible lessons about climate science. Chapter by chapter, her book teaches readers how to comprehend the significance of what researchers have discovered. For example, Kolbert writes about traveling to a research station on the Greenland ice sheet where scientists study ice cores drilled from the glacier. "A hundred and thirty-eight feet down," Kolbert writes, "there is snow that fell during the time of the American Civil War; 2,500 feet down, snow from the time of the Peloponnesian Wars; and, 5,350 feet down, snow from the days when the cave painters of Lascaux were slaughtering bison. At the very bottom, 10,000 feet down, there is snow that fell on central Greenland before the start of the last ice age, more than a hundred thousand years ago."

After having told readers about this amazing glacier, Kolbert shifts direction to discuss other scientific work taking place in Greenland. Researchers there are observing and measuring the gradual contraction of this massive glacier, which contains 8 percent of the world's fresh water supply. In 2006, it was shrinking by twelve cubic miles each year. You may be wondering why all these measurements are important. Why do these details — twelve cubic miles per year; 8 percent of the world's water—matter? Kolbert brings her point home when she explains that more than history will be lost if the Greenland ice sheet melts. The ice sheet, she reports, contains enough water to raise sea levels around the world by twenty-three feet! *That* will cause a global crisis.

Kolbert's determination to demonstrate that facts about climate change are, in fact, *facts* is only the beginning of the reader's journey toward understanding climate change. Her account of her physical travels sets the stage for preparing readers to think unthinkable thoughts about global catastrophe. She supplies them with irrefutable evidence that corporations and lobbyists spent decades influencing politics and discrediting scientific studies, and that those efforts discouraged governments from preparing for a warming planet with rising seawaters.

Those of you who write mostly for school may be struck by Kolbert's choice to present her strongest and most controversial claims in the final chapters of her book. Unlike an academic argument that begins with a thesis, Kolbert builds steadily toward her big ideas as the book progresses. She saves her biggest idea for the final chapter, where she argues that climate change is so far along, and the human behaviors that caused it are so deeply entrenched, that we may not be able to slow its destruction. Her next point is even more shocking: she asserts that human-caused climate change has launched the planet into a new geological era. We used to think that we were living in the Holocene epoch, which began at the end of the Pleistocene about 11,700 years ago. But we're not, she says. We are in the dawn of the "Anthropocene," a new epoch "defined by one creature—man—who [has] become so dominant that he [is] capable of altering the planet on a geological scale." Kolbert leaves one essential question unanswered: whether humans, who are destroying the only habitable planet we have, might be smart, creative, and lucky enough to come up with ways to ameliorate the consequences of this disaster.

. . . . .

Having read about Kolbert's intellectual and physical travels, you may be thinking that this approach to "argument as journey" is all well and good for her, but it's not going to fly in your environmental science class where the professor expects a "provable" thesis stated in the opening paragraph, et cetera. We'd say, however, that the way you get to having a thesis worth proving is by allowing the drafting process to include an intellectual journey in which you complicate your understanding of the question you've chosen to address. We can't count the number of times we've read a student's draft and discovered the best writing and the best ideas in the final paragraph. In traditional academic classes, our advice to the student is to bring the good ideas forward and to rewrite the rest of the essay to explain and develop those ideas. Students can be dismayed by this advice because they don't yet recognize that the time it took to write the draft was not wasted. The process of drafting is for figuring out what question you want to ask and how you want to answer it. The goal of revision, in this case, is to align your ideas with the expectations of academic writing. The insight achieved in the draft becomes the thesis of the final essay.

Practice Session One: Is There Hope for the Future?

Habits: connecting, exploring, speculating

Activities: analyzing, note taking, researching, writing

After reading our description of *Field Notes from a Catastrophe*, you now have a sense of Kolbert's view of the environmental challenges we face. The facts are menacing and disturbing, and they raise an important question: Can we construct rational hope in the face of climate change, and if so, how?

To compose an essay that offers a thoughtful answer to this question, you will need to spend at least an hour (preferably several hours) researching (1) examples of what people around the world are doing to slow the pace or lessen the effect of climate change, and (2) examples of what others are doing to increase the consumption of nonrenewable energy. Keep notes on your sources.

Given the evidence you've uncovered in your limited research, write a speculative essay about whether it is possible to construct a rational hope about the future. What compelling evidence would you point to that supports rational hope? What evidence undermines such hope? In composing your response, stick to evidence that you find persuasive. This isn't an invitation to trade in generalities about "human nature"; it's an opportunity to consider the relationship between evidence, reason, and the future. Take your reader on a journey that reveals your mind at work on this problem.

....

Practice Session Two: Are All Arguments Journeys?

....

Habits: connecting, speculating, working deliberately

Activities: analyzing, charting, note taking, writing

We've described how Elizabeth Kolbert takes a physical journey and transforms it into an intellectual journey for readers. To think more about the connection between arguments and journeys, we'd like you to read two of the readings at the end of the book: Rebecca Solnit's "Occupied Territory" (pp. 302–08) and Danielle Allen's "What Is Education For?" (pp. 270–81). Take notes on the authors' arguments and ideas as you read.

We could give you an easy assignment about whether the phrase "argument as journey" better describes one essay or the other, but the answer is too obvious. Solnit's essay both describes and enacts a journey, while Danielle Allen's is a traditional argument. Instead we'd like you to write a speculative essay about how Allen's essay could be seen as a journey and how Solnit's essay could be seen as an argument. In the end, consider whether all arguments are journeys.

Practice Session Three: What Do I Know?

Habits: paying attention, questioning, speculating
Activities: analyzing, reading, researching, thinking

The sixteenth-century writer Michel de Montaigne is known as the inventor of the essay. He called his writings *essais*, meaning "attempts," a name that suggests their speculative quality. They were often short, personal reflections that posed variations of the question, "What do I know?" We'd like you to read Montaigne's "How Our Mind Tangles Itself Up," which is included in the Readings section at the end of this book.

As you read, practice reading curiously, and therefore slowly. Look up references that are unfamiliar to you. Who were the Stoics, for example? What is the philosopher's stone? And what is "the squaring of the circle"? Take notes on what you learn.

Write an essay that speculates about Montaigne's mental journey as he wrote this essay.

On Imagining Alternatives

In December 2014, a visitor to Disneyland triggered a measles epidemic that eventually infected more than 125 people. Twelve of the infected were infants too young to be vaccinated and another twenty-eight were adults and children unvaccinated by choice. The Centers for Disease Control (CDC) concluded that the outbreak had spread because of the high number of parents who had chosen not to vaccinate their children. The recent resistance to immunizing children has increased the chances that vulnerable populations — including infants too young to be vaccinated, people whose immune systems are suppressed, and, of course, unvaccinated children — might get infected. And indeed, since 2014, there have been a growing number of outbreaks of mumps, measles, and pertussis (also known as whooping cough) in the United States despite the CDC's warnings about the mass effects of these individual parental decisions.

Why are parents choosing not to immunize their children? How did fear of vaccination take hold and become a movement? One explanation is that vaccination has become a victim of its success: diseases like measles and mumps have become so rare in the United States, Canada, and Europe that the general populace has forgotten how dangerous they can be. But that doesn't explain why people have gone from understanding that vaccines help to ward off epidemics to believing that vaccines are not only unnecessary, but are actually life-threatening in themselves.

One recent source of the fear of vaccines was the publication in 1998 of a fraudulent medical study that linked the measles, mumps, and rubella (MMR) vaccine, which is routinely recommended for children between twelve and fifteen months old, to an increase in autism (now called autism spectrum disorder). Although the article was retracted and the doctor who wrote it was barred from practicing medicine, the piece spread like a virus on the internet, where it continues to be cited to this day by "anti-vaxxers" who wish to dismiss the science behind immunization. Add to this the general suspicion about experts and expertise that characterizes life in the twenty-first century and the invocation of parental rights to raise their children free of governmental interference and you have the conditions necessary to significantly increase the number of intentionally unvaccinated children in the general population.

Essayist Eula Biss, who began to pay attention to the anti-vaxxers after she gave birth to her son, was struck by the intensity of people's feelings on both sides of the issue. As the daughter of a physician, she understood the science of vaccination and knew with complete certainty that only one side of the debate was grounded in fact: inoculation is an unquestionable good for society. She also knew that, in order to create mass immunity, pretty much everyone has to get vaccinated. To create what is called "herd immunity," members of a community have to commit to nearly universal vaccination against the most dangerous diseases. That's the only way to prevent the threat of epidemics. With a highly infectious disease like measles, for example, more than 90 percent of the population must be immunized to protect people who are not immune (infants, the elderly, the immune suppressed). In the absence of herd immunity, everyone is more vulnerable to infection.

Biss takes up this problem in her book *On Immunity: An Inoculation*, knowing that the only solution is for parents to return to vaccinating their children as a standard practice. But she also knows that feeding anti-vaxxers data from medical studies is unlikely to change many minds. Indeed, a study of parents opposed to or uncertain about vaccines found that providing these parents with information that debunked popular myths about vaccination actually made them *less* likely to agree to immunize their children! If facts are not convincing in and of themselves, what is the alternative?

Biss decided to dig into the reasons why people opposed vaccination. She listened to parents' stories to understand what fears and hopes motivated their decisions. As she listened to more and more parents tell their stories, she realized that all the stories shared a fear of human vulnerability, a fear, Biss knew, that could be traced back to the origins of human civilization. This fear is at the heart of the tale of the great warrior Achilles, a story that Biss's father told her when she was young. Achilles's mother Thetis, having been told that her son would die young, thought she could make her newborn baby immortal by immersing him in the River Styx, which the ancient Greeks believed flowed between the worlds of the living and the dead. When Thetis plunged Achilles into the river, she held firmly to the newborn's heel, inadvertently leaving her son exposed to danger at the one spot where the water did not touch him. Achilles lived to adulthood and did seem invincible during the ten years of the Trojan War, until he died on the battlefield, shot by an arrow in his heel. Despite Thetis's best intentions, she had failed to completely shield her son from death and the term "Achilles' heel" lives on to this day as a reminder of human vulnerability. What the tale of Achilles reveals, Biss tells her readers, is that "immunity is a myth . . . and no mortal can ever be made invulnerable," even though this is what parents everywhere, both those who vaccinate and those who don't, want for their children.

In her conversations with parents who opposed vaccination, Biss also observed their desire to preserve their children's purity by trusting in the benevolence of nature. At times, this trust expressed itself in the parents' reasonable efforts to keep their homes free from toxic chemicals. But Biss could also see that the parents' desires to keep their children's bodies unsullied by vaccines rested on magical thinking about the resilient powers of the human body unpolluted by modern medicine. In the grip of this myth about natural purity, the parents were unable to see how their decisions put their families at greater risk. Their idealization of nature obscured the reality that a natural world without antibiotics or effective medicine is far more dangerous than a world where vaccination is the norm. (Before 1900, for example, it was the norm in some US cities for 30 percent of infants to die within their first year of life.)

Biss imagines that one way to bridge the divide between the anti-vaxxer parents' fears and effective public health policy is to invent a story compelling enough to replace the myths of natural immunity and purity. Her antidote to the polarized argument is to explain that the reality of human health is actually very messy. We would all be better off, she explains, if we understood that purity is an illusion and that "we are all already polluted": "we have more microorganisms in our guts than we have cells in our bodies — we are crawling with bacteria and we are full of chemicals. We are, in other words, continuous with everything here on earth. Including, and especially, each other."

The world that Biss describes is not a new Eden. (Eden, after all, included the serpent). Nor is it an imagined retreat from reality. She describes instead a complicated, untidy world of mutuality, where nature and culture intersect. In her final chapter, Biss develops the metaphor of the garden to describe a place where people cultivate the world together. She invites readers to imagine our social body as a garden within a garden: "The inner garden of our bodies . . . host[s] fungi and viruses and bacteria of both 'good' and 'bad' dispositions. This garden is unbounded and unkempt, bearing both fruit and thorns. Perhaps we should call it a wilderness. Or perhaps *community* is sufficient." "However we choose to think of the social body," she concludes, "we are each other's environment. Immunity is a shared space — a garden we tend together." In this conclusion, the meaning of *community*, which normally refers to the social world, intersects with the term *environment*, which is typically associated with the natural world. Thus, when Biss writes, "we are each other's environment," she wants readers to imagine their porous bodies breathing with the world and the people around them, for good and for ill.

The subtitle of Biss's book is *An Inoculation*, a term she wants her readers to consider as a metaphor. Her book does not provide a medical cure for the problem she grapples with; it does, however, provide an alternative to false myths about human purity and a benevolent natural world. In a review of *On Immunity*, Parul Sehgal tells us that "knowledge isn't an inoculation. . . . There are things that must be learned and learned again, seen first with the mind and felt later in the body." There is no vaccination, in other words, that can keep us safe from the allure of myths about human invulnerability. Biss can't immunize us against "alternative facts," but she can teach us how we can learn to empathize with those whose fear of mortality drives them to embrace these "alternative facts." Once we learn how to do this, we can think in new ways about the relationship of the self to the world and imagine a community in which caring for others is an integral part of caring for one's self and one's family.

Practice Session One: Speculative Histories

Habits: connecting, playing, speculating, writing

Activities: being open to complexity and uncertainty, imagining, researching

The habit of speculation is acquired by rejecting the simple connection of *and* as well as the skeptical connection of *but*, and instead imagining the alternatives made possible by the word *or*, or the question *What if?*

Fiction writers have long played with the question What if? to invent alternative histories, which are also known as "speculative fiction." In *The Man in the High Castle* (1962; now a TV series), Philip K. Dick constructs a world in which the United States lost World War II and is occupied by Nazi Germany and Japan. In *The Plot Against America* (2004), Philip Roth imagines what would have happened if Charles Lindbergh, a hero of aviation and a political isolationist, had defeated Franklin D. Roosevelt in the 1940 presidential election. In *The Underground Railroad* (2016), Colson Whitehead imagines a world in which enslaved people escaped the Confederacy on a literal railroad.

For this practice session, we'd like you to write your own speculative history by imagining a different version of the Declaration of Independence (which can be found in the Readings section at the end of this book). How would you change the document if you wanted to alter the history and the arguments that have followed its signing?

Practice Session Two: Recognizing Imagined Alternatives

Habits: exploring, questioning, speculating

Activities: imagining, note taking, reading, writing

Select any one of the readings included in the Readings section at the end of this book and read or reread it, looking for places where the author imagines alternative responses to the problem she or he addresses. As you read, take notes on passages in which the writer imagines alternatives. How does Aviv provide alternatives to tragedy? How does Solnit posit alternative relationships to space and time? How does Allen offer alternatives to inequality in education? How does Montaigne imagine alternatives to philosophical discussions about the futility of choice? How do Jefferson and his cowriters invent an alternative form of government?

Using your notes, compose an essay that responds to one of the questions above. Conclude your essay by speculating about alternatives to the alternatives posed by the writer.

....

Practice Session Three: The Strange World of "Alternative Facts"

....

Habits: exploring, questioning, speculating

Activities: looking again, researching, writing

Imagining alternatives isn't necessarily an innocent habit of mind. At the time we were writing this, Alex Jones, an antigovernment conspiracy theorist and purveyor of political lies, had his shows and podcasts removed from iTunes, Facebook, YouTube, and Spotify. Among Jones's most outrageous lies are his claims that NASA filmed fake moon landings; that the US government was involved in both the Oklahoma City bombing and the 9/11 terrorist attacks; and that the Sandy Hook school shooting, in which twenty children and six adults were killed, was a hoax. Six Sandy Hook families sued Jones for his false claims that they faked their family members' deaths.

While it is generally fruitless to engage in an argument with someone who fervently believes something verifiably false, Eula Biss has demonstrated that it can be useful to try to understand the motives behind such counterfactual thinking. So for this practice session, we'd like you to choose an "alternative truth" regarding an issue you genuinely care about and then research explanations for this false belief. Dig deep; don't rely on a simple Google search. As you research, examine your own assumptions: Is it possible that the claim you thought was verifiably false might be true or partly true? Can you empathize with people who fervently believe something that you recognize to be wholly or partly false?

After you've done substantial research and taken notes on what you've discovered, write an essay about the motives (conscious or unconscious) of those who believe the particular "alternative fact" that interests you.

On Complexity

In "Why We Need Answers," Maria Konnikova explains the science behind the fact that the common response to uncertainty is to seek easy explanations and then to cling to them. Social psychologist Arie Kruglanski calls this tendency "cognitive closure": an "individual's desire for a firm answer to a question and an aversion to ambiguity." Konnikova expands on this: when we "rush for definition, we tend to produce fewer hypotheses and search less thoroughly for information. We become more likely to form judgments based on early cues . . . , and as a result become more prone to . . . using first impressions as anchors for our decisions and not accounting enough for situational variables." Psychologists call this behavior "seize and freeze": we grab hold of a quick and easy explanation and then we resist contradictory evidence. Quite simply, when we encounter complicated events or problems, we become sloppy thinkers.

Konnikova is concerned in her article with how people respond to highly stressful circumstances, but as writing teachers we're intrigued by this tendency because we see it all the time in our students' work. The simple, easily supported claim. The avoidance of controversy. The concealment of information that contradicts or complicates an assertion. And the absence of many of the habits of mind we discuss throughout this book. Students entering college meet a serious obstacle if they have only been taught to write in ways that reinforce cognitive closure, such as essays in which they are compelled to choose a side: true/false; pro/con; either/or. Ideally, as students learn more about their majors, the world, and themselves, they resist cognitive closure and become more open to uncertainty, ambiguity, and complexity.

Good professors model these more complex ways of thinking in lectures, class discussions, readings, and in their own writing. When your professors write, they pose problems and ask questions that can't be solved or answered simply. They aspire to produce writing that demonstrates complex and subtle thinking. And whether or not your teachers say so explicitly, this is the kind of writing they would like their students to produce. "Cognitive closure" is not a trait they value.

If you practice reading scholarly writing, you will become more familiar with how writers address complexity and uncertainty in their fields of study. You've already begun practicing how to read and write with complexity because many of the habits of mind we've written about are shared by nonfiction and scholarly writers: orienting, beginning, paying attention, questioning, exploring, connecting, working deliberately, reflecting, persisting, organizing, speculating, and even playing. What's different in scholarly writing, and what can be a source of frustration to students, is that writers who are experts in a field of study write primarily for other experts in that field. Scholars make references that their colleagues understand easily but that are obscure or unrecognizable to someone who is new to the conversation. A single word, such as *utilitarian*, signals a philosophical tradition; a single name, such as a reference to Max Weber, reminds experts of the life's work of an important social theorist. As we've discussed in the essays "On Joining the Conversation" and "On Reading in Slow Motion," it's important to get in the habit of taking the time to decode unfamiliar references in what you're reading. It's also worth knowing that reading academic writing really does get easier with time. Like most skills, it takes practice.

To help you get started learning how to unpack idea-rich academic arguments, we'd like to walk you through an example of a frequently cited article by political theorist Michael Walzer, "Political Action: The Problem of Dirty Hands," which appeared in *Philosophy & Public Affairs* in 1973. (The full article can be easily found online.) We've chosen this article in part because readers have admired its clarity, even as it addresses a vexingly difficult question.

In the introduction to his essay, Walzer immediately signals that he's joining an ongoing conversation. His first paragraph explains that he's interested in a disagreement about moral dilemmas that has already been addressed by three fellow philosophers—Thomas Nagel, Richard B. Brandt, and R. M. Hare. He describes how they disagree over the question of "whether or not a man can ever face, or ever has to face, a moral dilemma, a situation where he must choose between two courses of action, both of which it would be wrong for him to undertake." More specifically, they're concerned about whether it's possible for a leader to govern "innocently." In other words, can a political leader resolve moral dilemmas without ever having to choose a course of action that is immoral?

Nagel doesn't think so: he worries about moral dilemmas in which a person "must choose between two courses of action both of which it would be wrong for him to undertake." If this situation is possible, then leaders cannot govern innocently. Brandt disagrees. He argues that by following guidelines and logical reasoning, a leader can choose the right course of action under any set of circumstances. Thus, politicians can remain innocent. Hare agrees, but with a difference. He maintains that moral dilemmas in politics can and should be resolved at a higher level of moral discourse; he trusts that philosophers can resolve issues that are beyond ordinary politicians. In this scenario, the politician still remains innocent.

Walzer is not satisfied with any of these answers to the question of whether politicians can avoid immorality. In the third paragraph of his article, he writes:

> My own answer is no, I don't think I could govern innocently; nor do most of us believe that those who govern us are innocent—as I shall argue below—even the best of them. But this does not mean that it isn't possible to do the right thing while governing. It means that a particular act of government (in a political party or in the state) may be exactly the right thing to do in utilitarian terms and yet leave the man who does it guilty of a moral wrong. The innocent man, afterwards, is no longer innocent. If on the other hand he remains innocent . . . , he not only fails to do the right thing (in utilitarian terms), he may also fail to measure up to the duties of his office (which imposes on him a considerable responsibility for consequences and outcomes).

This argument is not easy to follow on a first, or even a second, reading. Read the passage again, slowly, and look up the terms that are unfamiliar to you. If you look up *utilitarianism*, for example, you'll find that it is the principle of doing the greatest good for the greatest number. A utilitarian evaluates choices on the basis of how useful they are; the *right* choice to a utilitarian is one that is beneficial for more people.

With this definition in mind, you might assume that calculating the greatest good for the greatest number is a straightforward business, but Walzer thinks that making a utilitarian decision can be both the right course of action and morally wrong at the same time. For example, suppose a political leader believes he can serve the greater good of his or her country by sacrificing the lives of bystanders in order to kill the head of a terrorist organization. Even if the "right" utilitarian choice is to kill the bystanders along with the terrorist for the greater good of the country, the political leader has still committed the immoral act of killing innocent people and now has dirty hands. If the leader refuses to commit this immoral act on behalf of the greater good and lets the terrorist live to fight another day, then the leader could well be risking what is good for a greater number of people through his or her inaction. With this choice, the leader commits a different moral wrong and likewise has dirty hands. Either way, dirty hands seem inevitable.

Six pages into the article, Walzer fully lays out this paradox that leaders "who act for us and in our name are often killers, or seem to become killers too quickly and too easily." Even good and decent people who choose politics as a vocation, he writes,

> are then required to learn the lesson Machiavelli first set out to teach: "how not to be good." Some of them are incapable of learning; many more profess to be incapable. But they will not succeed unless they learn, for they have joined the terrible competition for power and glory; they have chosen to work and struggle as Machiavelli says, among "so many who are not good." They can do no good themselves unless they win the struggle, which they are unlikely to do unless they are willing and able to use the necessary means. So we are suspicious even of the best of winners. . . . No one succeeds in politics without getting his hands dirty. This is conventional wisdom again, and . . . I repeat it only to disclose the moral dilemma inherent in the convention. For sometimes it is right to try to succeed, and then it must also be right to get one's hands dirty. But one's hands get dirty from doing what it is wrong to do. And how can it be wrong to do what is right? Or, how can we get our hands dirty by doing what we ought to do?

As this paragraph shows, Walzer doesn't rush to resolve the moral puzzle that fascinates him. Rather than being satisfied with the conclusion that successful leaders must have dirty hands, he continues to generate more and more questions: If having dirty hands is inevitable, when should dirty-handed leaders be held accountable? When are a politician's hands too dirty? Does holding leaders accountable, in turn, dirty the hands of citizens? Do we all have dirty hands? Walzer concludes his essay without having answered these questions definitively. And yet, forty years after it was written, "Political Action: The Problem of Dirty Hands" is still being cited by scholars and taught in politics classes. Why? For two reasons: because Walzer's article presents the complex puzzle of "doing bad to do good" with remarkable clarity; and because Walzer's way of engaging with this puzzle is so lively and original that readers from across the political spectrum feel invited to join with him as he wrestles with the unsolvable challenge of leadership.

Practice Session One: Cognitive Openness

Habits: persisting, questioning, speculating, working deliberately
Activities: analyzing, being open to uncertainty and complexity, writing

If it is inevitable that all politicians have dirty hands, as Walzer argues, then we may conclude that governments are always corrupt and therefore it's not worth paying attention or voting. But this response to the complex realities of government is too simple. It expresses a desire for cognitive closure. In this practice session, we want you to instead engage with this complex moral puzzle.

Write an essay that explores the implications of Walzer's argument. One option is to write about one of the questions posed above: If having dirty hands is inevitable, when should dirty-handed leaders be held accountable? When are a politician's hands too dirty? If citizens hold leaders accountable for immoral choices, does this action, in turn, dirty the hands of citizens? Or, you could address a different question: In a world in which all politicians have (or will have) dirty hands, how do we decide whether to vote for one candidate over another?

Your goal in this essay is not to answer quickly the question you've chosen. Instead, you should explore the complexities of the dilemma. Let the question you've chosen lead to speculation, and let speculation lead to new questions. You may not arrive at a completely satisfactory response but your essay should demonstrate that, having thought and written about your original dilemma at length, you better understand its complexity.

Practice Session Two: Can Killing Be Justified?

Habits: persisting, questioning, speculating, working deliberately

Activities: analyzing, openness to uncertainty and complexity, writing

We'd like you to think though a familiar moral, political, and religious dilemma. Many religions hold it as a moral absolute that it is wrong — even a sin — to kill another human being. Nations also have laws that prohibit murder. And yet, exceptions are made all the time. We wage wars. Deadly violence may be justified by law if a person's life was in danger. Some states now have stand-your-ground laws that allow the use of deadly force to protect oneself or others against a perceived threat.

Write an essay in which you speculate about when killing might be justified. Has the United States or your home state gone too far in permitting lethal violence against others? How do you decide? To what authorities do you turn for support in thinking about this problem?

Remember, the goal in your essay, as in the first practice session, is not to quickly resolve the dilemma you've chosen to write about. Instead, we want you to explore an instance in which killing creates a dilemma for your belief system. Let speculation lead to new questions. Although you may not arrive at a definitive answer, your essay should demonstrate that you understand the complexity of this moral dilemma.

Practice Session Three: What Is Educational Equality?

Habits: persisting, questioning, speculation, working deliberately
Activities: openness to uncertainty and complexity, questioning, reading, writing

Danielle Allen begins "What Is Education For?" (in the Readings section at the end of this book) with the complex question posed in her title. There's no easy answer to her question, but at the core of her answer is the ideal of equality. How, she wonders, could states or the nation design a system of education that "will offer the real possibility of equal educational attainment, if not achievement, to all students"? Read her essay with care and observe that Allen's essay also examines the meaning of *equality*. When we talk about equality in regard to education, she admits, "we generally don't bother to define it. Is it political equality that concerns us? Social equality? Or economic equality only?"

We'd like you to write an essay that speculates about this moment in Allen's argument. In your essay, consider the challenges of using education to advance civic equality, social equality, economic equality, or other types of equality. First define your terms, including the word *equality*. What version of equality would you prioritize in education? Which types of equality are you willing to set aside to prioritize others? Will there necessarily be educational winners and losers in the fight for equality?

12

·················

PLAYING

Two roads diverged in a wood, and I —
I took the one less traveled by,
And that has made all the difference.

···

If you were asked to gloss these lines from the final stanza of Robert Frost's "The Road Not Taken," you would likely say that the speaker is celebrating the fact that he's chosen a different path than most other people. But if you place those lines within the context of the entire poem, you can see that Frost is playing with a narrator who thinks that small, insignificant decisions made in the past were actually definitively important in giving shape and meaning to his life. This narrator has chosen between two paths that are not actually that different: the one he took was "just as fair" as the other; both paths were worn "really about the same"; and both were covered in "leaves no step had trodden black." Having made his choice, the narrator looks into the future and knows that he'll tell a more dramatic story, one that makes this decision seem momentous: "I shall be telling this [version] with a sigh. . . ."

Poetry isn't the only genre in which the writer can play with meaning; the essay form also encourages playing with ideas, with language, with structure, and with readers' expectations. This may seem like a surprising claim, but this is what we mean when we tell students that we are training them to be creative thinkers: we're teaching them to play with ideas. In this section, we'll discuss three different kinds of play: play that generates laughter (spoiler alert: our case study concerns laughing in the face of death); play that bends conventions; and play that becomes possible when writing under a pseudonym. In each instance, our goal is to show that play has an essential role in the life of the creative mind, providing one more way to explore what becomes possible when you veer from the common path.

On Laughter

"So, two writing teachers walk into a bar."

Could a joke that starts this way ever be funny?

What about this joke:

"How many writing teachers does it take to screw in a light bulb?"

Or a joke that begins,

"A writing teacher shows up at the Pearly Gates . . ."?

It all depends, right?

And not just on whatever the next line is, but also on the context — on who's telling the joke, how they're telling it, where they're telling it, why they're telling it, and, of course, on who's listening and/or watching. Humor is, we would argue, the most contextually dependent and the most contextually sensitive of all linguistic acts.

This is one reason why humor is the least likely of the habits of the creative mind to be taught in school: it is especially risky playing with audience expectations in a context where being playful is equated with being unserious. But being funny and being insightful have a common trait: they both involve seeing something from a different angle. When you successfully disrupt audience expectations by saying something surprising — perhaps by making connections between things that seem disconnected, or by pointing out an incongruity, or by unsettling typical ways of thinking about and seeing the world — you make it possible for your audience to shift perspectives, to see things in a new way. In our view, practicing being funny is a way to practice seeing a situation from multiple perspectives; it's also a way to practice gauging just how flexible your audience's expectations are.

Sometimes you will be wrong in your estimation of how much your audience will bend. One of us (we're not saying who) once made a joke in a paper in graduate school, and in the margin of the paper, next to the joke, the teacher wrote: "Humor has no place in academic discourse."

No place? *Really?*

Not even a very, very tiny one?

It is true that academic research on humor is unlikely to produce riotous laughter. It's also true that the tone and style of academic writing in general tends to fall somewhere on a spectrum that extends from the dispassionate to the gravely serious. But here's the thing: no government, institution, religion, or tradition is powerful enough to completely suppress the desire to laugh. Here's a case in point: the confirmation hearing on Jeff Sessions's appointment as attorney general of the United States in 2017. In that somber and serious setting, laughter would seem to have no place. And, indeed, when Desiree Fairooz, a protestor associated with Code Pink, laughed out loud after Senator Richard Shelby declared that Sessions's "extensive record of treating all Americans equally under the law is clear and well-documented," she was asked by the Capital Police to leave the building. When she refused, she was arrested for disorderly conduct and forcibly removed by three officers.

Shortly after Ms. Fairooz's arrest, the *Washington Post* ran an opinion piece by Dana Milbank entitled, "Apparently, It's Illegal to Laugh at Jeff Sessions." Milbank opens by saying he'd like to share a joke about the new attorney general, but he can't for fear of being arrested as an "accessory to mirth." Later, when Ms. Fairooz was convicted in a jury trial, Stephen Colbert specified that she had also been charged with "first-degree chuckling with intent to titter." The judge in the first trial, however, was so troubled by the prosecution's closing argument that Fairooz's laughter "in and of itself" was sufficient reason for the jury to find her guilty of disorderly conduct that he threw out the conviction. A week before Ms. Fairooz's second trial was set to begin, the prosecution dropped the case without explanation. For the time being, at least, it's still legal to laugh during the proceedings of the legislative branch in the most powerful democracy in the world.

There's a long history of writers using satire and absurdism to highlight political excesses. The value of humor in that context is straightforward: it exposes those in power to ridicule. But what about humor and the end of life? Surely that has to be out of bounds, right?

In *Romeo and Juliet*, Shakespeare's well-known (and some would say quite silly) play about star-crossed lovers, Romeo's best friend, the witty Mercutio, ends up being stabbed during a confrontation with a rival clan. When Romeo tries to determine whether his friend has been injured during the brandishing of swords, Mercutio won't give him a straight answer:

Ask for me to-morrow, and you shall find me a grave man.

A *grave* man? *Really?*

Yes, Shakespeare really does have his character make a joke about his own death while he is dying. Not only that, Shakespeare has Mercutio resort to a pun, which some define as the lowest form of humor, to both tell and not tell Romeo about the seriousness of his injury. Moments later, Mercutio exits and, we learn that he does indeed die of his wound. *Exeunt*, pursued by a pun.

But, you object, this is just a play. It's not real life. Real people wouldn't crack a joke when Death is *really* at their door, would they?

On August 3, 2012, the comedian Tig Notaro walked onto the stage at the *Largo*, a comedy club in Los Angeles, and said to the audience:

Good evening. Hello. I have cancer. How are you? Hi, how are you? Is everybody having a good time? I have cancer. How are you? Ah, it's a good time. Diagnosed with cancer. [Sighs] It feels good. Just diagnosed with cancer. Oh, God.

There was some uncomfortable laughter. Notaro repeated herself. More laughter followed, but it was the laughter of disbelief, of nervousness, of uncertainty. She can't be serious, can she? This seems beyond the pale, making jokes at the expense of people who really do have cancer—who would make light of such a thing?

As the routine continued, the audience slowly realized that Notaro was *both* telling the truth *and* joking about her diagnosis. She repeatedly paused to speak directly to audience members who didn't know how to respond to what she was telling them: a man who was laughing too much; a woman who was deeply troubled by what she was hearing.

It's OK. It's going to be OK. [Pause] It might not be OK. But I'm just saying, it's OK. You're going to be OK. [Pause] I don't know what's going on with me.

This set pushed Notaro's comedy career to a new level. She completely violated her audience's expectations in a way that virtually everyone would find unthinkable; and yet she made them laugh.

Notaro and Shakespeare show that you can joke about your own death; but that's different, you might say, from joking about a mass tragedy in which *thousands* of other people died horrific deaths. Surely no one would do such a thing. Well, at least not right away.

How much time has to pass before awful, unbearable, or unthinkable events can be redeployed in the service of comedy? What is the etiquette when one is making a joke that references the deaths of others? How soon is too soon? How do you know?

In *The Aristocrats*, a documentary we greatly admire, the filmmakers set out to understand the history of one particularly vulgar and offensive joke that comedians routinely tell each other. The triggering event for the documentary? The editors of the *Onion* and many comedy headliners were attending a roast of Hugh Hefner at the Friars Club in New York City on November 4, 2001, which was being filmed by Comedy Central for future broadcast. People are laughing and having a good time and then this happened: the comic Gilbert Gottfried took his turn at the podium and made a joke that alluded to 9/11. There was a nervous response, some boos, and then shouts of "too soon!" With the ruins of the Twin Towers still being sifted through for human remains, Gottfried had clearly crossed the invisible line of his audience's expectations about what constituted an appropriate topic for the occasion.

Gottfried's response?

He shifted gears and went straight into a joke known to all professional comics, a set piece that can be infinitely expanded between the setup (a family enters a talent agency) and the punch line ("We call the act 'The Aristocrats'!"). Soon enough, the room was filled with laughter; someone on the stage laughed so hard he fell out of his chair. Gottfried reminded everyone in the room that comedy's function is to make it possible to laugh in response to that which is surprising, incongruous, or dissonant, and that this necessarily includes laughing at the unimaginably horrific things that humans do to one another.

In the documentary about this joke (which includes footage of Gottfried's Friars Club appearance), no one gets hurt. There are no vivid scenes of murder or rape or humiliation. There's no nudity and no simulation of sex acts. There isn't, in other words, any of the kind of visual material that is common fare in movie theaters, TV shows, and music videos. All there is to see is comic after comic telling the same vulgar, obscene joke, though the language and the shape of the joke change with each telling. And after hearing this joke told over and over, we come to understand that the best jokes help us to see incongruities in the world and in ourselves, to make sense of nonsense, and to connect things that seem unconnectable. Or to put this another way, jokes give us access to the powers of the imagination in all of its unruliness.

But what about in the realm of the essay? Does humor have any place in writing that is research driven? Investigative? Exploratory? Thoughtful? We believe that humor provides a vital role in the deliberative process: when one line of thinking leads to an impasse, the introduction of humor can serve to open up access to another plane of thought, one in which the impasse gets reframed as the occasion for laughter. But we don't want to argue the point; we want you to be the judge.

In his short essay, "How Our Mind Tangles Itself Up" (pp. 268–69), Montaigne begins with a philosophical problem that amuses him: all things being equal, how do we decide which course of action to choose? In a playful state of mind, Montaigne presents the problem in a fanciful way: being equally hungry and thirsty, how does one choose between the ham and the bottle? With the desires being equal and there being no way to decide, what alternative is there "but to die of thirst and of hunger?"

Montaigne is enjoying himself here, playing with a paradox to create a situation that is laughable. What is the joke, though? Is it that philosophers try — but fail — to understand how humans make decisions, or that none of us is smart enough to know how our minds work? Montaigne's essay doesn't end with his evocation of a mind equidistant from two objects equally desired; that's how it opens. The rest of the essay is devoted to Montaigne's efforts to try to escape from the situation he's created for himself. With his humorous opening, Montaigne is trying to shake himself out of his usual pattern of thought so that he can see things differently. When humor is used in this way, it's obvious why it is central to curiosity-driven, creative work.

Practice Session One, Part One: Humor to the Rescue

Habits: paying attention, playing, questioning

Activities: reading, writing

We've just described how Montaigne used humor to help him shift his perspective. In "Occupied Territory" (which you can find in the Readings section at the end of this book), Rebecca Solnit offers another example of how laughter enabled her to think differently about the frustration of being made to wait. She was visiting a writer, Jarvis Masters, in San Quentin State Prison, where he had been imprisoned for three decades on death row for a crime that Solnit does not believe he committed. It is common practice in prisons for visitors to be locked in a small room with their guests. But when Solnit was ready to leave, no one was available to let her out. She waited for an hour before a guard arrived. Masters, she reports, "was amused at her impatience." She was delayed for an hour; "he'd been delayed more than thirty years." While this observation was funny to Masters, for Solnit, the humor caused her to see her impatience from a new perspective: Masters's joke reminded her of her privileged experience of time and space.

We want you to practice using humor to shift perspectives and advance your thinking. Select a piece you've written recently where you stalled or you repeated yourself at one or more points. Try introducing a contextual joke at one of the moments in the piece where you ran into trouble. Then keep writing for at least thirty minutes beyond the point where you've introduced the contextual joke, extending your paper into new territory. Where do you end up?

Practice Session One, Part Two: Transitional Humor

Habits: connecting, organizing, playing

Activities: revising

When you are happy with the results of your effort to get past a stalled point in your thinking, go back and try your hand at turning your contextual joke into a more conventional transitional sentence or paragraph.

Practice Session Two: Laughter on the Internet

Habits: exploring, playing, reflecting
Activities: researching, diagnosing

Humor is one of the primary modes for communicating online. But all jokes aren't for everyone and what's funny to one group can be baffling or offensive to another group. We'd like you to create a working file for storing online material you find humorous. This can be anything — from viral videos to memes to personal text exchanges, tweets, and fake Instagram posts — whatever best represents the various functions that humor plays for you and your community of friends.

When you have enough examples to provide a portrait of what you find funny, write an essay about the various functions humor plays in your online community. Make certain to use examples from your file as evidence. Assume that your readers won't see the humor in your examples; your job is to make clear how the humor works in context.

Practice Session Three: Explaining a Joke

Habits: organizing, playing, working deliberately
Activities: writing

For this exercise, we've adapted one of the essay prompts from the University of Chicago's 2013 admissions application: "Write out your favorite joke and then explain the joke without ruining it."

On Bending Conventions

Public speeches are, by definition, governed by convention. Take graduation speeches. They all more or less follow this predictable arc: the opening joke, the personal anecdote, praise for students' achievements, warnings about the challenges to come, and wise final words of encouragement about achieving success with integrity. Everybody in the audience knows that life after graduation is not that simple, but graduations are celebratory occasions, so it not the right time to point out the magnitude of the problems graduates are likely to face or the difficulties they will have in traveling the road ahead.

When the conventions are so rigid, is creativity possible? We've worked with many beginning creative writers who believe that all constraints, guidelines, and requirements are disabling intrusions; we even had a student who refused to read anyone else's work, published or unpublished, on the grounds that such exposure would taint the purity of his own writing. But thinking of creativity as the evasion of conventions is a mistake; creativity, we maintain, is better thought of as a way of playing with and within conventions.

David Foster Wallace's 2005 commencement speech at Kenyon College beautifully illustrates such creative play. Wallace began conventionally enough, with a parable about how much the young still have to learn:

> There are these two young fish swimming along and they happen to meet an older fish swimming the other way, who nods at them and says, "Morning, boys. How's the water?" And the two young fish swim on for a bit, and then eventually one of them looks over at the other and goes, "What the hell is water?"

Given the occasion, Wallace acknowledged that his audience was likely to see the point of the parable as introducing the moment when the "wise old fish" behind the podium shared his wisdom with the "younger fish" in the audience: "the most obvious, important realities are often the ones that are hardest to see and talk about." But, Wallace didn't sound much like a wise elder when he told the graduating seniors and their families that what he really wanted to talk about was "the value of the totally obvious." That's an odd topic for a commencement speech, but Wallace insisted that his unconventional choice made sense. "In the day-to-day trenches of adult existence," he said, "banal platitudes can have a life-or-death importance."

Life-or-death importance?

Coming from a more conventional writer, those words might have served only as a laugh line, an over-the-top exaggeration. But Wallace wasn't kidding. He was utterly, disarmingly sincere. Having posed the problem of how we all can become numb to our own lives and surroundings and our shared tendency "to be deeply and literally self-centered, and to see and interpret everything through this lens of self," he challenged his audience to consider other options:

> Twenty years after my own graduation, I have come gradually to understand that the liberal arts cliché about teaching you how to think is actually shorthand for a much deeper, more serious idea: learning how to think really means learning how to exercise some control over how and what you think. It means being conscious and aware enough to choose what you pay attention to and to choose how you construct meaning from experience. Because if you cannot exercise this kind of choice in adult life, you will be totally hosed.

In other words, we can put our brains on their default settings and glide along thinking we are the center of the universe, or we can be deliberate about how we think and what we pay attention to. Choosing to pay attention takes practice and effort. It is, Wallace stated at the end of his address, "unimaginably hard to do this, to stay conscious and alive in the adult world day in and day out." And this means, he concluded, that "yet another grand cliché turns out to be true: your education really *is* the job of a lifetime." The ultimate value of an education, he continued, has almost nothing to do with knowledge, and everything to do with simple awareness; awareness of what is so real and essential, so hidden in plain sight all around us, all the time, that we have to keep reminding ourselves over and over:

"This is water."

"This is water."

When Wallace sat down to write this commencement speech, he knew the basic conventions of the genre, but in order to write a *good* speech, a *memorable* speech, he needed the habits of a curious and creative mind. He gave the families of the Kenyon graduates what they came for by hitting most of the marks of a conventional graduation speech—the parable, the words of wisdom, and so on. But he also invited his audience to join him in conscious reflection about the artificiality of those conventions when they are deployed without creativity, and about the authenticity that can be generated when those same conventions are used to say something unexpected. He asked all those present to contemplate the possibility that the adult lives these graduates were about to commence could well become so consuming in their dull everydayness that personal experience itself might stop being meaningful.

Wallace didn't end his speech on this ominous note, though: this is a commencement speech, after all. Instead, almost in spite of himself, he offered the audience some wise advice—that it's possible to become aware again of what's real and essential, and that reacquiring and maintaining this awareness never stops being work. Or to put it another way, he encouraged his audience to practice the habits of the creative mind, day in and day out, fully aware that the practice never ends.

. . . . .

David Foster Wallace's speech is worth reading and listening to in full, so we'd like you to find a copy of *This Is Water* at the library, or find transcripts and audio files of the speech online. We recommend reading the transcript while following along with Wallace's voice on a recording before you move on to the practice sessions.

Practice Session One: A Case Study

Habits: paying attention, playing, working deliberately
Activities: analyzing, listening, writing

In our discussion of convention, we said that thinking of creativity as the evasion of conventions is a mistake, and that creativity is better thought of as a way of playing with conventions. In this practice session we want you to explore how Wallace plays with, rather than evades, conventions. Listen to the speech — ideally with a transcript in hand — and find at least five specific examples, other than the ones we've discussed above, of Wallace playing with conventions. Then take at least thirty minutes to write about how his play with words, style, ideas, and the tradition of the commencement speech contributes to your experience as a reader.

Note: At times you may not like Wallace's playfulness, so feel free to write about the full range of ways his approach to convention contributes to your experience.

Practice Session Two, Part One: Seeing the Water

Habits: paying attention, playing, reflecting
Activities: listening, observing, writing

Wallace's commencement speech points out that it's conventional for adults to be governed by an inner monologue that ends up preventing them from thinking new thoughts. For this practice session we'd like you to set aside three fifteen-minute periods over a span of several days during which you consciously try to silence your automatic inner monologue and practice being aware of your surroundings — the people around you, the scene unfolding before you, the questions or ideas you might normally tune out. After you've practiced awareness over the three fifteen-minute periods, spend at least thirty minutes writing about what you saw, heard, or sensed that was new to you.

Practice Session Two, Part Two: Making Sense of the Everyday

Habits: paying attention, playing, reflecting
Activities: writing

Wallace says in his speech that, when we are no longer numb to our surroundings, we have the opportunity to make choices about the meaning of our experience. After reviewing your notes from the first part of this practice session, write a meditative essay that makes your experience of paying attention meaningful. We invite you to play with conventions of thought and form as you write. Don't imitate Wallace's voice — just his habits of mind.

Practice Session Three: The Artist and the Person

Habits: exploring, playing, reflecting
Activities: note taking, reflecting, researching

One of the most powerful social movements of our time centers on victims of sexual predation publicly sharing their experiences. #MeToo has raised awareness about the metaphorical water that surrounds women and has compelled a cultural reckoning with the ordinariness of gender-based harassment, abuse, and violence. (It has also made it possible for men who have been assaulted to give voice to their stories, but no one would claim that this is a threat that surrounds men at all times.)

We'd like you to research how David Foster Wallace has figured in the #MeToo movement. You'll need to deploy your creative research skills, drilling down past the Wikipedia entries to the reflective pieces on how writers and teachers have responded to the revelations about Wallace's behavior. Once you feel you have a handle on the facts and the positions others have taken in relation to those facts, we'd like you to write an essay on what you think it means to read responsibly. We're not asking you to argue either for or against assigning Wallace's work: he is just one instance of a pervasive reality that the #MeToo movement has brought to light. Instead we want you to reflect on the complex problem of how one reads or watches movies or listens to music or looks at art or reads poetry in light of such revelations.

On the Joys of Pseudonymous Writing

Seven years ago, I[1] threw in the towel on academic publishing. The precipitating event was, I readily admit, a ridiculous disagreement I had with an editor I admire over an article I had been invited to write. This debacle happened to coincide with some equally ridiculous developments in my home department. My decision to shift my energies to self-publishing online wasn't particularly well thought out. I was just tired of fighting and I needed to head in a different direction if I was going to write at all.

What I didn't realize at the time I made this decision was that I was also tired of me—the author-function me, the me who thought X, argued X, wrote about X, could be counted on to say X. I found that the academic arguments I got pulled into were dull, and I had to admit that I was bored because I already knew what I was going to say. I already knew the critiques that would be made about what I was going to say, and I also knew how I was going to respond. I didn't want to give up writing, but I also didn't want to keep on writing the same thing, making the same argument, pounding my head against the same wall for the remaining years of my career. Moving to writing exclusively for my public blog solved this problem for me, but not in the ways I had expected.

I started out wanting to move beyond the conventions and the commonplaces of what I have come to call "the paper-based world," to see what writing full-time in "the screen-centric world" entailed. When I would speak about this decision publicly, invariably someone would say, "Fine for you to fool around writing online—with the luxury of tenure. But what about the rest of us?" And, like that, the conversation would move back into its familiar ruts. I'd say that I'd never been motivated to write by the famous dictum of the tenure system: publish or perish! And that my feeling has always been that if you're just publishing so as not to perish, you've been conned into sacrificing what is most important about having a job with writing at its center: the opportunity to think new thoughts. There'd be more back and forth and then the conversation would end where it began: with one person trying to learn to write online and the other person seeing the decision as misguided and unnecessary. Such is the nature of argument.

---

[1] The I in this piece is Richard. Or is it?

While some assumed I had some natural affinity for technology, the truth is that when I started I knew nothing about how to begin writing online: how to get a web address; how to get a hosting service (or what that service did); how to code in html (or whether that was even necessary); or pretty much anything else about the technical side of writing in and for the screen-centric world. I figured, though, that these things had to be learnable. After all, by the time I was entering the game, there were already a gazillion websites in existence, a fact that suggested to me that the learning curve couldn't be that steep.

I stumbled along, starting a Google blog with the address critical_optimist. Back then, though, a Google blog couldn't accommodate more than text and images and all the blogs looked pretty much the same on the screen, so I eventually graduated to getting my own URL and committed myself to learning how to think outside the template. As I was coming to understand the project I had embarked on, I didn't just have the alphabet to compose with anymore; I had everything that was available on the web: music, videos, interviews, lectures, libraries around the world, image banks, maps. It was more like sitting at a giant pipe organ than at a typewriter; and more like producing an illuminated manuscript than typing out my thoughts as they made their way into language. Every search I did could turn out to be a rabbit hole; any question could lead me to sources and resources I never knew existed. While there were stints of insane frustration, overall I felt like I'd been released into a playground for the curious mind.

It turned out, though, that for me the most momentous part of changing venues really had nothing to do with the shift from paper to screen; it had to do with assuming a new writing persona, an option that really was only theoretically available to me in the paper-centered world. In my previous writing life, I was Richard E. Miller; in my new writing life, I was text2cloud, the lead for the URL on my website. Putting some distance between myself and my history, text2cloud became a way for me to think new thoughts, to try on new sentences, to call on a different vocabulary, to explore a world of concerns that fell outside the frame of my other writing life. And text2cloud gave rise to Professor Pawn, the central figure in a graphic narrative I composed about the absurdities of working at a university that had become an afterthought of the athletic program. The pseudonyms proliferated. I created a character called Hieronymous Paunch, a big-data humanist and founder of Sadness Studies, and later still I invented an anonymous voice for "Tales of the White Knight," a Facebook diary about the 2016 presidential debates that turned into a mashup of Don Quixote, King Arthur, King Lear, Monty Python, and the Marx Brothers.

Somewhere along the line, the liberating effect of writing pseudonymously also led to my writing, along with Ann Jurecic, the book on how to make creativity a habit that you are reading right now. In this book, there's a collaborative pseudonym that made it possible for us both to rethink our futures as teachers of writing: "we" became a way of allowing us to write not as a unified, coherent entity, but in dialogue, animated by the desire to get beyond the template, the formula, the step-by-step approach to making sense of the world.

Obviously, I eventually made my way back to writing under my own name and have returned to the work of getting my words to appear on paper. But the journey changed me, changed my writing, and changed my teaching. It also taught me that I can invite my students to embark on this same journey. I can invite them to write under a pseudonym, one that allows them to escape, for a moment, writing and thinking as they always have. Anonymity makes it possible for them to write passionately about ideas without embarrassment, to follow their thoughts wherever they might lead; and to write as if their very lives depended on it.

Practice Session One: What's in a Name?

Habits: exploring, playing, speculating
Activities: imagining, researching, note taking

What does your name say about you? How was it chosen? Do you have a nickname or nicknames? We'd like you to embark upon a two-pronged research project into the history and the significance of your own name. For one prong of the research, you'll need to get access to the story of how your name was decided on. Why was it chosen? What did the choice mean to the person or the people who chose it? For the other prong of your research, you'll need to explore the history associated with your name. What etymological roots can be traced to your name? Can you create a family tree that follows your last name back a generation? Two? How far back can you go?

When you've completed your research, write up what you've discovered. Are there experiences that your name makes possible? Are there experiences your name prevents?

Practice Session Two, Part One: The Right Pseudonym

Habits: exploring, playing, speculating
Activities: brainstorming, revising

If you were to write under a pseudonym that allowed you to be a more creative thinker, what would it be? Spend some time generating possibilities. We don't want you to assume someone else's identity. This isn't an invitation to write *as if* you were an already established author; it's an opportunity to choose a name that gives you a little more room to breathe, a little more space between what you think you have to say and what you might want to try out saying. It's best if you pick a name that your friends won't recognize. After all, your pseudonym should make it possible for you to experiment without having to conform to their expectations.

When you've settled on a name, write up a profile of your pseudonym's habits of mind. How will your pseudonym's thinking style differ from the thinking style that is evident in writing that appears under your name?

Practice Session Two, Part Two: Putting the Pseudonym to Work

Habits: beginning, exploring, playing
Activities: revising

Select an essay you wrote in the past, one that you feel didn't reflect your actual investment in what you handed in. Rewrite the paper from scratch using your pseudonym. Make sure the habits of mind you attributed to your pseudonym in the first part of this practice session are in evidence in your revision. Your goal is to revise the original in such a way that your investment in your writing is clear and the way your mind works on a problem is in the foreground. You're aiming to get your writing to help you think new thoughts and to invent new ways of communicating thoughts to your readers.

READINGS

THE DECLARATION OF INDEPENDENCE

Thomas Jefferson, et al.

IN CONGRESS, JULY 4, 1776
The unanimous Declaration of the
Thirteen United States of America

When in the Course of human events it becomes necessary for one people to dissolve the political bands which have connected them with another and to assume among the powers of the earth, the separate and equal station to which the Laws of Nature and of Nature's God entitle them, a decent respect to the opinions of mankind requires that they should declare the causes which impel them to the separation.

We hold these truths to be self-evident, that all men are created equal, that they are endowed by their Creator with certain unalienable Rights, that among these are Life, Liberty and the pursuit of Happiness. —That to secure these rights, Governments are instituted among Men, deriving their just powers from the consent of the governed, —That whenever any Form of Government becomes destructive of these ends, it is the Right of the People to alter or to abolish it, and to institute new Government, laying its foundation on such principles and organizing its powers in such form, as to them shall seem most likely to effect their Safety and Happiness. Prudence, indeed, will dictate that Governments long established should not be changed for light and transient causes; and accordingly all experience hath shewn that mankind are more disposed to suffer, while evils are sufferable than to right themselves by abolishing the forms to which they are accustomed. But when a long train of abuses and usurpations, pursuing invariably the same Object evinces a design to reduce them under absolute Despotism, it is their right, it is their duty, to throw off such Government, and to provide new Guards for their future security. — Such has been the patient sufferance of these Colonies; and such is now the necessity which constrains them to alter their former Systems of Government. The history of the present King of Great Britain is a history of repeated injuries and usurpations, all having in direct object the establishment of an absolute Tyranny over these States. To prove this, let Facts be submitted to a candid world.

He has refused his Assent to Laws, the most wholesome and necessary for the public good.

He has forbidden his Governors to pass Laws of immediate and pressing importance, unless suspended in their operation till his Assent should be obtained; and when so suspended, he has utterly neglected to attend to them.

He has refused to pass other Laws for the accommodation of large districts of people, unless those people would relinquish the right of Representation in the Legislature, a right inestimable to them and formidable to tyrants only.

He has called together legislative bodies at places unusual, uncomfortable, and distant from the depository of their Public Records, for the sole purpose of fatiguing them into compliance with his measures.

He has dissolved Representative Houses repeatedly, for opposing with manly firmness his invasions on the rights of the people.

He has refused for a long time, after such dissolutions, to cause others to be elected, whereby the Legislative Powers, incapable of Annihilation, have returned to the People at large for their exercise; the State remaining in the mean time exposed to all the dangers of invasion from without, and convulsions within.

He has endeavoured to prevent the population of these States; for that purpose obstructing the Laws for Naturalization of Foreigners;

refusing to pass others to encourage their migrations hither, and raising the conditions of new Appropriations of Lands.

He has obstructed the Administration of Justice by refusing his Assent to Laws for establishing Judiciary Powers.

He has made Judges dependent on his Will alone for the tenure of their offices, and the amount and payment of their salaries.

He has erected a multitude of New Offices, and sent hither swarms of Officers to harass our people and eat out their substance.

He has kept among us, in times of peace, Standing Armies without the Consent of our legislatures.

He has affected to render the Military independent of and superior to the Civil Power.

He has combined with others to subject us to a jurisdiction foreign to our constitution, and unacknowledged by our laws; giving his Assent to their Acts of pretended Legislation:

For quartering large bodies of armed troops among us:

For protecting them, by a mock Trial from punishment for any Murders which they should commit on the Inhabitants of these States:

For cutting off our Trade with all parts of the world:

For imposing Taxes on us without our Consent:

For depriving us in many cases, of the benefit of Trial by Jury:

For transporting us beyond Seas to be tried for pretended offences:

For abolishing the free System of English Laws in a neighbouring Province, establishing therein an Arbitrary government, and enlarging its Boundaries so as to render it at once an example and fit instrument for introducing the same absolute rule into these Colonies:

For taking away our Charters, abolishing our most valuable Laws and altering fundamentally the Forms of our Governments:

For suspending our own Legislatures, and declaring themselves invested with power to legislate for us in all cases whatsoever.

He has abdicated Government here, by declaring us out of his Protection and waging War against us.

He has plundered our seas, ravaged our coasts, burnt our towns, and destroyed the lives of our people.

He is at this time transporting large Armies of foreign Mercenaries to compleat the works of death, desolation, and tyranny, already begun with circumstances of Cruelty & Perfidy scarcely paralleled in the most barbarous ages, and totally unworthy the Head of a civilized nation.

He has constrained our fellow Citizens taken Captive on the high Seas to bear Arms against their Country, to become the executioners of their friends and Brethren, or to fall themselves by their Hands.

He has excited domestic insurrections amongst us, and has endeavoured to bring on the inhabitants of our frontiers, the merciless Indian Savages whose known rule of warfare, is an undistinguished destruction of all ages, sexes, and conditions.

In every stage of these Oppressions We have Petitioned for Redress in the most humble terms: Our repeated Petitions have been answered only by repeated injury. A Prince, whose character is thus marked by every act which may define a Tyrant, is unfit to be the ruler of a free people.

Nor have We been wanting in attentions to our British brethren. We have warned them from time to time of attempts by their legislature to extend an unwarrantable jurisdiction over us. We have reminded them of the circumstances of our emigration and settlement here. We have appealed to their native justice and magnanimity, and we have conjured them by the ties of our common kindred to disavow these usurpations, which would inevitably interrupt our connections and correspondence. They too have been deaf to the voice of justice and of consanguinity. We must, therefore, acquiesce in the necessity, which denounces our Separation, and hold them, as we hold the rest of mankind, Enemies in War, in Peace Friends.

We, therefore, the Representatives of the united States of America, in General Congress, Assembled, appealing to the Supreme Judge of the world for the rectitude of our intentions, do, in the Name, and by Authority of the good People of these Colonies, solemnly publish and declare, That these united Colonies are, and of Right ought to be Free and Independent States, that they are Absolved from all Allegiance to the British Crown, and that all political connection between them and the State of Great Britain, is and ought to be totally dissolved; and that as Free and Independent States, they have full Power to levy War, conclude Peace, contract Alliances, establish Commerce, and to do all other Acts and Things which Independent States may of right do. — And for the support of this Declaration, with a firm reliance on the protection of Divine Providence, we mutually pledge to each other our Lives, our Fortunes, and our sacred Honor.

New Hampshire:
Josiah Bartlett, William Whipple, Matthew Thornton

Massachusetts:
John Hancock, Samuel Adams, John Adams, Robert Treat Paine,
Elbridge Gerry

Rhode Island:
Stephen Hopkins, William Ellery

Connecticut:
Roger Sherman, Samuel Huntington, William Williams, Oliver
Wolcott

New York:
William Floyd, Philip Livingston, Francis Lewis, Lewis Morris

New Jersey:
Richard Stockton, John Witherspoon, Francis Hopkinson, John Hart,
Abraham Clark

Pennsylvania:
Robert Morris, Benjamin Rush, Benjamin Franklin, John Morton,
George Clymer, James Smith, George Taylor, James Wilson,
George Ross

Delaware:
Caesar Rodney, George Read, Thomas McKean

Maryland:
Samuel Chase, William Paca, Thomas Stone, Charles Carroll of
Carrollton

Virginia:
George Wythe, Richard Henry Lee, Thomas Jefferson, Benjamin
Harrison, Thomas Nelson Jr., Francis Lightfoot Lee, Carter Braxton

North Carolina:
William Hooper, Joseph Hewes, John Penn

South Carolina:
Edward Rutledge, Thomas Heyward Jr., Thomas Lynch Jr.,
Arthur Middleton

Georgia:
Button Gwinnett, Lyman Hall, George Walton

HOW OUR MIND TANGLES ITSELF UP

Michel de Montaigne

It is a pleasant thought to image a mind exactly poised between two desires, for it would indubitably never reach a decision, since making a choice implies that there is an inequality of value; if anyone were to place us between a bottle and a ham when we had an equal appetite for drink and for food there would certainly be no remedy but to die of thirst and of hunger![1]

In order to provide against this difficulty the Stoics, when you ask them how our souls manage to choose between two things which are indifferent and how we come to take one coin rather than another from a large number of crowns when they are all alike and there is no reason which can sway our preference, reply that this motion in our souls is extraordinary and not subject to rules, coming into us from some outside impulse, incidental and fortuitous.

It seems to me that we could say that nothing ever presents itself to us in which there is not some difference, however slight: either to sight or to touch there is always an additional something which attracts us even though we may not perceive it.

Similarly if anyone would postulate a cord, equally strong throughout its length, it is impossible, quite impossible, that it should break. For where would you want it to start to fray? And it is not in nature for it all to break at once.

Then if anyone were to follow that up with those geometrical propositions which demonstrate by convincing demonstrations that the container is greater than the thing contained and that the center is as great as the circumference, and which can find two lines which ever approach each other but can never meet and then with the philosopher's stone and the squaring of the circle, where reason and practice are so opposed, he would perhaps draw from them arguments to support the bold saying of Pliny: "*Solum certum nihil esse certi, et homine nihil miserius aut superbius.*" [There is nothing certain except that nothing is certain, and nothing more wretched than Man nor more arrogant.][2]

---

[1] The dilemma of Buridan's ass: it starved to death when equidistant from identical food. [Footnote provided by translator.]

[2] A saying of Pliny's (*Hist. nat.*, II, vii) which Montaigne inscribed in his library; until [C] he translated it in his text.

COMME NOSTRE ESPRIT S'EMPESCHE SOY-MESMES

Michel de Montaigne

C'est une plaisante imagination de concevoir un esprit balancé justement entre-deux pareilles envyes. Car il est indubitable qu'il ne prendra jamais party, d'autant que l'application et le chois porte inequalité de pris; et qui nous logeroit entre la bouteille et le jambon, avec egal appetit de boire et de menger, il n'y auroit sans doute remede que de mourir de soif et de fain.

Pour pourvoir à cet inconvenient, les Stoïciens, quand on leur demande d'où vient en nostre ame l'election de deux choses indifferentes, et qui faict que d'un grand nombre d'escus nous en prenions plustost l'un que l'autre, estans tous pareils, et n'y ayans aucune raison qui nous incline à la preference, respondent que ce mouvement de l'ame est extraordinaire et déreglé, venant en nous d'une impulsion estrangiere, accidentale et fortuite.

Il se pourroit dire, ce me semble, plustost, que aucune chose ne se presente à nous où il n'y ait quelque difference, pour legiere qu'elle soit; et que, ou à la veue ou à l'atouchement, il y a tousjours quelque plus qui nous attire, quoy que ce soit imperceptiblement.

Pareillement qui presupposera une fisselle egalement forte par tout, il est impossible de toute impossibilité qu'elle rompe; car par où voulez vous que la faucée commence? et de rompre par tout ensemble, il n'est pas en nature.

Qui joindroit encore à cecy les propositions Geometriques qui concluent par la certitude de leurs demonstrations le contenu plus grand que le contenant, le centre aussi grand que sa circonference, et qui trouvent deux lignes s'approchant sans cesse l'une de l'autre et ne se pouvant jamais joindre, et la pierre philosophale, et quadrature du cercle, où la raison et l'effect sont si opposites, en tireroit à l'adventure quelque argument pour secourir ce mot hardy de Pline, *solum certum nihil esse certi, et homine nihil miserius aut superbius.*

WHAT IS EDUCATION FOR?

Danielle Allen

In 2006, the highest court in New York affirmed that students in the state have a right to civic education. It was a decision thirteen years in the making, and it spoke to a fundamental question: What is an education for? Lawyers representing the Campaign for Fiscal Equity (CFE), which brought suit, argued that the purpose of education is to develop not only vocational capacities, but also civic agency. Students, in other words, are entitled to learn in public schools the "basic literacy, calculating, and verbal skills necessary to enable children to eventually function productively as civic participants capable of voting and serving on a jury."

The state, in the position of defendant, did not disagree with the need for civic education. But it argued that once students had completed eighth grade, the public schools had met their responsibility to enable children "to eventually function productively as civic participants." Not coincidentally, the state argued that this education level was adequate preparation for minimum-wage labor.

CFE disagreed, arguing that the standard should be set higher. "Capable" civic participation, Judge Leland DeGrasse finally ruled, includes, for instance, the ability to make sense of complex ballot propositions and follow argumentation about DNA evidence at trial. The court agreed that "meaningful civic participation" and prospects for "competitive employment," not simply minimum-wage employment, demanded a twelfth-grade level of verbal and math skills and similarly advanced competence in social studies and economics. The court ordered New York City to increase school funding with these goals in mind.

In part because of the Great Recession, the state and city failed to deliver, and a new lawsuit is underway. But the economic downturn cannot be blamed for the fact that citizenship remains effectively absent from discussions of education policy, not only in New York but also generally. The dominant policy paradigm attends almost exclusively to education's vocational purpose: the goal is to ensure that young people, and society generally, can compete in a global economy. This view is tightly

connected to a technocratic economic policy that focuses on the dissemination of skills as a way to reduce inequality in a technology-dependent
economy. The result has been massively increased investment in science,
technology, engineering, and mathematics education—STEM—and
correspondingly reduced outlays for the humanities.

Yet this is not the only possible response to contemporary inequalities. As economists such as Dani Rodrik have pointed out, gross economic inequalities do not result from an inexorable forward march of
technology or globalization or from the nature of markets. They are
products of policy choices, which are themselves the outcome of politics. "Inequality," as Joseph Stiglitz argues in *Rewriting the Rules of the
American Economy* (2015), "has been a choice." Achieving an economy
with more egalitarian outcomes will require different political choices
and economic policies. It will require that we choose different rules to
govern labor, housing, and financial markets.

Where does education enter the picture? At the most fundamental
level.

When we think about education and equality, we tend to think first
about distributive questions—for example, how to design a system
that will offer the real possibility of equal educational attainment, if
not achievement, to all students. The vocational approach imagines
that this equal attainment will translate into a wider distribution of
skills, which will reduce income inequality.

The civic conception of education suggests a very different way to
understand the link between education and equality. This understanding begins with the recognition that fair economic outcomes are aided
by a robust democratic process and, therefore, by genuine political
equality. Thus an education focused not merely on technical skills, but
also on what I call *participatory readiness*, provides a distinct and better
way to promote equality through schooling.

Moreover, the aspiration to educate for civic participation and not
merely work has important distributive implications. The participatory
paradigm demands a higher educational standard than the vocational,
and meeting that standard requires that more resources be allocated
for schools.

It should not be necessary to argue for a vigorous public commitment to civic education in our society. The vast majority of state

constitutions include a right to education tied either explicitly or through legislative history to a civic purpose. In addition, as scholar and litigator Michael Rebell writes, twenty-four state courts "have explicitly held that preparation for capable citizenship is a primary purpose of public education, and no state court has disputed this proposition."

And yet, the argument for civic education is now indispensable. To see why, we should begin by exploring more deeply how the vocational paradigm arose and why it can neither vindicate our rights nor overcome the challenge of inequality.

EQUALITY AND THE VOCATIONAL PARADIGM

The language of work and global competitiveness did not always dominate public conversations about education. Its recent ascendancy can be traced to 1957. The Soviet launch of Sputnik, the first satellite, provoked a sense that the United States was falling behind in a Cold War scientific contest. The response was the National Defense Education Act, signed into law in 1958, which increased funding for science and math education, as well as vocational training. The 1983 Reagan administration report *A Nation at Risk* deepened the country's anxiety: "If an unfriendly foreign power had attempted to impose on America the mediocre educational performance that exists today, we might well have viewed it as an act of war," reads one provocative sentence. Although its data were later debunked, *A Nation at Risk* is generally understood to have kicked off the era of school reform that currently shapes education discussion and policy. Tellingly, the commission that produced the report held hearings on "Science, Mathematics, and Technology Education" and "Education for a Productive Role in a Productive Society," but none concerning the humanities, social sciences, or civic education.

By 2007, when the National Academy of Sciences' *Rising above the Gathering Storm* again emphasized the need for significant improvements in science and technology education, these disciplines had already been consolidated under the umbrella of STEM, a concept that has been employed with equal gusto by education reformers and politicians. "An educated, innovative, motivated workforce — human capital — is the most precious resource of any country in this new, flat world," the report asserts. "Yet there is widespread concern about our K–12 science and mathematics education system, the foundation of that human capital in today's global economy."

Consensus thus emerged in the 1980s around vocational education's essential role in global economic competitiveness. At the same time, economists drew closer connections between education and inequality. By the early 1990s, economists had identified technological change, which biased available jobs toward high-skilled workers, as the primary culprit. It was a short step from this diagnosis to the argument that education was the remedy. That was the lesson of Claudia Goldin and Larry Katz's important book on *The Race between Education and Technology* (2008). In *Capital in the Twenty-First Century* (2014), French economist Thomas Piketty writes, "Historical experience suggests that the principal mechanism for convergence [of incomes and wealth] at the international as well as the domestic level is the diffusion of knowledge. In other words, the poor catch up with the rich to the extent that they achieve the same level of technological know-how, skill, and education." Broad dissemination of skills is expected to drive down the wage premium on expertise and compress the income distribution. To the degree that Piketty's recommendations turn to educational policy, he focuses on access. When he considers curriculum, he is explicit only about vocational goals. Thus he argues that educational institutions should be made broadly accessible; elite institutions, which serve mainly privileged youth from the highest income brackets, should draw students from other backgrounds; schools should be run efficiently; and states should increase investment in "high-quality professional training."

Such arguments from economists — that vocationalism generally and STEM in particular are the solutions both for inequality and for America's ostensibly precarious global economic standing — have been widely adopted at the highest levels of government. President Obama, in his 2013 State of the Union address, announced a competition to "redesign America's high schools." Rewards would go, he said, to schools that develop more classes "that focus on science, technology, engineering, and math — the skills today's employers are looking for to fill jobs right now and in the future." More recently, in his 2016 State of the Union address, the president announced a Computer Science for All initiative that would make students "job-ready on day one."

Today, these technologically oriented, vocational approaches to education and the problem of inequality leave almost no room for the civic alternative. It is not that civic education is incompatible with professional training, but policymakers, education specialists, and many parents—including low-income parents, whose children are most likely to see their civic education shortchanged—have narrowed their focus exclusively to the economic field. In the process, they have lost sight of the full range of inequalities from which our society suffers and which well-rounded education could alleviate.

EQUALITY AND THE PARTICIPATORY PARADIGM

When we invoke the concept of equality in conversations about education, we generally don't bother to define it or to identify which concept of equality pertains. Is it political equality that concerns us? Social equality? Or economic equality only?

The technology-based analysis of inequality and the vocational paradigm focuses specifically on economic equality. Questions of political equality have no place in this picture. Indeed, the purely technocratic treatment of income and wealth inequality as problems of technology to be solved through the dissemination of skills is blind precisely to politics.

This is shortsighted because economic inequality is an outgrowth of politics. "Today's world economy is the product of explicit decisions that governments had made in the past," Rodrik writes. "It was the choice of governments to loosen regulations on finance and aim for full cross-border capital mobility, just as it was a choice to maintain these policies largely intact, despite a massive global financial crisis." Or, as Daron Acemoğlu and Jim Robinson argue, "It is the institutions and the political equilibrium of a society that determine how technology evolves, how markets function, and how the gains from various different economic arrangements are distributed."

Piketty agrees that the wage premium on skill can explain only part of growing US income inequality: political forces shape distributive outcomes, and there are limits to how much the advantages of education can be moderated through the dissemination of technological skills. Income growth at the highest end, accruing to what he calls "supermanagers," reflects social acceptance of sky-high executive pay. In his argument, such social norms constitute and reinforce a political ideology endorsing "hypermeritocracy." Reining in income inequality therefore requires not only the dissemination of skill but also social and political change. If political choices determine the rules that shape distributive patterns, it makes sense to focus first on political, not economic, equality. And if we choose political equality as our orienting ideal—empowering all to participate capably in the life of a polity—a different view of education's purpose, content, and consequence comes into view.

In an important 2006 paper, "Why Does Democracy Need Education?" economists Edward L. Glaeser, Giacomo Ponzetto, and Andrei Shleifer argue that education is a causal force behind democracy. Specifically, they point to the relationship between education and participation, considering three hypotheses for why the former might be a source of the latter: through indoctrination, through the cultivation of skills that facilitate participation (reading and writing and "soft skills" of collaboration and interaction), and through the increased material benefits of participation. (On the last, the idea is that education increases income, and participation correlates to socioeconomic status.) The authors reject the first and third hypotheses in favor of the second. Education, they argue, fosters participation because it prepares people for democratic engagement. Reading, writing, and collaboration are, after all, the basic instruments of political action.

An education that prepares every student for civic and political engagement not only supports political equality but may also lead to increased economic fairness. As Acemoğlu and Robinson argue, the expansion of political participation drove egalitarian economic reforms in Britain in the nineteenth century and the United States in the early twentieth. We are currently seeing a resurgence of participation on both the right and left. These movements, dubbed populist by many commentators, are putting issues of distributive justice on the agenda once again.

This resurgence increases the stakes for participatory readiness. It also raises the question of how best to prepare students for their lives as civic agents. While the technological view of the link between education and equality reinforces a vocational approach to curriculum and pedagogy, a participatory view demands a renewed focus on the humanities and social sciences.

PARTICIPATORY READINESS

So what exactly is participatory readiness, and how can education help people achieve it? To answer these questions, we first need to understand what students should be getting ready for: civic agency. While there is no single model of civic agency dominant in American culture, we can identify a handful at work.

Following philosopher Hannah Arendt, I take citizenship to be the activity of co-creating a way of life, of world-building. This co-creation can occur at many social levels: in a neighborhood or school; in a networked community or association; in a city, state, or nation; at a global scale. Because co-creation extends beyond legal categories of membership in political units, I prefer to speak of civic agency instead of citizenship.

Such civic agency involves three core tasks. First is disinterested deliberation around a public problem. Here the model derives from Athenian citizens gathered in the assembly, the town halls of colonial New Hampshire, and public representatives behaving reasonably in the halls of a legislature. Second is prophetic work intended to shift a society's values; in the public opinion and communications literature, this is now called "frame shifting." Think of the rhetorical power of nineteenth-century abolitionist Harriet Beecher Stowe, of Martin Luther King Jr., or of Occupy Wall Street activists with their rallying cry of "we are the 99 percent." Finally, there is transparently interested "fair fighting," where a given public actor adopts a cause and pursues it passionately. One might think of early women's rights activists such as Elizabeth Cady Stanton, Susan B. Anthony, and Matilda Joslyn Gage.

The ideal civic agent carries out all three of these tasks—disinterested deliberation, prophetic frame shifting, and fair fighting—ethically and justly. Stanton is an example of this ideal at work. At the Seneca Falls Convention, she was in deliberative mode for the debate about the text of the Declaration of Sentiments. However, before the convention's deliberations, when she drafted that text, she was in the prophetic mode, just as she was in her innumerable speeches. Finally, in campaigning for legal change, as in the adoption of the Woman's Property Bill in New York and similar laws in other states, she was operating as an activist.

Yet if these three are the rudimentary components of civic agency, they do not in themselves determine the content of any given historical moment's conception of citizenship. There is no need for each of these functions to be combined in a single role or persona, nor is there any guarantee that all three will be carried out in each historical context. These tasks can also become separated from one another, generating distinguishable kinds of civic roles. This is the situation today, as roles have been divided among civically engaged individuals, activists or political entrepreneurs, and professional politicians.

The civically engaged individual focuses on the task of disinterested deliberation and actions that can be said to flow from it. Such citizens pursue what they perceive to be universal values, critical thinking, and bipartisan projects. Next comes the activist, who seeks to change hearts and minds by fighting fairly for particular outcomes, often making considerable sacrifices to do so. Finally, the professional politician, as currently conceived, focuses mainly on fighting, not necessarily fairly. In contemporary discourse, this role, in contrast to the other two, represents a degraded form of civic agency; for evidence one has only to look at Congress's all-time-low approval ratings.

In the current condition, we have lost sight of the statesman, a professional politician capable of disinterested deliberation, just frame shifting, and fighting fair. And, even more importantly, we have lost sight of the ideal ordinary citizen, who is not a professional politician but who has nonetheless developed all of the competencies described above and who is proud to be involved in politics.

If we are to embrace an education for participatory readiness, we need to aim our pedagogic and curricular work not at any one of these three capacities but at what lies behind all of them: the idea of civic agency as the activity of co-creating a way of life. This view of politics supports all three models of citizenship because it nourishes future civic leaders, activists, and politicians. Such an education ought also to permit a reintegration of these roles.

The United States has a history of providing such an education: it is called the liberal arts. How, you may ask, can the seemingly antique liberal arts be of use in our mass democracies and globalized, multi-cultural world? Let us consider where we find ourselves and how we got here.

Science, technology, engineering, math, and medicine have done much to create the contemporary condition. Thanks to the industrial, aeronautical, biomedical, and digital revolutions, the world's population has grown from one to seven billion in little more than 200 years, a profound historical transformation. We surely need the STEM fields to navigate this new landscape. But if the STEM fields gave us the mass in "mass democracy," the humanities and social sciences gave us the democracy.

The Europeans and American colonists who designed systems of representative democracy capable of achieving continental scale — while employing genocidal techniques in the process — were broadly and deeply educated in history, geography, philosophy, literature, and art. The pithiest summary of the intellectual demands of democratic citizenship that I know appears in the second sentence of the Declaration of Independence, especially the final clause:

> We hold these truths to be self-evident, that all men are created equal; that they are endowed by their Creator with certain unalienable Rights; that among these are Life, Liberty and the pursuit of Happiness—That to secure these Rights, Governments are instituted among Men, deriving their just Powers from the Consent of the Governed; *that whenever any Form of Government becomes destructive of these Ends, it is the Right of the People to alter or to abolish it, and to institute new Government, laying its Foundation on such Principles and organizing its Powers in such Form, as to them shall seem most likely to effect their Safety and Happiness.*

This final clause summarizes the central intellectual labor of the democratic citizen. Citizens must judge whether their governments meet their responsibility, spelled out earlier in the sentence, to secure rights. If a government fails in its core purposes, it is the job of the citizen to figure this out and decide how to change direction. This requires diagnosing social circumstances and making judgments about grounding principles for the political order and about possible alternatives to the formal organization of state power. Properly conducted, the citizen's intellectual labor should result in a probabilistic judgment answering this critical question: What combination of principle and organizational form is most likely to secure collective safety and happiness?

To make judgments about the course of human events and our government's role in them, we need history, anthropology, cultural studies, economics, political science, sociology, and psychology, not to mention math—especially the statistical reasoning necessary for probabilistic judgment—and science, as governmental policy naturally intersects with scientific questions. If we are to decide on the core principles that should orient our judgments about what will bring about safety and happiness, surely we need philosophy, literature, and religion or its history. Then, since the democratic citizen does not make or execute judgments alone, we need the arts of conversation, eloquence, and prophetic speech. Preparing ourselves to exercise these arts takes us again to literature and to the visual arts, film, and music.

In other words, we need the liberal arts. They were called the free person's arts for a reason.

To say that we need all these disciplines in order to cultivate participatory readiness is not to say that we need precisely the versions of these disciplines that existed in the late eighteenth century. To the contrary, it is the job of today's scholars and teachers, learning from the successes and errors of our predecessors, to build the most powerful intellectual tools we can. Where their versions of the tools were compatible with preserving patriarchy, enslaving black Africans, and committing genocide against indigenous peoples, ours must not be. This revision of the liberal arts curriculum is controversial but necessary, for we want to retain the purposes and intellectual methods of the liberal arts, if not all of its content. We still need to cultivate capacities for social diagnosis, ethical reasoning, cause-and-effect analysis, and persuasive argumentation.

Given that the liberal arts are especially useful for training citizens, it should come as little surprise that attainment in the humanities and social sciences appears to correlate with increased engagement in politics. There is a statistically significant difference between the rates of political participation among humanities and STEM graduates. Data from the Department of Education reveal that, among 2008 college graduates, 92.8 percent of humanities majors have voted at least once since finishing school. Among STEM majors, that number is 83.5 percent. And, within ten years of graduation, 44.1 percent of 1993 humanities graduates had written to public officials, compared to 30.1 percent of STEM majors. As college graduates, the students are generally of similar socioeconomic backgrounds, suggesting that other distinctions must account for the difference in political engagement.

Of course, the self-selection of students into the humanities and STEM majors may mean that these data reflect only underlying features of the students rather than the effects of teaching they receive. Yet the same pattern appears in a study by political scientist Sunshine Hillygus, which controls for students' preexisting levels of interest in politics.

Hillygus also finds that the differences in political engagement among college graduates are mirrored in K–12 education. High SAT verbal scores correlate with increased likelihood of political participation, while high SAT math scores correlate with decreased likelihood of participation. Again, since socioeconomic effects on SAT scores move both verbal and math scores in the same direction, this difference between how high verbal and high math scores affect the likelihood of participation must be telling us something about the relationship between attainment in specific subject domains and participatory readiness. Moreover, the SAT effect endures even when college-level curricular choices are controlled for. Just as Glaeser, Ponzetto, and Shleifer conclude, it is attainment in the verbal domain that correlates with participatory readiness.

To identify a correlation is not, of course, to identify, let alone prove, causation. But those with more sophisticated verbal skills and with more skills at socio-political analysis are clearly more ready to participate in civic life. Another source of motivation may have engaged them in politics, leading them, once engaged, to seek out the verbal and analytical skills needed to thrive as civic participants. Or verbal competence and social analytical skills may make engagement easier in the first place. We don't have a study that considers levels of engagement before and after significant increases in these kinds of competence. Nonetheless, data suggest that the work of the humanities and social sciences on verbal empowerment and social analysis is intrinsically related to the development of participatory readiness. The riches of the liberal arts of course extend well beyond verbal empowerment and social analysis, but these core activities are themselves of immense value. Such equality as the world has managed to achieve — whether political or economic — can often be traced to the operations of these human capacities.

. . . . .

Few among us pay adequate attention to the fact that almost all of our state constitutions guarantee a right to education. We pay even less attention to the fact that we have a right to civic education. Our state constitutions, in other words, are directed at the pursuit of equality. Through the acquisition of participatory readiness, a great diversity of citizens could tap into the power to challenge oligarchical social and political arrangements.

In the final analysis, the reliance on an exclusively vocational paradigm as the sole guide to education policy-making is a failure to meet the legal standard for securing a basic right. Precisely those parts of the K–12 curriculum most vulnerable during a recession — humanities, social studies, arts, and extracurricular activities such as debate and model UN — deserve rights-based legal protection. What is more, defending the right to civic education, and the kind of curriculum that delivers it, would benefit not only individual students but also society as a whole, advancing both political equality and distributive justice. This is an untapped source of advocacy around educational rights and on behalf of an egalitarian America.

THE EDGE OF IDENTITY

Rachel Aviv

Hannah Upp had been missing for nearly two weeks when she was seen at the Apple Store in midtown Manhattan. Her friends, most of them her former classmates from Bryn Mawr, had posted a thousand flyers about her disappearance on signposts and at subway stations and bus stops. It was September, 2008, and Hannah, a middle-school teacher at Thurgood Marshall Academy, a public school in Harlem, hadn't shown up for the first day of school. Her roommate had found her wallet, passport, MetroCard, and cell phone in her purse, on the floor of her bedroom. The *News* reported, "Teacher, 23, Disappears Into Thin Air."

A detective asked Hannah's mother, Barbara Bellus, to come to the Thirtieth Precinct, in Harlem, to view the Apple Store surveillance footage. Barbara watched a woman wearing a sports bra and running shorts, her brown hair pulled into a high ponytail, ascend the staircase in the store. A man stopped her and asked if she was the missing teacher in the news. Barbara said, "I could see her blow off what he was saying, and I knew instantly it was her—it was all her. She has this characteristic gesture. It's, like, 'Oh, no, no, don't you worry. You know me, I'm fine.'" Another camera had captured Hannah using one of the store's laptops to log in to her Gmail account. She looked at the screen for a second before walking away.

The sighting was celebrated by Hannah's friends, many of whom were camping out at her apartment. They made maps of the city's parks, splitting them into quadrants, and sent groups to look in the woods and on running paths and under benches.

According to the Myers-Briggs personality test, which Hannah often referenced, she was an E.N.F.P.: Extraverted Intuitive Feeling Perceiving, a personality type that describes exuberant idealists looking for deeper meaning and connection. Five of her friends used the same phrase when describing her: "She lights up the room." A friend told the *News* reporter, "Everyone you talk to is going to say she is their closest friend. She has no barriers. She was raised to trust and care for everyone, and she did."

Two days after Hannah was seen at the Apple Store, she was spotted at a Starbucks in SoHo. By the time the police arrived, she had walked out the back door. The police recorded sightings of her at five New York Sports Clubs, all of them near midtown, where the detective on the case presumed she had gone to shower. In an article about her disappearance, the *Times* wrote, "It was as if the city had simply opened wide and swallowed her whole."

On September 16th, the twentieth day she'd been missing, the captain of a Staten Island ferry saw a woman's body bobbing in the water near Robbins Reef, a rocky outcropping with a lighthouse south of the Statue of Liberty. Two deckhands steered a rescue boat toward the body, which was floating face down. "I honestly thought she was dead," one of the men said. A deckhand lifted her ankles, and the other picked up her shoulders. She took a gasp of air and began crying.

The woman was taken to Richmond University Medical Center, on Staten Island. For three weeks, her own biography had been inaccessible to her, but when the medical staff asked her questions she was suddenly able to tell them that her name was Hannah and to give them her mother's phone number. Barbara arrived within an hour. (Hannah's father was living in India, where he taught at a seminary; her brother, a Navy officer, was stationed in Japan.) Barbara said that Hannah looked "both sunburned and pale, like she'd been pulled behind a boat for three weeks." The first thing she said was "Why am I wet?"

She was treated for hypothermia, dehydration, and a severe sunburn on the left side of her body, and her condition rapidly improved. Four friends came to the hospital that afternoon. Manuel Ramirez, her roommate, said, "She saw me and smiled and said something like 'I hope they release me soon, because I have to set up my classroom.' She clearly didn't get that three weeks had passed."

Later that day, the police interviewed Hannah privately. Barbara stood outside the room. "I could hear her trying to respond to their questions—she was really working at it, trying to give them what they wanted—but she didn't have any explanation." Her last memory was of taking a run in Riverside Park, near her apartment, the day that she went missing.

Barbara, a United Methodist pastor, slept in a chair beside Hannah's hospital bed. In the middle of the night, Hannah jolted awake. "I was at a lighthouse," she said, then immediately fell asleep again. In the morning, when Barbara asked about the lighthouse, Hannah said that she had no memory of it.

. . . . .

Hannah was transferred to a psychiatric unit run by Columbia University Medical Center. She underwent a series of brain-imaging tests, but the doctors couldn't find any neurological condition that would cause her to forget her identity. They concluded that the episode was psychological in nature. As soon as she was lifted from the river, she remembered all the details of her life prior to her disappearance.

She was given a diagnosis of dissociative fugue, a rare condition in which people lose access to their autobiographical memory and personal identity, occasionally adopting a new one, and may abruptly embark on a long journey. The state is typically triggered by trauma — often sexual or physical abuse, a combat experience, or exposure to a natural disaster — or by an unbearable internal conflict. Philippe Tissié, one of the first psychiatrists to study fugue, characterized it as a kind of self-exile. In 1901, he wrote, "The legend of the Wandering Jew has become a reality, proved by numerous observations of patients or unbalanced persons who suffer from an imperious need to walk, on and on."

Hannah was hypnotized, to see if she could recall a traumatic event that triggered her fugue, but she couldn't remember anything unusual. Hannah and her mother, father, and brother said that as a young child she hadn't endured anything that they considered trauma. Hannah's roommate, Ramirez, said that, when he visited her on the psychiatric unit, "she was her normal, upbeat, funny self. I remember her rattling off all these possibilities: 'Was I in a hit-and-run? Was I mugged? Was I assaulted?'" The beginning of the school year was always stressful — her students struggled with problems, such as hunger and unstable housing, that she couldn't address within the confines of her classroom — but her colleagues had the same dilemmas.

In the hospital, Hannah read the news articles about her disappearance and the comments from readers, some of whom accused her of staging it. She was so embarrassed that she contemplated changing her name. But, her friend Piyali Bhattacharya said, "she ultimately decided—and she was very clear on this—that she did not want to run away from who Hannah Upp was."

One of the psychiatrists on Columbia's psychiatric unit, Aaron Krasner, now a professor of clinical psychiatry at Yale, described the comments in the news as "very condemning and discrediting. I think this speaks to the rage that dissociative conditions incur in certain people. There is an ineffable quality to dissociative cases. They challenge a conventional understanding of reality." He told me that he was troubled by the narrowness of medical literature on these states; there are no medications that specifically target the problem. "Dissociative fugue is the rare bird of dissociation, but dissociation as a phenomenon is very common," he said. "I think as a field we have not done our due diligence, in part because the phenomenon is so frightening. It's terrifying to think that we are all vulnerable to a lapse in selfhood."

. . . . .

Freud explored dissociative states in his early writings, but the phenomenon did not fit easily into his sweeping theory of human behavior. Most of the dissociative patients he saw said that they had been sexually abused as children, but he ultimately concluded that their memories were fantasies. He proposed that unacceptable wishes were repressed into the unconscious, and that traces of them resurfaced in people's fantasy lives. Theorists of dissociation disagreed, arguing that some events were so traumatic that, afterward, the mind was unable to develop as an integrated whole. The French philosopher and psychologist Pierre Janet, who developed the first formal theory of dissociation, in 1889, wrote, "Personal unity, identity, and initiative are not primitive characteristics of psychological life. They are incomplete results acquired with difficulty after long work, and they remain very fragile." After Freud's success, Janet's work fell into obscurity.

Cases of dissociation had a whiff of the mystical, and doctors tended to stay away from them. Dozens of articles from the turn of the twentieth century, published in the *Times*, recount miraculous, inexplicable transformations: a Minnesota reverend, missing for a month, realized that he had traveled across the county and enlisted in the Navy, "though never before in his life had he even gazed on the ocean"; a professor thought to have drowned was discovered, three years later, using a new name and working as a dishwasher; a deacon in New Jersey woke up and "realized the room he has occupied for more than a year was strange to him" and his Bible was marked with someone else's name. He had been missing for four years.

The most famous American fugue patient was Ansel Bourne, a preacher who, in 1887, left his home in Rhode Island with a vague sense that he had fallen from "the path of duty." He traveled to Norristown, Pennsylvania, two hundred and forty miles away, and opened a shop selling stationery and candy. He went by the name Albert Brown. His neighbors found his behavior perfectly normal. Two months after leaving home, he knocked on his landlord's door and asked, "Where am I?"

The philosopher and psychologist William James offered to treat him by using hypnosis to "run the two personalities into one, and make the memories continuous." But the two identities could not be merged. Bourne returned to his wife in Rhode Island with almost no memories of his life as Albert. In an essay that James wrote shortly before treating Bourne, he argued that science would advance more rapidly if more attention were devoted to unclassifiable cases—"wild facts" that threaten a "closed and completed system of truth." Understanding splits in consciousness, he wrote, is "of the most urgent importance for the comprehension of our nature."

But, in the decades after Bourne's disappearance, the study of dissociation largely vanished. The prevailing schools in psychology and psychiatry—behaviorism and psychoanalysis—adopted models of the mind that were incompatible with the concept. Then, in the nineteen-eighties, several thousand people claimed that, having been abused as children, they had developed multiple selves. The public responded to these stories much as it had to the surge of dissociative cases at the turn of the century: this sort of mental experience was considered too eerie and counterintuitive to believe. Whatever truth there was to the condition was lost as hyperbolic stories circulated in the media: tales of feuding selves and elaborate acts of sexual abuse, such as torture by satanic cults. The legacy of that time is that people with similarly radical alterations of self are viewed with distrust.

Richard Loewenstein, the medical director of the Trauma Disorders Program at Sheppard Pratt, in Towson, Maryland, may have worked with more fugue patients than any other psychiatrist in the country. He said that modern psychiatry and psychology still fail to "pay much attention to the self or to the complexities of subjectivity." When he encounters people in fugues, often in emergency rooms, he finds it nearly impossible to treat them in that state. He said that, in conversation, "there's a quality of them running away from whatever you are trying to ask them. If you begin to hold on to them and try to get them to stay in one place, they go—they're gone."

.   .   .   .   .

The first time I spoke with Hannah's mother, early this year, she told me it was important that an article about her daughter's experience "let it stay a mystery." She felt that Hannah's condition lay at the "edges of knowledge," and she didn't want to impose false connections. The more she read about fugue, the less she felt she understood it. Hannah's father, David Upp, wrote in an email, "I suspect they will need a new paradigm, before Fugues can fit ANY theories." He suggested that "magical realism comes closer" than any current psychological theory, and said that one of Hannah's favorite authors is Isabel Allende. "Perhaps a book like 'El Plan Infinito'?" he wrote. The book's hero spends decades wrestling with the teachings of his father, who, like Upp, became an itinerant preacher.

As a child, Hannah was "the princess of her church," as a friend described her. She grew up in Japanese-American churches in Oregon, where her parents served as pastors. (Both of her parents are American, but Barbara taught in Japan and is fluent in Japanese.) When she was young, her parents' perspectives on theology sharply diverged. Upp characterized himself with the phrase *homo unius libri*, "man of the one book." In monthly newsletters sent to colleagues, congregants, and friends, he argued that "there is no such human as a natural homosexual." He urged his readers to "fully support Biblical Morality and to oppose any compromise with sexual deviance/perversion."

Barbara filed for divorce when Hannah was fifteen. Upp moved abroad and taught the Gospel, often to indigenous tribes, in Fiji, Palau, Guam, Malta, India, Zimbabwe, Guyana, and the Philippines, where he now lives in a one-room house in a remote village. In 2007, Barbara took a leave from her position as a pastor and moved to Pendle Hill, a Quaker retreat outside Philadelphia. She and Upp stopped speaking to each other.

Hannah was a creationist when she arrived at Bryn Mawr, and she joined the InterVarsity Christian Fellowship, an evangelical campus ministry. Her friend Piyali Bhattacharya, who was raised Hindu, once asked Hannah, "Do you think I'm going to Hell?" She said that Hannah began crying. "Hannah lost it. She couldn't answer the question. Whereas another person might try to defend her beliefs, Hannah is the kind of person who would take a question like that and turn it in on herself and think about it and come out the other end being a different person." Bhattacharya went on, "She knew she was loving and openhearted, but beyond that I think she had zero idea of who she actually was. She wanted to give herself over to someone or some idea."

In the spring of her sophomore year, Barbara said, Hannah called her, crying, after going to a talk by Beth Stroud, a United Methodist minister who was defrocked after telling her congregation that she was in a relationship with a woman. "Hannah was troubled that something that she'd thought was part of her faith was cruel," Barbara said. By her junior year, Hannah was dating a woman.

Although she found herself drawn to Quakerism, she still traveled with her father at least once a year in whatever part of the world he was teaching. Her friend Hannah Wood wondered what it meant for Hannah to "swallow a part of herself down while she was traveling," but Hannah always spoke fondly of her father. Her friends liked to joke that she resided in "Hannah Land." Her friend Amy Scott said, "She lives in this separate place where there are butterflies and birds, and they follow her around. Everything is good and everyone is happy, and there's no conflict, ever."

. . . . .

Hannah thought that her fugue may have begun with a liminal phase: there were two days when she slept in her apartment but communicated with no one. Her bank records showed that she had gone to a movie in Times Square which she had no memory of seeing.

During the weeks that Hannah spent wandering, her family believes that she understood on some level that people were searching for her. "She characterized her recollections of that time as just being continually roaming," her brother Dan said. "We think that maybe she had this sense that she was being hunted and didn't know why."

A few months before her disappearance, Hannah and a friend had gone to a meeting for "freegans," a group that tries to minimize its consumption of resources, and they'd visited grocery stores on the Upper East Side, collecting discarded food. Dan said that the family believed Hannah "remembered what she'd learned on the tour and was eating perfectly good food that the stores were not able to legally sell the next day. She seemed to have access to those memories. Even if she didn't understand why at that time, she gravitated to places that were familiar."

Dan met with the captain of the Staten Island ferry and analyzed the currents in the Hudson River. They surmised that Hannah must have entered the river in lower Manhattan before the tide took her south. Hannah and Dan walked along the piers downtown, and when they got to Pier 40, a former marine terminal on the west end of Houston Street, Hannah told him that the place felt familiar. She remembered lights floating on the water.

Dan learned that there had been a Japanese floating-lantern ceremony on the pier on September 11th, to honor the victims of the World Trade Center attacks. As a child, Hannah had danced in an annual Obon festival, which has a floating-lantern ceremony, the lights representing the souls of the departed. Barbara said, "Something about that powerful ritual registered."

Based on the condition of her body the day she was found, she and her family concluded that she had been at the floating-lantern ceremony and, three days later, had returned to the pier and entered the water. Barbara said, "Maybe when Hannah was getting alarmed or upset because people kept saying her name, it felt more comfortable to go back to that place."

It is likely that Hannah spent the night in the river. She later checked the lunar calendar and was able to confirm her memory that there had been a full moon that night. Her skin showed signs of prolonged immersion. Barbara said that Hannah vaguely remembered "holding on to the hull of a barge—she may have wanted some rest—and then she realized that she was being sucked toward the propeller, which is a very dangerous thing, so she swam away." It was as if her body, undirected by what we typically conceive of as consciousness, were still intent on survival.

Hannah and her family concluded that she either swam to or was washed up onto Robbins Reef. She scraped her knees on its rocks. She slept there the following day, long enough to get a sunburn. Then she returned to the water.

· · · · ·

Bhattacharya said that when she and Hannah spoke about the experience they often lapsed into silence. "It felt like the words we have in the English language were not sufficient to describe this," Bhattacharya said. Hannah saw a few therapists, but found conversations with her friends more helpful. She described the mental-health system as dogmatic and overly attached to its diagnostic models. She felt as if her experiences had to be reshaped to fit within the diagnoses. Barbara said that Hannah told her, "If people want to spend a lot more time figuring out what set this off, they can, but I'm not going to spend the rest of my life focusing on it." Barbara found the same tendencies within psychiatry as she had in the church: an emphasis on what she described as "the letter of the law, rather than the spirit of it." She didn't think it "left room for the reality of individual unique experience."

Hannah's fugue seemed to fit what Etzel Cardeña, a professor of psychology at Lund University, in Sweden, describes as "anomalous psychological experience." Cardeña has published a textbook on phenomena that "fall between the cracks of the house built by contemporary mainstream psychology." He told me, "In our culture, we have a nice narrative that personality is stable. That is a fiction. When a person enters a fugue and becomes someone else—or isn't there—it's an exaggerated version of the way we all are."

Cardeña has done research on altered states of consciousness in religious practice, and he found that some people who would otherwise be given a diagnosis of dissociative disorder have been able to channel their tendencies into rituals of spirit possession, trance, speaking in tongues, or intimate experiences of God. He said, "There is a cultural context for surrendering themselves. It's not about getting rid of the dissociative state so much as giving it a syntax, a coherence, a social function." In an article in the journal *Spiritus*, T. M. Luhrmann, a Stanford anthropologist who studies religion and psychiatry, suggests that there is a "shared psychological mechanism" in dissociation and evangelical worship: the capacity to withdraw from the everyday and become entirely absorbed by interior experience. "Trance-like responses to great distress have occurred throughout history and across culture," she writes.

Nearly all the medical literature suggests that people in fugue states adopt new identities, but Barbara said that, for Hannah, "it was more like the complete absence of identity," a kind of "dangerous nothingness." None of Hannah's friends or family had ever seen her in a fugue state, beyond the surveillance footage from the Apple Store. Barbara said, "Nothing we know indicates that she built a new identity—unless she did and it was lost when she came back."

David Spiegel, a professor of psychiatry at Stanford who has spent his career studying dissociation, told me that he'd never heard of someone navigating the world without something that resembles an identity. "It may be sparse, with far less structure or detail to it, but I don't know if you can be a functioning human without something that passes for a self," he said. "You need some kind of orientation for understanding who you are and what you are doing here."

. . . . .

A little more than a year after her disappearance, Hannah left New York, joining Barbara at Pendle Hill. Sometimes called Mecca for Quakers, the institution was founded in 1930 as a retreat for people of all religions. Hannah worked in the kitchen and attended daily meetings for worship, a half hour of silence.

Quaker practice operates according to the premise that a single person cannot see the entire truth, and the people at Pendle Hill never asked Hannah for answers about her disappearance. Patrick Roesle, an intern at Pendle Hill whom Hannah dated there, said that he viewed the episode as a "freak accident." He believed that "Hannah gives so much to other people that at a certain point there is literally nothing left, and she departs from herself." When friends had celebratory occasions or setbacks, however minor, she would write them cards by hand. To a friend at Pendle Hill who broke an arm, she wrote, "It's an honor to fold your laundry or crawl under your bed, for, you see, that's what community is all about!" Her friend Hannah Herklotz said that Hannah was so attentive to other people's needs that it sometimes felt impossible to reciprocate. "You'd come out of a two-hour conversation that you'd feel was incredibly deep, and you'd feel heard and known and seen, and then you'd realize later: she didn't tell me a thing about herself."

After working at Pendle Hill for three years, Hannah was hired as a teaching assistant at a Montessori school for underserved children in Kensington, Maryland. She was drawn to Maria Montessori's notion of an "education capable of saving humanity": by protecting the autonomy of children, society would become more loving, peaceful, and unified. Roesle said, "She flung herself—all of her weight—into learning Montessori, internalizing Montessori, loving Montessori."

On the morning of Hannah's first day of class, Barbara got a phone call from the police. They told her that Hannah's purse, wallet, and cell phone had been found on a wooded footpath in Kensington. A colleague reported that as she was driving to school she had seen Hannah walking quickly in the wrong direction. Hannah's mother and friends from Pendle Hill drove to Maryland and looked for her in the woods and put up flyers around town. They discovered that she hadn't slept at her apartment the night before. In the previous twenty-four hours, no one had talked to her.

The next day, at 10:30 P.M., Barbara received a call from an unknown number. "All she said was 'Mom?'" Barbara said. Hannah had found herself in a dirty creek in a residential area in Wheaton, Maryland, a mile and a half from her school. There was a shopping cart beside her. Barbara's housemate at the time, Jennifer Beer, recalled that Hannah "regathered herself instantly—it was sort of like her soul getting sucked back in." Hannah walked to the closest commercial area and borrowed a stranger's phone. She realized that she had been walking for more than two days.

Later, Hannah reviewed the text messages she'd sent the day that she disappeared. "We could see in the texts where she had made that transition," Barbara said. "She could remember sending some of the texts, but then there came a point where she said, 'I don't remember writing any of this.'"

Barbara said that after each fugue she felt a kind of "awe at where Hannah had been." The ancient Greeks had two words for time: *kronos*, chronological time, and *kairos*, which is often translated as "the right time" and cannot be measured. Barbara said, "I imagined her as having entered more fully into *kairos*—the appointed time, the fullness of time. There's a suspension of certainty."

Hannah's friends were struck by the similarities between her two disappearances. In both instances, she had disappeared at the beginning of the school year, after traveling with her father. David Upp had pondered whether the vacations had been a trigger for her, but he wasn't satisfied with that explanation. "Travel? That's just 'what we do,'" he wrote me. "Hannah and I have been to twenty-five nations together, so it is 'normal' not disruptive." In an article for *Bryn Mawr Now*, a campus newsletter, Hannah had once described the "violent surprise" and loneliness of returning home from a trip to Ghana. "I thought I was coming 'home,' but was surprised at the longing for a new place that had grown so comfortable," she wrote.

In both fugues, she had been drawn to water. Her friend Amy Scott said, "The way she describes it is she finds herself in a body of water and realizes who she is."

. . . . .

Hannah returned to her job within a few days. The following year, she was hired as a teaching assistant for preschoolers at a Montessori school in St. Thomas, in the US Virgin Islands. When she disclosed her condition, the administrators at the school were warm and accepting. She joked with friends that she was moving to paradise.

After the Maryland disappearance, Barbara said that friends asked her, "Couldn't you put a chip in her, like you would in a schnauzer?" The police in Maryland had proposed using the type of ankle bracelet designed for people who are under house arrest. "She didn't want to pursue it—she refused to be defined by this—and I chose to honor her decision," Barbara said. "I had to be clear that I'm not living my daughter's life—she's living it, and she needed to have the freedom to make choices."

Hannah moved to the east end of St. Thomas, away from the docks for cruise ships, which bring tens of thousands of tourists to the island every week. She could see the British Virgin Islands from the balcony of her apartment, which she called her "island palace." A parent of one of her students described her as a "modern-day Mary Poppins." The head of the school, Michael Bornn, said, "Whenever a parent showed up for a tour, we took them to Hannah's classroom."

After a year of teaching, the school paid for her to take summer classes at a Montessori training center in Portland, Oregon, so that she could eventually become certified and lead her own class. One of the school's directors, Norma Bolinger, said, "She totally absorbed the Montessori theory, to the point where I could see her becoming a mover and shaker in politics and trying to get Montessori into all schools globally." Hannah made a pilgrimage to Maria Montessori's grave, on the Dutch coast. Bhattacharya said, "It was Hannah's new church. There's a book; there are rules. If you follow the rules, good things happen to good people. Her desire to worship never left her."

In St. Thomas, she attended a few meetings devoted to the Bahá'í faith, a Persian religion that teaches the unity and equality of all people, but she was put off by what she saw as the community's negative judgment of nontraditional families. She saw a therapist on the island, but she put more stock in tending to her physical health. She swam in the ocean nearly every day, becoming so strong that she could reach cays more than two miles away. "She found the world underwater just so peaceful and so magical," Scott said. "Her solace was always the majesty of the island."

. . . . .

Hurricane Irma hit St. Thomas on September 6, 2017, a week after Hannah began her fourth year of teaching. That summer, she had completed her Montessori degree. She and her roommates huddled in the laundry room of their apartment. The wind reached a hundred and eighty-five miles an hour, shattering one of their windows. With each new gust, a power line, dislodged by the storm, smacked the roof.

The next morning, the island had turned brown, the trees stripped of their leaves. Suzanne Carlson, a reporter at the Virgin Islands *Daily News*, told me, "I heard a lot of people say, 'This is it—St. Thomas is over.'" Hannah texted friends that she was safe but the island was devastated. "I don't recognize anything," she wrote.

Since her 2008 fugue, Hannah's roommate from New York, Manuel Ramirez, had used a code phrase to check up on her. After her first disappearance, they had made fun of an ABC News story that characterized her as a "friendly vegetarian who constantly experimented with new dishes." After the storm, Ramirez texted her "friendly vegetarian." Hannah wrote back, "I like to try new dishes."

Six days after the storm, Hannah drove to the house of an ex-boyfriend, Joe Spallino, a scuba instructor, and saw that his belongings were gone. Hannah learned from his landlord that he had rushed to the marina to get on one of the "mercy ships" giving people free rides off the island. Hurricane Maria, another Category 5 storm, was forecast to hit the island the following week.

Hannah drove to the marina to say goodbye. Spallino was waiting to board a cruise ship to Puerto Rico, and they talked for several hours. Spallino said, "I kind of jokingly asked, 'What if you come along?' She thought about it and said that, in reality, she wouldn't want to."

After Hannah left the marina, she never used her phone again. The next day, she helped Norma Bolinger prepare the school for Hurricane Maria by taking pictures off the walls. Bolinger said, "She responded to everything I asked with 'Yes, Norma.' 'Yes, Norma.' 'Yes, Norma.' Which normally wasn't her tone of voice to me. Hannah was not a 'yes' sort of person. If you asked her to do something, she would want to know why."

That night, Hannah's three roommates told her that they were all trying to leave the island. One of them, Leslie Bunnell, said that Hannah told her, "I'm staying—that's where my heart is. School is going to be the first step toward normality for these kids." The next morning, Hannah said that she was heading to school, and a roommate watched her get in her car. She never showed up at the school. The following day, there was a faculty meeting, and she wasn't there. Her friend Maggie Guzman called Hannah's closest friends, on the island and in the States, but no one had spoken to her for three days. It was the same time of year as her previous two fugues, and they told Guzman to search near the water.

Guzman and other friends started with Hannah's favorite beach, Sapphire, where she often snorkeled. Near the water, there was a small bar that served hamburgers and mimosas. On a stool, they found Hannah's sundress, her sandals, and her car keys. Workers said that they had discovered the belongings in the sand when they were clearing debris from the storm. Hannah's car was in the parking lot. Inside were her purse, wallet, passport, and cell phone.

Given Hannah's strength as a swimmer, her friends assumed that she could survive for several days in the water. By boat, they searched the shoreline and a small island nearby, where the current might have taken her. The Coast Guard sent three helicopters. Her friends also checked the manifests of people evacuated on mercy ships, but her name wasn't listed. The storm had exacerbated deep divisions on the island—some people could leave, while others had no means to travel and nowhere to go—and Hannah's family and friends felt self-conscious about the fact that they were searching "for one white gal in a sea of troubles and suffering," as one put it.

After three days, they had to call off the search to prepare for Hurricane Maria, which brought heavy rain to the island. When the storm subsided, an EMT named Jacob Bradley, who had set up a makeshift emergency-medical-services station on the island, organized another search. If Hannah had drowned, her body would likely float to the surface within a few days. Bradley circled the island and all its cays in a rescue boat and also canvassed the airport, the homeless shelters, the beaches, and the hospitals, and interviewed captains who came in and out of the island's marinas. He went to the morgue and looked at ten unclaimed bodies. None of them were Hannah.

Hannah's friends developed a range of theories for what had happened, all of which they acknowledged were unlikely. But her survival in New York had been improbable, too. One friend from St. Thomas said, "There are pockets of communities in the bush, and she could be living there." Others thought that Hannah, who is fluent in Spanish, might have got on a boat to Puerto Rico or St. Croix or Miami without ID and integrated into a community of displaced people. "Even if she doesn't have a grip on her past, she's still Hannah, and she's probably doing what she can to be of service to the people around her," Roesle, her ex-boyfriend, said. Hannah Wood said, "Even if she's not aware that she's herself, she's a very charming person. If someone was inclined to do a good deed, she'd be the kind of person who would persuade someone to do it."

. . . . .

After her first fugue, Hannah gave her mother *Traveling with Pomegranates: A Mother-Daughter Story*, a memoir framed as a modern version of the myth of Persephone and Demeter. Hannah rarely spoke about her fugue, but Barbara was touched by what she felt was an allusion to the experience. Demeter searches the earth for her daughter, Persephone, who has been taken into the underworld. "I remember reading that Persephone falls into an abyss, and that just hit something close to my heart," Barbara said. Even when Persephone is saved, Hades requires that she return to the underworld for a portion of each year. With each fugue, Barbara found more solace in what she described as "the primal archetype of the daughter descending and the mother seeking her, whatever that takes."

After Bradley's search failed to turn up any bodies, Barbara's clearness committee, a group of Quakers appointed to guide someone facing a dilemma, bought her a one-way ticket to St. Thomas. She asked the Red Cross if she could do volunteer work in exchange for a bed. "I didn't want to take up precious resources," she said. The Red Cross put her in touch with the owner of the Windward Passage Hotel, in downtown St. Thomas, which was providing rooms to recovery workers and hotel employees who had lost their homes in the storms.

Barbara arrived on the island on November 21st, more than two months after Hannah disappeared. Her room looked out on the part of the harbor where seaplanes take off. The cruise ships had begun to return, and the businesses devoted to their passengers — on a street behind the hotel were Dynasty Dazzlers, Ballerina Jewelers, Jewels Forever, and a dozen other jewelry stores — were reopening.

Barbara is constitutionally optimistic, and she tried to cast away the idea of negative outcomes. She drove Hannah's car — a black Suzuki, whose back window had been blown out by Hurricane Irma — and went to Hannah's favorite beaches, restaurants, and shops. "I do have the sense sometimes that she's around any corner," Barbara told me. She talked to Hannah's friends and colleagues, trying to understand her last known interactions. Barbara believed that this fugue, too, may have started with a prelude in which Hannah was still home and communicating with people in a rudimentary way, without encoding the interactions into memory.

Barbara called Richard Loewenstein, the psychiatrist who specializes in fugues, and was struck by his conviction that dissociative fugues are organized and purposeful, operating according to some internal logic. The person's thinking is dominated by a "single idea that symbolizes or condenses (or both) several important ideas and emotions," Loewenstein writes.

Barbara tried to imagine what thought could be motivating her daughter to journey to water. She contemplated the symbolism of baptism. "One rises from the water reborn," she said. But, in the United Methodist tradition in which Hannah was raised, believers are not required to be fully immersed. Barbara also considered the imagery of creation in the Old Testament. "The water is a vast chaos, formless — a void," she said. "Could it be a kind of metaphor for the primeval chaos out of which creation comes?" The description in Genesis reads, "Now the earth was formless and empty, darkness was over the surface of the deep, and the spirit of God was hovering over the waters." But, Barbara added, "we don't generally get so literal about it as to charge off into the briny deep or the creek."

She said that, one day, shortly before she filed for divorce, she, too, had entered a kind of dissociative state, in part, she believes, in response to a medication that she had just started taking. She had been on her way to teach a class, at a United Methodist church, about the women who worshipped at the church at Corinth. The women's existence is recorded only because Paul admonished them for preaching and prophesying in public. "The husband is the head of his wife," he wrote.

The last thing Barbara remembered was driving south on the highway. She found herself beside the Willamette River. "Why did I go to the water?" she asked. "I do remember feeling comfort finding myself there." She sat in her car for several hours. "I had lost the ability to understand categories," she said. "I no longer had a chronological measure of time. I no longer experienced myself in a specific place. I didn't have an understanding of the mechanisms by which this world fits together." After several hours, she drove home. She said, "I fully came to when I saw my children's faces, and I thought, Oh, my God — they're worried."

· · · · ·

The front-desk manager of the Windward Passage Hotel, Vedora Small, is a middle-aged mother from St. Thomas whose home was destroyed in the storm and who lives in a room on the same floor of the hotel as Barbara. She often lies in bed at night wondering where Hannah could be. "I know St. Thomas is a small place and it looks simple," Small told me. "But you can live here for years and I don't see you and you don't see me."

Small took Barbara to shelters and abandoned buildings where people who are homeless or mentally disturbed often turn up. On the island, there are only thirty-two beds for psychiatric patients — the shortage is so severe that a judge recently ordered a mentally ill man to live in his pickup truck — and a large number of people are chronically adrift. After the storms, more people joined their ranks. Barbara was repeatedly directed to the same circuit of buildings: a night club downtown that had been the site of several crimes, a car wash on a side street near Frenchtown, and a house where people from the car wash always told her to go. It was owned by a man who was rarely home. Under his door, Barbara slipped a flyer with Hannah's face on it that warned she "may not know who she is."

When I visited these sites with Barbara, people who were drunk, high, or unhinged seemed to engage with reality for long enough to tell her that they were praying for her. One woman, who was struggling to stay upright, told Barbara, "I love you, you will find her — even if she's dead, you're still going to find her." A woman who worked at a farm on the Estate Bordeaux, a former sugar plantation, said that she understood why someone might forget her identity during the storm. "There was a lot of trauma," she said softly. "It cracked things wide open." A man making hamburgers at the bar at Sapphire told Barbara that a few people had drowned near the beach in the past. "I don't think she went out into the water," he said. "Everything that goes out comes back this way. She would have washed up already."

Every few weeks, there was another sighting. It was often the same women: a white teacher at a different private school on the island, or an older, homeless woman from Massachusetts who panhandled in an open-air mall near the marina.

On January 23rd, two caseworkers at the Bethlehem House Shelter for the Homeless, in downtown St. Thomas, reported that they had just seen Hannah at an abandoned building where people often smoked crack. Barbara and a detective from the Virgin Islands Police Department, Albion George, drove to a peach-colored, crumbling three-story structure close to Market Square, a produce market that was once the site of some of the largest slave auctions in the world. They climbed a steep flight of concrete steps with no railings. Detective George reached the third floor and saw the woman. "I thought, My God, that's her," he told me. "My heart was beating. I grabbed her right away and handcuffed her."

The woman was thin and had acne, and her light-brown hair was in a bun. Her eyes were a striking sea green. Barbara reached the top of the stairs a minute later, and told George that it was not Hannah. The woman was shouting about police accountability—she said that she needed George's badge number. George went to release the handcuffs, and Barbara touched the woman's shoulder and apologized over and over. She explained that she was searching for her daughter. The woman had seen the flyers for Hannah. She told Barbara, "I wish I were her for you."

An emergency call came over George's radio, but Barbara was reluctant to leave. She was moved by the woman's compassion and wondered if her mother was looking for her, too. After she returned to the hotel, she wished she could go back and help the woman somehow. She realized that in the time it had taken to drive to the building and climb to the top she had conditioned herself to fully accept a daughter who would find herself in such surroundings. "That sort of gift is at the heart of religion," she told me. "To love your neighbor as yourself. To love that woman as I love Hannah."

. . . . .

Barbara went to a number of religious services on the island, including at the Reformed church, at the Methodist church, and at the island's only Jewish temple, built in 1833 by Spanish and Portuguese settlers. It is one of the oldest synagogues in the Western Hemisphere. Barbara started going to services every Sabbath, and described the synagogue as an "unlikely spiritual home in the wilderness." The tile floor of the temple was covered in sand; according to legend, the sand symbolized the desert in which the Israelites wandered for forty years.

On a recent Sabbath, the rabbi, a transplant from Chevy Chase, Maryland, warmly welcomed Barbara. He had added Hannah's name to the list of people whose recovery the congregation prayed for every week. By most counts, Hannah is one of five people still missing in the Virgin Islands in the wake of the storms. When the rabbi recited the prayer for healing, Barbara closed her eyes and bowed her head, remaining motionless long after it had ended. For much of the sermon, she gazed at the temple's domed ceiling. The rabbi's words were punctuated by frogs chirping outside the open door.

At the end of the service, we were all asked to stand in a circle and greet the person next to us. There were about twenty people there, most of them wearing shorts and sandals. Barbara introduced herself to a blond woman, a tourist, and explained why she was on the island. The woman said, automatically, "That's terrible."

After the service, Barbara and I went to dinner, and she seemed unusually deflated. "There's a whole range of how people deal with the unknown," she said. Hannah's father told me in an email, "I am sure that Hannah is alive . . . but I do not know IF she is 'Safe in the Arms of Jesus' or IF she is still walking around on this earth with the rest of us."

When Barbara feels impatient for an answer, she reminds herself of a Quaker adage: "Live up to the light thou hast, and more will be granted thee." The quest for her daughter—she described it as "navigating the realms of the watery unknown"—seemed to have also become a kind of end in itself. She and Hannah have always been close, but she felt she was accessing new facets of her daughter's experience. "Sometimes, when I come to the end of the day, I just have to take some deep breaths, remember the things I heard, and be grateful for them and let them go," she told me. "I have to realize that no matter how much I know about her, no matter how much more I learn, there's still a mystery."

Hannah's two closest friends told me that they wondered if Barbara would stay on the island forever. She often described phases of her life using the word "journey," and the search for her daughter had taken on a new dimension: she was connecting with the many lost women on the island who were not Hannah. "I need to be here, and I trust I'll know when I need to be back home," she told me. She felt that she was still piecing together clues and connections. She quoted a line from an Emily Dickinson poem, one of her favorites: "Not knowing when the dawn will come / I open every door."

OCCUPIED TERRITORY

Rebecca Solnit

One morning, as I walked on the quiet, mostly wooded King Mountain trail above San Francisco Bay, a dog not much smaller than I and possessed of much sharper teeth made straight for me, growling. I tried to get away; it butted me roughly. When its owner came around the bend with a second dog, I said, the snot from the first still gleaming on my pants, "You need to keep your dogs under control." "My dogs are under perfect control," the woman replied with asperity. The point was clear: She could control them but didn't care to. She didn't share my belief that a person should have exclusive jurisdiction over her body.

Indignant, I strode away through the live oaks and the bay trees and the coyote brush. My mind was on its own track. Decades ago, I spent several minutes with my left thigh inside the jaws of a boxer, an episode that left me jumpy about dogs in the same way that a series of threats and assaults has left me anxious about strange men. The encounter on the trail hadn't just alarmed me—it had offended my principles. I passed by wood ferns, maidenhair ferns, sword ferns, without seeing them. All power, I reflected, can be understood in terms of space. Physical places, as well as economies, conversations, politics—all can be conceived of as areas unequally occupied. A map of these territories would constitute a map of power and status: who has more, who has less.

At the start and end of that particular trail, you can look out across the bay to San Quentin State Prison, whose old stucco walls from that distance can look inappropriately idyllic, shining golden against the blue water. Up close, however, the penitentiary—the oldest in California—is a grim, ramshackle place, draped in razor wire and surrounded by gun towers. Every so often, I go inside those walls to visit Jarvis Masters, a writer who is doing his third decade on death row for a crime that the evidence convinces me he did not commit.

When I went earlier this year, Masters and I sat in the little cage into which prisoners are always locked with their guests. After an hour and a half or so, I needed to leave, but nobody came to usher us out—the staff were busy with the basketball playoffs, Masters told me. A further sixty minutes passed before a guard arrived to perform the elaborate rite of departure. Masters, in a familiar routine, turned around, put his hands behind his back, and was cuffed and led away; I was allowed to exit the cage on my own, then buzzed out at the fortified doorway and released into the open air. Masters was amused at my impatience—I'd been delayed by a mere hour, he pointed out; he'd been delayed more than thirty years.

On the trail, I turned away from the view. There are two kinds of borders: those that limit where we can go and those that limit what people can do to us.

. . . . .

Masters, who is confined to a cage most of the time, has a knack for calling me when I'm out in the world and reminding me, simply with his presence on the phone, of my considerable freedom. As it happens, he called me on January 28, when I was at the international terminal of the San Francisco airport. I was protesting, along with more than a thousand other people, the executive order Donald Trump had just signed, a week into his presidency: "Protecting the Nation from Foreign Terrorist Entry into the United States." The order summarily denied people from seven countries, all of which have majority-Muslim populations, the right to enter the United States. The administration's rationale was that these people posed a threat to the safety of US citizens, but the measure was clearly just the first part of a broad campaign to expand the space available to a select group of people while curtailing that available to everyone else. As human rights lawyers circulated inside the terminal, the rest of us filled the road outside, blocking it to through traffic to protest the blockage of the travelers, some of whom had been caught midair when the order came down and were now being held at the airport. I put my phone on speaker so Masters could listen to the crowd shouting and chanting. He was delighted—for the duration of the phone call, he was part of the multitude.

It felt strange to be, for that brief time, a bridge between a person who couldn't get out and others who couldn't get in; it felt good to be in a throng of people who wanted to aid and support the latter. One of the fundamental arguments in this country is about whether there's enough to go around, about whether we can lift everyone up, to use one spatial metaphor—or, to use another, whether we must live by a sort of lifeboat ethics, not letting certain people on, as if there were room only for a few. At our best, we invite people into spaces that belong to us and defend their right to sovereignty over their own. At our worst, we invade or shut out, whether by land grabs or street harassment or travel bans.

Many men and white people fear that they are on the losing end of social change. The anxiety is at once well founded—after all, moving toward equality requires them, us, to cede territory—and wrongheaded. It is an analysis predicated on scarcity, on the notion that abundance depends on exclusion. Why consider this a zero-sum game? Must one person's gain be another's loss?

. . . . .

The King Mountain trail is in a part of northeastern Mount Tamalpais where the wealthy locals haven't yet restricted access by preventing street parking near trailheads. The route traversing this foothill of Mount Tam is circular once you summit a steep and sometimes muddy fire road, and a sudden right turn onto a narrow trail leads into the forest. Repeatedly, the trees thin and a vista appears, then they close in again, enfolding you in green shade and the world nearer at hand. This opening and closing of vistas is one rhythm of the trail; the other is its undulations uphill and downhill after the initial ascent. In the late 1970s and early 1980s, a rapist and serial murderer known as the Trailside Killer roamed the area, one of myriad assailants who curtailed my sense of freedom as a young woman. He, too, is now a death-row inmate at San Quentin.

You can start at any point and make connections that constitute a story about where we are and why, though the pursuit of those connections can feel like bushwhacking through a thicket. Yet there are a few clear trails, a few undeniable facts that shape our experience. Some of my freedom comes from my race. Jarvis Masters is black; I am white. The writer Garnette Cadogan, who is also black, responds quizzically when I talk about hiking and camping, because he feels unsafe in such spaces—wide open, but not to people like him. However, he often walks all night around New York City alone, an unthinkable exercise for me. My race and gender determine the borders I can cross, the places I can go, just as yours do for you.

Feminism has long been a campaign to open closed spaces — to provide women access to education, employment, political power, to enable us to move freely in the world. And to close spaces that groping bosses and domineering husbands have historically treated as open. Misogyny is territorially expressed in ways both trivial — men manspreading, say, or monopolizing the conversation — and violent. What is a rape but the insistence that the spatial rights of a man — and by implication all men — extend to the interior of a woman's body, the insistence that her rights don't extend even over her own person? As Danielle L. McGuire relates in *At the Dark End of the Street*, her counterhistory of the civil rights movement, for centuries Southern white men used the rape of women to intimidate black communities. The fight against sexual violence and interracial rape "became one crucial battleground upon which African Americans sought to destroy white supremacy and gain personal and political autonomy."

Rape is a common tool of war and even of genocide. During the recent conflict in Sudan, for example, it has been documented that mass rape has been used by the Janjaweed to torture and intimidate the population. Women have been beaten and taunted with slurs such as "I will give you a light-skinned baby to take this land from you," according to a 2007 report by Refugees International. But the women were also vulnerable to being punished and stigmatized by their own communities. In Syria, the threat of rape is among the reasons some families have fled their country.

Just as fear of assault keeps women out of too many spaces too much of the time, whether it be the corner store at midnight or the wilderness alone, the threat of hostile entry of bodies can define the space that entire groups are allowed to occupy; an attack on an individual can lead to a collective retreat, on a scale that ranges from a neighborhood to a nation.

. . . . .

The domination of space by the powerful might be called structural violence. We are still a nation that, despite the lip service to representative government and equality under the law, has never managed to elect a governing body that is remotely representative of the population. Around 70 percent of Americans are not white men, but about 80 percent of Congress is, as were forty-four of our forty-five presidents. Our only non-white president saw his right to govern continually challenged, notably by baseless charges that he was born overseas, a proxy for the sense that he could not possibly claim legitimate ownership of the seat of power, did not belong inside the institutions he presided over. Though the views of politicians vary, and certainly some endeavor to represent the interests of people unlike them, a case can be made that equal people would take up equal space in government.

Even when women do rise to power, their right to occupy that arena is contested in any number of ways. Exclusively male for almost two centuries, the Supreme Court is still two-thirds male. (The first two women on the court have numerous stories of the obstacles placed in their paths.) Male Supreme Court justices interrupt their female colleagues three times as often as they interrupt one another, according to scholars Tonja Jacobi and Dylan Schweers, who observe that this is not merely unpleasant for the female justices—it is consequential. Not being given room to speak often prematurely terminates a person's arguments and renders her less effective in shaping the course of justice.

When I was young, some people argued that women were fundamentally better than men, kinder and less bellicose, and that governments led by women would be less inclined to aggression and invasion. Others cited conservative, hawkish female politicians such as Margaret Thatcher and Indira Gandhi to disprove the claim. (Today, of course, we have Marine Le Pen and Ivanka Trump among the women who support right-wing policies and are, like conservative blacks opposed to affirmative action, useful counterweights to any argument that demographic differences matter.) You can argue either side: We won't actually know what women might do with power until they're a majority in the House or the Senate or the Supreme Court, though there's evidence that it might lead to change.

Worldwide, women hold barely more than 20 percent of parliamentary seats—a vast improvement that is nevertheless inadequate and changing so slowly that at its current rate another half-century may pass before parity is reached. In no country do women constitute a legislative majority. Political scientists Tali Mendelberg and Christopher F. Karpowitz found that it was only when women were a majority in decision-making bodies—when they made up 60 to 80 percent of a group—that they spoke up as much as men and were heard. Under these conditions, they tended to emphasize the needs of the vulnerable and to argue for redistribution of wealth. But equal space and equal security should not be considered rewards for virtue; they are rights in and of themselves, unrealized in innumerable ways as yet.

· · · · ·

Almost twenty years ago, while taking care of a friend's dog, I took the animal out for a stroll. Along the way, three tall young men came walking directly toward us, a situation in which I always give way, step aside. But I had a pit bull on a short leash. I walked right through those men like Moses parting the Red Sea. I never tried that again, but I never forgot what I learned in that moment: So deeply had I known who owned the sidewalk that I'd always yielded, without even noticing. Since then, I've read accounts of trans women who found, after their transition, that they were constantly bumping into people or being bumped into—as women they no longer owned the right of way.

As a child, I somehow absorbed the idea that getting in the way of other people or wasting their time was a terrible offense. I have been scrupulous about standing to the right on escalators, not blocking aisles, not showing up late. Underlying my anxiety are implicit assumptions about whose time and space matters, perhaps matters more than mine. Yet in recent years I've become overloaded with work, and a contrary impulse has taken hold of me: to move as fast as possible through crowds or traffic, sometimes through conversations and social obligations. When Jarvis laughed at me for being anxious about an hour's delay, he wasn't thinking about the press of deadlines and obligations hanging over me, or rather hovering behind me, urging me onward. It's easy to see how readily this feeling of urgency could become a sense that everyone else is in your way, that your rights and needs matter more—could become, ultimately, the sort of self-absorption that renders others invisible. To believe that my important business is more important than others' is the path of entitlement, the antithesis of any ideal of equality.

As a writer, I've been given more and more space to occupy, and my voice reaches further and further. The only justification I can think of for such disproportionate influence is to use it to advocate for others, to invite in those who have been excluded. And to listen, because when you're not a conduit you may as well be a dead end. The woman I met on the trail with the dog was approximately the same race, age, gender, and, presumably, class as me, yet we disagreed profoundly about the one thing we discussed. As my own status has risen and shifted, I've felt the pull of something that isn't exactly conservatism but may fuel it. Sometimes the force you need to resist is yourself.

ACKNOWLEDGMENTS (continued)

Allen, Danielle. "What Is Education For?" *Boston Review*, May 9, 2016. http://bostonreview.net/forum/danielle-allen-what-education. Reprinted with permission from the author.

Aviv, Rachel. "How a Young Woman Lost Her Identity," *The New Yorker*, Apr. 2, 2018. Reprinted by permission of the author.

Council of Writing Program Administrators. Bulleted list of points taken verbatim from p. 1 of "Framework for Success in Postsecondary Writing." Council of Writing Program Administrators. wpacouncil.org. Reprinted by permission.

De Montaigne, Michel. "That Our Mind Hinders Itself" from *The Complete Essays*, by Michel de Montaigne, translated by M. A. Screech (Penguin Classics, 1993). Copyright © M. A. Screech, 1993. Reproduced by permission of Penguin Books Ltd.

Solnit, Rebecca. "Occupied Territory," *Harper's Magazine*, July 2017, pp. 5–7. Reprinted with permission of the author.

Webster, Daniel W., and Jon S. Vernick, eds. Foreword by Michael R. Bloomberg. *Reducing Gun Violence in America: Informing Policy with Evidence and Analysis*, pp. xxv–xxviii. © 2013 Johns Hopkins University Press. Reprinted with permission of Johns Hopkins University Press.

WORKS CITED

Abumrad, Jad, and Robert Krulwich. "An Equation for Good." *Radiolab*, WNYC, 15 Dec. 2010, www.wnycstudios.org/story/103983-equation-good.

Allen, Danielle. *Our Declaration: A Reading of the Declaration of Independence in Defense of Equality.* W. W. Norton, 2014.

Anderson, Sam. "The Mind of John McPhee." *The New York Times*, 28 Sept. 2017, www.nytimes.com/2017/09/28/magazine/the-mind-of-john-mcphee.html.

The Aristocrats. Directed by Paul Provenza, Think Film Company, 2005.

Aviv, Rachel. "What Does It Mean to Die?" *The New Yorker*, 5 Feb. 2018, www.newyorker.com/magazine/2018/02/05/what-does-it-mean-to-die.

Bain, Ken. *What the Best College Students Do.* Harvard UP, 2012.

Beard, Jo Ann. "The Fourth State of Matter." *The New Yorker*, 24 Jun. 1996, www.newyorker.com/magazine/1996/06/24/the-fourth-state-of-matter.

Berger, John. "Why Look at Animals?" *About Looking*, Random House, 2011.

Berthoff, Ann E. *Forming/Thinking/Writing: The Composing Imagination.* Boynton/Cook, 1982.

Biss, Eula. *On Immunity: An Inoculation.* Graywolf Press, 2014.

Blake, William. "Auguries of Innocence." *The Poetry Foundation*, 16 Jan. 2014, www.poetryfoundation.org/poems/43650/auguries-of-innocence.

Burke, Kenneth. *The Philosophy of Literary Form.* UP of California, 1941.

Cain, Susan. *Quiet: The Power of Introverts in a World That Can't Stop Talking.* Crown, 2012.

Carnegie, Dale. *How to Win Friends and Influence People.* Simon & Schuster, 1936.

Carroll, Lewis. *Alice's Adventures in Wonderland.* Project Gutenberg, 8 Mar. 1994, www.gutenberg.org/files/11/11-0.txt. Accessed 28 Mar. 2019.

Colette. Quoted in Emily Temple, " 'My Pencils Outlast Their Erasers': Great Writers on the Art of Revision." *The Atlantic*, 14 Jan. 2013, www.theatlantic.com /entertainment/archive/2013/01/my-pencils-outlast-their-erasers-great-writers -on-the-art-of-revision/267011/.

Covey, Stephen. *The 7 Habits of Highly Effective People.* Free Press, 1989.

Crutchfield, Susan. " 'Play[ing] her part correctly': Helen Keller as Vaudevillian Freak." *Disability Studies Quarterly*, vol. 25, no. 3, Summer 2005, dsq-sds.org /article/view/577/754.

"Diane Arbus." *Wikipedia*, 8 Dec. 2013, en.wikipedia.org/wiki/Diane_Arbus.

Dissanayake, Ellen. "The Arts After Darwin: Does Art Have an Origin and Adaptive Function?" *Ellendissanayake.com*, www.ellendissanayake.com/publications/pdf /EllenDissanayake_ArtsAfterDarwinWAS08.pdf. Accessed 16 Jan. 2014.

Donne, John. *Devotions upon Emergent Occasions*. 1624. Project Gutenberg, www.gutenberg.org/ebooks/23772. Accessed 28 Mar. 2019.

Duncker, Karl. "On Problem Solving." *Psychological Monographs*, vol. 58, no. 5, 1945, pp. i–113, doi:10.1037/h0093599.

Edwards, Betty. *Drawing on the Right Side of the Brain: A Course in Enhancing Creativity and Artistic Confidence*. Tarcher, 1979.

Ericsson, K. Anders, Ralf Th. Krampe, and Clemens Tesch-Römer. "The Role of Deliberate Practice in the Acquisition of Expert Performance." *Psychological Review*, vol. 100, no. 3, 1993, pp. 363–406, doi: 10.1.1.169.9712.

Fitzgerald, F. Scott. "Appendix A: Fitzgerald's Correspondence about *The Great Gatsby* (1922–25)." *The Great Gatsby*, edited by Michael Nowlin, Broadview Press, 2007, pp. 185–87.

Framework for Success in Postsecondary Writing. *Council of Writing Program Administrators*, wpacouncil.org/files/framework-for-success-postsecondary -writing.pdf. Accessed 27 Jan. 2014.

Frost, Robert. "The Road Not Taken." *The Poetry Foundation*, www .poetryfoundation.org/poems/44272/the-road-not-taken. Accessed 4 Jun. 2015.

Gaiman, Neil. "Advice to Authors." *Neilgaiman.com*, www.neilgaiman.com/FAQs /Advice_to_Authors. Accessed 6 Nov. 2014.

Gazzaniga, Michael S. "The Split Brain in Man." *Scientific American*, vol. 217, no. 2, Aug. 1967, pp. 24–29, www.scientificamerican.com/article/the-split-brain-in-man/.

"Genesis." *The English Standard Version Bible*. Crossway, 2015, www.esv.org/Genesis+1/.

Gibson, William. *The Miracle Worker*. Playhouse 90, 1957. Teleplay.

---. *The Miracle Worker*. Directed by Arthur Penn, Playfilm Productions, 1962.

---. *The Miracle Worker*. Samuel French, 1961.

---. *Monday After the Miracle*. Dramatists Play Service, 1983.

Gladwell, Malcolm. *Outliers: The Story of Success*. Little, Brown, 2008.

---. *The Tipping Point*. Little, Brown, 2000.

---. *Blink: The Power of Thinking without Thinking*. Little, Brown, 2005.

Gladwell, Malcolm, and Robert Krulwich. "Secrets of Success." *Radiolab*. WNYC, 26 Jul. 2010, www.wnycstudios.org/story/91971-secrets-of-success.

Gonzales, Laurence. *Deep Survival: Who Lives, Who Dies, and Why*. Norton, 2004.

Gopnik, Adam. "Life Studies: What I Learned When I Learned to Draw." *The New Yorker*, 27 Jun. 2011, www.newyorker.com/magazine/2011/06/27/life-studies.

Hochschild, Adam. " 'Why's This So Good?' No. 61: John McPhee and the Archdruid." *Nieman Storyboard*, Nieman Foundation for Journalism at Harvard, 2 Oct. 2012, niemanstoryboard.org/stories/whys-this-so-good-no-61-john-mcphee-and-the -archdruid/.

Johnson, Harriet McBryde. "Unspeakable Conversations." *The New York Times Magazine*, 16 Feb. 2003, www.nytimes.com/2003/02/16/magazine/unspeakable -conversations.html.

Keefe, Patrick Radden. "The Detectives Who Never Forget a Face." *The New Yorker*, 22 Aug. 2016, www.newyorker.com/magazine/2016/08/22/londons-super -recognizer-police-force.

Keller, Helen. *The Story of My Life*. Project Gutenberg, 4 Feb. 2013, www.gutenberg .org/files/2397/2397-h/2397-h.htm. Accessed 28 Mar. 2019.

---. *Teacher: Anne Sullivan Macy*. Doubleday, 1955.

---. "Vaudeville Speech." Quoted in Dorothy Hermann, *Helen Keller: A Life*. University of Chicago Press, 1998.

---. *The World I Live In*. Project Gutenberg, 1 Jan. 2009, www.gutenberg.org /files/27683/27683-h/27683-h.htm. Accessed 28 Mar. 2019.

Kolbert, Elizabeth. *Field Notes from a Catastrophe: Man, Nature, and Climate Change*. Bloomsbury, 2006.

Konnikova, Maria. "Why We Need Answers." *The New Yorker*, 30 Apr. 2013, www .newyorker.com/tech/annals-of-technology/why-we-need-answers.

Lamott, Anne. *Bird by Bird: Some Instructions on Writing and Life*. Anchor, 1995.

Lepore, Jill. "Battleground America: One Nation, Under the Gun." *The New Yorker*, 23 Apr. 2012, www.newyorker.com/magazine/2012/04/23/battleground-america.

---. *Book of Ages: The Life and Opinions of Jane Franklin*. Knopf, 2013.

---. Interview by Sasha Weiss and Judith Thurman. "Out Loud: Jane Franklin's Untold American Story." *The New Yorker*, 30 Jun. 2013, www.newyorker.com /culture/culture-desk/out-loud-jane-franklins-untold-american-story.

---. "Poor Jane's Almanac." *The New York Times*, 23 Apr. 2011, www.nytimes .com/2011/04/24/opinion/24lepore.html.

---. "The Prodigal Daughter: Writing, History, Mourning." *The New Yorker*, 8 Jul. 2013, www.newyorker.com/magazine/2013/07/08/the-prodigal-daughter.

Lincoln, Abraham. "Lincoln's Gettysburg Address." Project Gutenberg, www.gutenberg.org/0/4/4-h/4-h.htm. Accessed 24 Jan. 2014.

The Matrix. Directed by Andy Wachowski and Lana Wachowski, Warner Brothers, 1999.

McPhee, John. "John McPhee, The Art of Nonfiction No. 3." Interview by Peter Hessler, *Paris Review*, vol. 192, Spring 2010, www.theparisreview.org /interviews/5997/john-mcphee-the-art-of-nonfiction-no-3-john-mcphee.

---. "Structure." *The New Yorker*, 14 Jan. 2013, www.newyorker.com/magazine /2013/01/14/structure.

---. "Travels in Georgia." *The New Yorker*, 28 Apr. 1973, www.newyorker.com /magazine/1973/04/28/travels-in-georgia.

Milbank, Dana. "Apparently, It's Illegal to Laugh at Jeff Sessions." *The Washington Post*, 5 Sept. 2017, www.washingtonpost.com/opinions/apparently-its-illegal-to-laugh -at-jeff-sessions/2017/09/05/86b6e48a-9278-11e7-aace-04b862b2b3f3_story. html?noredirect=on&utm_term=.6b8ed50b78a0.

Morrison, Toni. "Toni Morrison, The Art of Fiction No. 134." Interview by Elissa Schappell. *The Paris Review*, vol. 128, Fall 1993, www.theparisreview.org /interviews/1888/toni-morrison-the-art-of-fiction-no-134-toni-morrison.

Nelson, Maggie. *The Argonauts*. Graywolf Press, 2016.

Notaro, Tig. *LIVE*. Secretlycanadian.com, 3 Aug. 2012, secretlycanadian.com/artist /tig-notaro/.

Osifchin, Chris. "Abu Ghraib Ruminations." Personal Correspondence, 29 Jan. 2014.

Pink, Daniel. "The Puzzle of Motivation." *TED*, Jul. 2009, tedsummaries.com/2014/06/06/dan-pink-the-puzzle-of-motivation/.

---. *A Whole New Mind: Why Right-Brainers Will Rule the Future*. Riverhead, 2005.

Plato. "Apology." *Project Gutenberg*, www.gutenberg.org/files/1656/1656-h/1656-h.htm. Accessed 29 Mar. 2019.

Pollan, Michael. "An Animal's Place." *The New York Times*, 10 Nov. 2002, www.nytimes.com/2002/11/10/magazine/an-animal-s-place.html.

Prose, Francine. "Close Reading: Learning to Write by Learning to Read." *Atlantic*, 1 Apr. 2006, www.theatlantic.com/magazine/archive/2006/08/close-reading/305038/.

Robinson, Ken. "Do Schools Kill Creativity?" *TED*, Feb. 2006, www.ted.com/talks/ken_robinson_says_schools_kill_creativity?language=en.

Rose, Erik. Student Writing, Rutgers University, Apr. 2012.

Rossano, Julianna. "Choose Your Own Adventure." Student Writing, Rutgers University, Dec. 2017.

Sacks, Oliver. "The Mind's Eye." *The New Yorker*, 28 Jul. 2003, www.newyorker.com/magazine/2003/07/28/the-minds-eye.

Sagan, Carl. *Cosmos*. Ballantine, 2013.

Saint Anselm. *Basic Writings: Proslogium, Mologium, Gaunilo's In Behalf of the Fool, Cur Deus Homo*. Translated by S. N. Deane, 2nd ed., Open Court, 1998.

Scully, Matthew. *Dominion*. Macmillan, 2002.

Sehgal, Parul. "Ripple Effects." Review of *On Immunity*, by Eula Biss, *The New York Times*, 3 Oct. 2014, www.nytimes.com/2014/10/05/books/review/on-immunity-by-eula-biss.html.

Shakespeare, William. *Romeo and Juliet*. Project Gutenberg, 25 May 2012, www.gutenberg.org/cache/epub/1112/pg1112-images.html. Accessed 28 Mar. 2019.

Shimazu, Donald. "The Good News Cult." Student Writing, Rutgers University, Apr. 2012.

Singer, Peter. *Animal Liberation: A New Ethic for Our Treatment of Animals*. Random House, 1975.

Skloot, Rebecca. "How Rebecca Skloot Built *The Immortal Life of Henrietta Lacks*." Interview by David Dobbs, *The Open Notebook*, 22 Nov. 2011, www.theopennotebook.com/2011/11/22/rebecca-skloot-henrietta-lacks/.

---. *The Immortal Life of Henrietta Lacks*. Crown, 2010.

Smith, Zadie. "Fail Better." *The Guardian*, 13 Jan. 2007, www.scribd.com/doc/73273033/Zadie-Smith-s-Fail-Better-Read-Better.

---. *NW*. Penguin Books, 2012.

Solnit, Rebecca. "The Mother of All Questions." *Harper's*, Oct. 2015, harpers.org/archive/2015/10/the-mother-of-all-questions/.

Sontag, Susan. "America Seen through Photographs, Darkly." *On Photography*. Farrar, Straus and Giroux, 1977, pp. 27–50.

---. "Regarding the Torture of Others." *New York Times Magazine*, 23 May 2004, www.nytimes.com/2004/05/23/magazine/regarding-the-torture-of-others.html.

Stern, Daniel. "Life Becomes a Dream." Review of *The Benefactor,* by Susan Sontag, *The New York Times,* 8 Sept. 1963, movies2.nytimes.com/books/00/03/12/specials /sontag-benefactor.html.

Stiver, Annie. "The Time Is Ripe." Student Writing, Rutgers University, Apr. 2012.

Thoreau, Henry David. "Walden." *Walden, and On the Duty of Civil Disobedience.* Project Gutenberg, Jan. 1995, www.gutenberg.org/files/205/205-h/205-h.htm.

Toy Story. Directed by John Lasseter, Pixar Animation Studios, 1995.

Trainer, Laureen. "The Missing Photographs: An Examination of Diane Arbus's Images of Transvestites and Homosexuals from 1957 to 1965." *American Suburb X,* 2 Oct. 2009, www.americansuburbx.com/2009/10/theory-missing-photographs -examination.html.

Tremmel, Michelle. "What to Make of the Five-Paragraph Theme: History of the Genre and Implications." *TETYC,* Sept. 2011, pp. 29–41.

van der Hart, Onno. "Pierre Janet, Sigmund Freud, and Dissociation of the Personality: The First Codification of a Psychodynamic Depth Psychology." *The Dissociative Mind in Psychoanalysis: Understanding and Working with Trauma.* Edited by Elizabeth Howell and Sheldon Itzkowitz, Routledge, 2016.

Waking Life. Directed by Richard Linklater, Fox Searchlight, 2001.

Walk, Kerry. "Teaching with Writing." *Princeton Writing Program.* Princeton U, writing.princeton.edu/sites/writing/files/teachingwithwriting.pdf. Accessed 27 Dec. 2013.

Wallace, Amy. "An Epidemic of Fear: How Panicked Parents Skipping Shots Endanger Us All." *Wired,* 19 Oct. 2009, www.wired.com/2009/10/ff-waronscience/.

Wallace, David Foster. *This Is Water: Some Thoughts, Delivered on a Significant Occasion, About Living a Compassionate Life.* Transcription of 2005 Kenyon Commencement Address, 21 May 2005, Purdue U, web.ics.purdue.edu/~drkelly /DFWKenyonAddress2005.pdf. Accessed 23 Dec. 2013.

Walzer, Michael. "Political Action: The Problem of Dirty Hands." *Philosophy and Public Affairs,* vol. 2, no. 2, 1973, pp. 160–80.

Webster, Daniel W., and Jon S. Vernick. "Introduction." *Reducing Gun Violence in America: Informing Policy with Evidence and Analysis,* edited by Daniel W. Webster and Jon S. Vernick, Johns Hopkins UP, 2013.

Winkler, Adam. *Gunfight: The Battle over the Right to Bear Arms in America.* W. W. Norton, 2011.

Woolf, Virginia. Letter to Vita Sackville-West, 26 Feb. 1939. *Woolf in the World: A Pen and Press of Her Own.* Mortimer Rare Book Room, Smith College. Accessed 31 Dec. 2013.

---. *A Room of One's Own.* Project Gutenberg Australia, Oct. 2002, gutenberg.net .au/ebooks02/0200791.txt. Accessed 28 Mar. 2019.

---. "Street Haunting: A London Adventure." *Virginia Woolf: Selected Essays.* Oxford UP, 2008, pp. 177–87.

"WPA Outcomes Statement for First-Year Composition." Council of Writing Program Administrators, 17 Jul. 2014, wpacouncil.org/positions/outcomes.html.

INDEX

Work spaces, 195, 213–222
  digital, 216–218
  physical, 213–216
  practice in, 211–212
  solitude and, 13–16
Working deliberately, 127–148
  Practice Session, 17–20, 47–49,
    54, 55–56, 61–62, 77–78, 87,
    88, 103–104, 119, 120, 127,
    132–133, 137–139, 145–148,
    168–169, 222, 230, 242–244,
    253, 257
  reading as a writer and, 134–139
  reading in slow motion and,
    140–148
  seeing as a writer and, 129–133
World I Live In, The (Keller),
    161–162
Writing
  as composing, 5
  getting your act together and,
    213–222
  humor in, 247–253
  as intellectual journey, 223,
    225–231
  Practice Session, 25–26, 35–36,
    42, 47–50, 76–78, 102–104,
    125–126, 257–258
  predictable, 32–35
  pseudonymous, 259–262
  question-driven, 74–78

reading as a writer and, 135–139
revising and, 204–212
as a tool, 9–10
work spaces for, 195, 213–222
Writing about problems, puzzles, or
    questions, 6–7
  confronting the unknown in,
    37–41
  connecting in, 107–114
  context of words and, 43, 57–61
  curiosity-driven versus formula-
    driven, 30–32
  examples of (Webster and Vernick),
    33–35
  learning from failure in,
    187–188
  making sense of the world through,
    43, 51–54
  by unlearning rules, 21, 22–25
  writing to a question, 70–73
  See also Curiosity; Questioning
Writing to learn, 6
  examples of, 52–54
  organizing, 195–222
  Practice Session, 54–55, 62, 73,
    96, 127
  writing through difficulties
    and, 185
  writing to a question, 70–73

Zotero, 18, 19